Thank You India

A German Woman's Journey To The Wisdom Of Yoga

MARIA WIRTH

First published in India 2018

ISBN: 978-1-942426-09-7
Cover Design: Rakesh Chaudhary

Garuda Prakashan Private Limited
Gurugram, Bharat
www.garudaprakashan.com
www.garudabooks.com

Printed in India

ॐ श्री गणेशाय नमः

Dedicated To The Rishis Of Ancient & Modern Times !

Contents

Prologue

India is a huge country and has many faces. Over 1300 million to be precise. It is natural that opinions concerning India vary vastly. They depend on the faces one meets.

"How did you like India?" I once asked a German woman sitting next to me in the plane to Frankfurt. She was part of a tourist group. I had already noticed this group in the departure hall at Delhi airport, because all members, men as well as women wore the same outfit, different only in colours: shorts and T-shirt.

"What can one expect from such a country?" she asked back without really waiting for an answer. Probably she thought that everyone, like herself, would reply, "Nothing!"

"For me, India is the best country of all, and I have lived there for over thirty years", I surprised her. She looked astonished, "Really? That long? Can you tell me what you like about this country?"

It had not been love at first sight in my case, too. India hides her positive sides. Whoever expects comfort, will probably be disappointed, even on a luxury tour in five-star hotels. At some point one will be confronted with hawkers, beggars, potholes, dirt, noise, cockroaches or heat and face situations, which are not the way as one would like them to be.

Indians, too, have to face situations that are far from ideal. Life is hard in India. People are much closer in touch with poverty, illness and death than we in the West are. Competition for jobs and seats in colleges are unimaginable. For example, over one million students sat for the screening test for the prestigious Indian Institutes of Technology (IIT) in 2018 and only 11,000 are finally accepted. And when the railways started the process of filling up 88,000 posts, over 23 million people applied!

In spite of it, a smile comes easily to Indians, and they are quick to recover even after horrendous catastrophes. They are experts in accepting difficult situations and difficult people. Surely, in this field, if it were part of the Olympic Games, they would win the gold medal. There is comparatively little complaining in India. People seem to realise that complaining and whining serve no purpose except spoiling one's mood. This wise, accepting attitude gives India a special position in the world, and it shows in daily life.

Once I visited a friend in Delhi. It was in the peak of summer. "What heat!" I sighed, even before I sat down. I felt that my complaining was the most natural thing to do in that situation; after all, the temperature measured 43 degrees Celsius! "Yes, it is hot", my friend calmly confirmed. In that moment it struck me that there was a vast difference between his remark and my remark. He just stated a fact while I complained about it. His attitude was definitely preferable to mine, provided I have a choice. Sighing makes neither me nor others happy, on the contrary. And it doesn't bring down the heat either.

India is traditionally the land of wisdom. This wisdom is a treasure that is spreading more and more to the West and is valued there. It is today the only tradition worldwide that reaches back in an unbroken line for many thousands of years. It was persecuted under Muslim rule and ridiculed and demonised by Christian missionaries under British rule. Nevertheless, it remained intact to a great extent. This shows its power. It still shines from many faces in India.

To be still and look inwards is not considered a waste of time in India. "Inside" is more important. "Outside" is secondary and mirrors the 'inside'. Questions regarding the meaning of life are not pushed aside. India knows how one can be peaceful and content in life.

This spiritual side of India hides behind the exterior of a developing nation with its negative aspects like poverty and corruption. Yet India is no doubt spiritually more highly developed than other countries. This affects the general atmosphere in the country.

Indians call their country Bharat Mata, 'Mother India'. For them India is alive, like a mother, who bears and nourishes her children. Even to me India seems to be alive by now, although I grew up in the West where the dividing line between living beings and 'dead' matter is considered to be clear and taken as a matter of fact. If India wasn't alive, how could I love her?

Mother India or Bharat Mata is generous and shares her treasure with all human beings. She shows to everyone, how to make life joyful and worthwhile, provided he is interested in knowing it. But she is not pushy and doesn't try to convince others of her wisdom. "There are many paths to the peak of a mountain", she explains, and such tolerant view is unfortunately rather unique in this world. She even allows others to denigrate or misinterpret her. "Truth will be victorious" is her motto. And she seems not in a hurry.

Therefore, it can easily happen that tourists are put off by the exterior appearance of India and do not discover her strength. It happened to the woman who sat next to me in the plane. It happened also to me during my first visit during my studies. "Never again India!" my mother claims I have said when coming back from there after six weeks.

During that visit, the beggar children of Mumbai (former Bombay) were mainly responsible for spoiling my stay. Hardly had I left my small hotel near the sea avenue, they stuck to my heels, kept touching me, patted their naked bellies and whined away. If I wanted to sit down somewhere quietly, I could forget about 'quiet'. No chance. I simply was no equal to those rascals and did not know how to react. I didn't get rid of them no matter whether I gave something or pretended to be deaf. They were far more confident than I was. Of course, I felt sometimes pity for them. Yet often I felt weak, in the minority, helpless and was angry with myself, because I allowed them to push me into a corner.

Only years later, when I lived in India, I discovered another way to be with beggar children, whose number has by now come down considerably. There is a big difference, whether I take them to be a nuisance, which I blindly try to escape from, or whether I see them as children whom I wish from my heart all the best. Whether I give money or not is suddenly not that important anymore. The connection is now on another, more humane level.

It was accidental that in spite of my "Never again India!" I flew once more to India five years later. I had finished my studies in psychology and had enough money in my pocket that I had earned by selling Crepes Suzettes on markets in Hamburg. I wanted to go to Australia.

Then I met Juergen, an acquaintance. I told him that I am soon on my way to Australia. "Oh, at the same time I am flying to India" he said surprised. "Come with me to the wildlife sanctuaries in Kerala", he suggested. "India is on your way, and from there you can continue to Australia."

Juergen had an assignment for a wildlife magazine. We would stay right in the jungle, would trace elephants and tigers, and wildlife guards would accompany us. He painted a colourful, tempting picture. In my imagination I saw us riding on elephants in the thick, inaccessible jungle and sleeping in hammocks next to a protecting bonfire.

I planned a stopover in India.

This stopover lasts now for over 38 years. Juergen flew back to Germany after four months, and I am still in India, and still have not gone to Australia.

On this second visit, India threw a spell on me. The country was vast, bright and warm and the people were helpful, friendly and well meaning. Just a hint of a smile from my side and a big smile would flash back to me.

During this second visit, I also came into contact with India's wisdom and realised how alive it was in the country. I felt immediately familiar with it and it kept me in India. I delved deep into it and started to write articles about it. Though Indian wisdom is proverbial, and I had read the Bhagavad-Gita while still in school,

I had not understood what India's wisdom was really about. I did not know that self-realisation meant to naturally identify with our divine essence. I also did not know the big role that yoga plays in helping us to consciously unite (yoga means unite) with what we truly are. Like most Westerners, I had wrongly assumed that yoga is only about asanas or postures. Yet when I met sages, who explained yogic wisdom, it made immediately so much sense and it was just what by intuition I had always felt to be true.

For the first seven years, I travelled through the country without a permanent place and with minimal luggage. I was roaming in spiritual India, stayed often in ashrams and met many enlightened or supposedly enlightened masters. When after seven years I made a list of the gurus, whom I had met, 36 names were on it. There were famous names such as Osho, Anandamayi Ma and Haidakhan Baba, and lesser-known gurus who were not less impressive like Devaraha Baba, who, people said, was at least 300 years old. He looked it, yet was present and alert, and I liked him. I also had the opportunity for a long conversation with the Dalai Lama.

It was an intense and inspiring time, and my worldview changed in the light of Indian wisdom and so did my attitude towards God, love, life and death.

Actually, it was a hard life. I travelled in full buses or trains in second class, slept in not so clean beds in Spartan rooms, never ate at home since I did not have a home, got hepatitis and malaria, yet I would not have exchanged my life with anybody.

After seven years, I stayed with a guru—Satya Sai Baba—lived seven years in his ashram and got to know the mentality of a devotee first-hand. I went through the ups and downs of a guru-disciple relationship and was convinced that I was lucky to have such a great guru and nobody and nothing could have changed this conviction.

Yet, one day my strong faith in him suddenly slipped away and I felt relieved.

After that and without any intention I became once more attached to another, though unknown guru. He was a wealthy coffee planter with family. I stayed near his centre for almost five years. Yet one day, my faith in him also fell away and again, I felt relieved and free.

Ever since, I live a 'normal' life at the feet of the Himalayas on the outskirts of Dehradun, unconnected to any guru or ashram. I realised only then how many Indians had been weaned away from their valuable tradition due to the English education system. So far I had written articles only in German, but now I also wrote in English as my English had improved over the years. Still, it is not flawless and I hope native English speakers are generous enough to overlook those flaws.

I still travel occasionally and spend the winters often in the ashrams of Sri Aurobindo in Puducherry and of Ramana Maharshi in Tiruvannamalai. I still met gurus, for example Amma, Sri Sri Ravi Shankar and Baba Ramdev, and am grateful to these gurus, yet there is no desire to cling to a guru, because that, what is in them and what makes them attractive, compassionate and competent, is also in me and in everyone, always ready to emerge, if only allowed.

The trust, common in India, that all that happens is ultimately for the best, took hold of me, as well. Indians generally live more in the present than Westerners do. This attitude seems to rub off. By now, I am also more likely to be present in the now.

India and her wisdom changed the quality of my life. I do not believe in God anymore, but I know that there is a divine Presence within. Trust in this Presence has grown over the years and is still growing further. Another important change is not dramatic, yet fundamental: I am not intertwined so closely with my thoughts and feelings anymore. They are still there, but have lost their power, and cannot order me around. As a result, I do not 'have to' be unhappy or angry or hurt or whatever else, but can be myself, including my inadequacies and shortcomings.

Thank you, India!

CHAPTER 1

With Osho in Pune and Kriya Yoga

During my studies at Hamburg University, several of my friends, including the professor who supervised my thesis, were followers of Bhagavan Rajneesh, as Osho was known at that time. They had visited him in Pune, and had come back from there full of enthusiasm and robed in red.

Rajneesh was radical and refreshing in his thinking. He himself had probably not expected that he would have such decisive influence on a whole generation of young Westerners, when, in 1969, he shared his views for the first time with a small group of foreigners in Kashmir. The foreigners were participating in a meditation camp of Maharishi Mahesh Yogi, who had already achieved some fame thanks to the Beatles, and they had invited Rajneesh.

Maybe they regretted their invitation, because Rajneesh did not mince words. He told them that he considered the so-called Transcendental Meditation (TM) of Maharishi as a sleeping pill. It may be calming and good for people who are nervous or cannot sleep. But it is neither transcendental nor meditation. Meditation does not make you sleepy but wakes you —from sleep and dream into reality. It destroys every kind of illusion and reveals that you are god.

Whatever a guru says is usually taken as truth by his followers, yet even gurus may not always be right. I personally had a very good experience with TM, into which I was initiated when I was just 20. However, I also got influenced and stopped meditating after some two years, influenced not by Osho, but by German media which portrayed TM as dangerous and asked parents to watch out that their children don't fall for this 'sect', as they may go mad. The Church had even appointed special officials to have an eye on sects. I loved those 20 minutes of meditation daily morning and evening, but then, I was young and not sure…

Back to Bhagavan Rajneesh. He was a rebel and did not shy away from confrontation. He knew a lot about different spiritual traditions and did not think much of conventions and nothing at all of hypocrisy and sexual repression—fully in tune with the hippy movement. He was nicknamed 'sex guru', after his book 'From Sex to Super Consciousness' made waves. However, he felt misunderstood. "Rather I am an anti sex guru", he once claimed and gave the comparison of coal and diamond. "I am rather against sex, in the sense that I am in favour of the transformation of coal into diamond. I want to transform sex." According to him, this is possible only if one does not suppress it but considers it sacred and is friendly with it. The 'flower children' as the hippies were called, could not have agreed more.

Yet the amazing wave of admiration, which in the seventies and eighties rolled from the West towards Bhagavan Rajneesh might have overwhelmed, if not spoiled him. If nothing else, those many Rolls-Royces, which he owned, point towards it. One of the equivalents for 'God' is 'Bhagavan'. How would it feel to be addressed as Bhagavan in all earnestness and full of devotion, if one has not completely gone beyond good and bad, and beyond the ego?

I did not feel attracted to Bhagavan Rajneesh or Osho, as he called himself later, and wouldn't have made a trip to India because of him, but since I was going to India now anyway, I wanted to make use of the opportunity and see him. Therefore, I flew one week before Juergen to India.

I reached Pune on the evening of 10th December 1979. All hotels near the ashram were full, and I came to know why: Osho's birthday would be celebrated on the next day. Without intention, I had arrived just in time and finally slept on a mattress in the corridor of a hotel.

The programme started in the morning with a talk by Osho. Everybody had to pay ten Rupees and then pass two people who were sniffing at each person's head. Osho was allergic against several synthetic odours, especially shampoos that were not produced by the ashram. I had washed my hair in the morning and did not pass the sniffing test.

A red scarf for another ten Rupees was prescribed and a woman pulled my hair tightly together and made it disappear under the scarf. I saw other people with similar red headgear and we met in the lecture hall in a special enclave that was reserved for us—at a respectable distance from Osho's seat.

Then he came. He drove around the hall a few times in one of his many Rolls-Royces. Then he got down and walked towards his seat, dressed in a long robe and with his trademark cap on his head.

He talked in a low voice and what he said made sense. He interspersed his talk with humorous anecdotes and was a good orator. Nevertheless, I dozed off towards the end of his talk. I was no doubt tired from the flight, yet wondered later how I could have fallen asleep in the presence of a possibly enlightened master and not recall anything he had said. Yet I do not remember my idea of an enlightened master at that time.

In the afternoon, we—around 600 mostly young people from around the world—were packed into buses and driven through the countryside to a hill, to which the ashram was supposed to move in near future. There were no buildings yet, only plans. However, things took a different turn. A couple of years later Osho went to the United States and settled in Oregon. A Newspaper headline screamed "Bhagawan left the country."

The ashram in Pune looked to me as I imagined a university campus in America—young, good-looking people with long hair (women as well as men) in red, flowing robes met everywhere friends and embraced each other. Couples kissed, and everyone seemed so modern, open, extrovert. I did not feel modern, open, extrovert and withdrew into myself. On boards there were advertisements for encounter and other therapeutic groups, and the reason that I did not sign up was not only because the fees were steep. Years later, I saw a video of an encounter group which was highly abusive. The motto seems to have been: what does not kill you makes you stronger.

However, I participated in free 'dynamic' meditations. The intense, fast breathing and the dancing afterwards increased the energy level.

The few people I talked to were all mesmerised by Osho. They felt a close connection with him due to the energy darshan, when he had pressed his thumb against their third eye on the forehead. I was new to the spiritual scene, though during my studies, there were occasionally meditations on weekend retreats and I had read a few books on the topic. Yet most of the time, during meditation, thoughts carried me off. At that time I thought this happened only to me, because during the feedback sessions others recounted how wonderful they had felt and that they had seen light or something else. I believed it. I did not know that thoughts are quick and fleeting like the wind not only in me but in others, too, and that it is not easy to still them. Maybe some of the feedback did not mirror facts but rather wishful dreams.

In Pune, I considered it as possible that the energy darshan created a connection between Bhagawan and his disciple and made meditation easier. I could not test it, because there was a condition attached for being granted the energy darshan: one had to become a sanyasi or rather a neo-sanyasi—Osho had given the traditional, strict Indian sanyas (renouncing the world) a more lenient form. However, I did not want to join a club and dress henceforth in red. So Osho's thumb imprint on my third eye remained out of reach. I deliberately dressed in yellow or blue and avoided red, even if it meant that I miss enlightenment. Strangely, in Pune around Osho, I felt more resistance against the guru veneration than I had felt in Hamburg, and I preferred to remain an outsider.

I was just not mature enough, declared a batch mate from Hamburg University, whom I met by chance in the canteen of the ashram. She could not understand that I didn't recognize Osho as an enlightened master at first sight, and she embraced a woman dressed in red like herself sitting next to her and confided, "I can't talk anymore with non-sanyasis."

The canteen was the place I liked best in the ashram. The food was delicious. There, I made contact with a Canadian woman. After finishing her meal, she took a jar of peanut butter out of her handbag, and began spooning her desert straight from the jar. I laughed. She also laughed and we started talking.

"Have you ever heard of Babaji and Kriya Yoga?" she asked.

I was all attention. "Yes", I replied.

Only a few months ago I had read the 'Autobiography of a Yogi' by Paramahansa Yogananda. He wrote about Babaji and Kriya Yoga, a form of yoga, which Babaji had taught. Babaji fascinated me so much, that I straight away wrote to the organisation in California, which Yogananda had founded. I wanted to learn Kriya Yoga and thereby symbolically connect with Babaji. Subsequently, a long enrolment form came by mail. They would send me monthly lessons that I would have to learn. After one year, my knowledge would be tested and if I passed the test, I would be initiated into Kriya Yoga. It sounded complicated. Furthermore, I was soon to leave for Australia and had no address. I dropped the idea.

Babaji is a great yogi in the Himalayas who over the centuries, and supposedly even today, appears to disciples. He was the guru of Lahiri Mahasaya who lived in the 19th century. Babaji taught him Kriya Yoga. Lahiri Mahasaya was the guru of Sri Yukteswar and Yukteswar in turn was the guru of Yogananda. So, Yogananda stood in direct lineage to Babaji. The stories about Babaji in his autobiography are simply incredible.

Babaji, for example, had promised Lahiri Mahasaya that he would always appear whenever he called him. On his return journey from the Himalayas, Lahiri stayed overnight with friends in Moradabad. He told them how Babaji had once materialised a palace for him. His friends were understandably sceptical and Lahiri's trustworthiness was at stake. He remembered Babaji's promise and called him. Babaji appeared. He allowed himself to be touched and ate with them. However, he reproached Lahiri, "Don't call me for petty things. From now on I will only come if you really need me."

On one hand, the story sounded incredible; on the other hand, I felt that Yogananda would not tell lies. Whatever the case, for me Babaji was the ideal yogi.

And now, in the canteen of Osho's ashram, the woman from Canada mentioned him out of the blue. She continued, "There is a yogi here in Pune, who stands in direct lineage to Babaji and is authorised to give initiation into Kriya Yoga. I am going there this afternoon. Would you like to come?"

"Yes", I answered without thinking twice.

The Canadian stayed in the Blue Diamond Hotel, a rather expensive hotel nearby and we would meet there in the late afternoon. After three days, my visit in Pune had taken an unexpected turn and I felt much better.

On my way to the Blue Diamond Hotel, I saw an astonishing bit of the traditional India:

A young man was sitting by the roadside in front of the ashram. He had spread a bed sheet on the ground. In one corner of it, there was a small altar with a kind of doll. He explained to the spectators that it was his grandmother who helped him. For a couple of rupees from us who were squatting around the sheet he performed astonishing feats. He produced for example two chuckling hens from a hat and I wondered how they could have been so quiet earlier and where they suddenly came from. There was a wire mesh fence behind him.

A trick with my ring astonished me even more. He asked for my ring, wrapped it in a handkerchief and made me touch the hidden ring. Then he gave me a thin stick that I was to hold tight with my hands on both ends, which I did. He then hit the middle of the stick a few times with the ring inside the handkerchief. And lo, I didn't believe my eyes: the ring was suddenly dangling on the stick in between my fists.

The Canadian waited for me already and we took an auto rickshaw into town. She introduced me to Sidoji, a friendly, about 40-year old man. He was a disciple of Hariharananda, who was younger to Yogananda and his 'guru-brother'—they had the same guru: Shri Yukteswar. Yukteswar had sent Yogananda to America to make Kriya Yoga known to the West. Hariharananda stayed with Yukteswar in India and took over the ashram in Puri at the Bay of Bengal after his guru's death. While Yogananda died in America in 1952, Hariharananda died only in 2002.

Sidoji lived in an old house with an inner courtyard and verandas surrounding it. Two boys—his sons—were sitting there engrossed in homework.

We were five foreigners gathered around Sidoji. All of us had come to Pune to see Osho and now we sort of went astray. Sidoji taught us Surya Namaskar, the yogic salutation to the sun, and some breathing exercises as a preparation for the Kriya. He also spoke generally about the Indian spiritual tradition and the importance of Kriya. I did not keep a diary and do not remember the details. Yet one thing I still remember: 'my wife and I have two sons and that is enough for us', he said. 'I know you Westerners will consider it strange, but ever since, my wife and I live together like sister and brother. This is in harmony with our tradition.'

We were amazed. It was in stark contrast to the atmosphere a few kilometres away—in Osho's ashram, where the process of transformation from coal to diamond seemed to take time or perhaps had been forgotten altogether.

I requested Sidoji to give me initiation into Kriya Yoga soon, before I go to Bombay, because I had to meet a friend there at the airport. He hesitated at first, but then agreed and instructed me how I should meditate, breathe and where to put my attention. I was grateful and happy that a connection to Babaji, which I had greatly wished for after reading the 'Autobiography of a Yogi', had come about so unexpectedly.

Soon after I had a beautiful dream. I stood at the bottom of a staircase and saw Babaji at the top, looking at me. On the railing a mala was hanging, which suddenly turned into a snake. I was frightened and called out to Babaji for help. He stretched out his hand and took my hand into his. All fear was gone. I tried hard to imprint his face on my mind so that I would recognize him again. The dream felt very real, yet I woke up from it twice, till I finally reached this worldly reality.

CHAPTER 2

In the jungle and Swami Vivekananda

Juergen came straight from the German winter. I had already forgotten all about the cold and had adapted quickly to India, especially to the warm climate. It seemed normal.

We wanted to take the train from Mumbai to Kerala but could not get a reservation for the sleeper class. It was fully booked. The train left in the evening and was to arrive in the morning. We decided to sit through the night in the general compartment, for which no reservation was required. After a tough, wakeful night in an over-crowded coach on hard, wooden benches, we discovered to our dismay that the journey lasted not one, but two nights.

We reached our limits and it probably showed. A co-passenger graciously offered us his luggage rack. The first travellers to enter the train had occupied those racks. Up there one could stretch out and Juergen and I took shifts. It certainly was a sacrifice for our co-passenger to forgo the luxury of lying flat, but he apparently did not mind. He did not put on any airs of being selfless and suffering silently. He was simply hospitable, and I asked myself whether we deserved it.

Anyway, I noticed that the Indians took those forty hours on wooden benches rather coolly. Do Indians, especially poor Indians, feel hard benches less acutely? I don't think so, because all of them were thinner than we were. However, I guess that their mind gave them less trouble. They just sat there, in the moment, and hardly thought about the forty hours, which they would continue to sit there, whereas we made life difficult for ourselves by fretting over the long time we would still have to survive on those hard benches and by internally resisting the situation. Strangely, it did not strike us, that by resisting we did not improve the situation, but made it much worse.

Ever since those nights in the general compartment right in the beginning of my stay in India, I never spent a night under similar circumstances, but always slept in reserved compartments. By now, there are even fully air-conditioned trains and every night-train carries at least a few air-conditioned coaches. Yet I am glad about the experience of those nights and have sympathy for the people who crowd in front of the general compartment trying to rush in first—to occupy the luggage racks.

The jungle was fascinating and our stay there not as hard as I had imagined. The simple accommodations in the middle of nowhere turned out to be rather comfortable. There were no hammocks and no bonfire. Juergen got permission to stay in forest rest houses, which the British colonial masters had built for their forest officials.

We saw many elephants from close quarters and had often almost overlooked them, because they stood rooted like grey, massive rocks in the thick jungle. It probably was our luck that we did not encounter a tiger or leopard, even though we looked for them, followed their tracks and courageously went in the evenings to the waterholes where they were supposed to be. Strangely, it never occurred to me that it was dangerous to trek through the sanctuary without the protection of a vehicle.

There is no all-India statistics about the number of humans killed or injured by wildlife. If it existed, in all likelihood the numbers would be shocking. With a population now of over 1300 million, the animal man conflict has become a big issue. The international wildlife lobby wants India to increase the number of

In the grassland of Eravikulam wildlife sanctuary in Kerala at an altitude of over 2000 metres (in February 1980).

tigers from around 1700 today and in recent years indeed the numbers increased. Those people in the planning committees abroad are, however, not in danger. In danger are the villagers. Of course, I also hope that tiger, leopards, etc. will survive in India, but Westerners, who have far more space and still have killed off almost all their wildlife, certainly have no right to make any demands on India.

Most people do not realise how densely populated India is. If the USA were as densely populated, the country would have to have 3800 million inhabitants instead of its 320 million! Or reversely, if India was as scarcely populated as the US, only the state of Bihar with its 110 million would be populated in India. The rest of the country would be without any humans…

India is amazingly generous. Here millions (or are they billions?) of monkeys and dogs, apart from tigers, leopards, bears, elephants, snakes, etc. live side by side with human beings. Every living creature is given space. The dictum is not the biblical (Genesis 1.26): "The earth and the creatures on it shall be subservient to man", but a harmonious living together.

Maybe this is the reason why in India miracles do happen. Or should it not be called a miracle, when for several months a leopard regularly visits a cow at night, they both play with each other and the cow licks the leopard's head in all friendship? This actually happened in the village Antoli in Gujarat, in western India. In May 2003, newspapers published an amazing photo, which showed the leopard and the cow cuddling close to each other. One of their clandestine rendezvous was filmed with a camera hidden in the house of the farmer, who owned the cow, and shown on Indian television.

From Times of India on 14.5.2003 - a truly miraculous friendship between a cow and a leopard.

Juergen and I had finally visited all main wildlife sanctuaries in Kerala and neighbouring Tamil Nadu, even the grassland of Eravikulam, which lies at an altitude of above 2000 meter in the mountains and is home to the Nilgiri Tahr. Jürgen suggested we travel to the Southern tip of India, called Kanyakumari, which is a place of pilgrimage. At a little distance off the coast, there is a huge rock. In December 1892, a young man swam to this rock to meditate for a couple of days all alone. He had wandered around India and was a disciple of the spiritual master Ramakrishna, who had died in Calcutta some years earlier, in 1886. The young man had fire in his belly. He realised that his compatriots had fallen into torpor under British colonial rule. He wanted to wake them up, give them back their self-worth and pride of their tradition.

During his meditation, he felt that he should participate at the World Congress of Religions in 1893 in Chicago, as advised by a Maharaja friend of his. There, he wanted to present Advaita Vedanta, probably the most beautiful flower among the different Indian philosophical systems. Advaita Vedanta is contained in the last part (anta = end) of the Vedas (Veda = knowledge), the most ancient scriptures of humanity, and postulates that the manifold appearances in this universe are a sense deception. Basically, everything is a unity (a-dwaita = not two)—a view to which quantum physics meanwhile also subscribes and which radically questions our traditional worldview.

He went to America and his presentation became a huge success. There he sat on the dais and was soon to give his talk. He got up, a young man of 30, dressed in a long silk robe, with a silk turban on his head—both given to him by the Maharaja—and began his talk, "Sisters and brothers of America". He could not continue to speak. Thunderous applause greeted him for several minutes. What had happened? "He was the only one who *meant* what he said", a commentator explained it at that time.

This man became world famous as Swami Vivekananda. He contributed significantly to the renaissance of Indian wisdom in India and the West. His photo is prominently displayed in many Indian houses: his arms crossed, a proud, bold glance from huge, dark eyes under a turban.

Juergen and I did not have to swim. We boarded a ferry, which was packed to capacity with pilgrims. The tiny island is now a memorial for Swami Vivekananda. At a bookstall, I bought 'Jnana Yoga', the 'Yoga of wisdom' and 'Raja Yoga', the 'Royal Yoga'. The books contained talks that Vivekananda had given in America.

First, I studied 'Jnana Yoga' and was amazed. Swami Vivekananda expressed exactly what I somehow always felt to be true. For example, he questioned the reality of the world that we perceive with our senses. As a child, I had often had very vivid dreams and when I was awake, I would sometimes ask myself, whether, maybe, I am dreaming now? How could I know? I could not. And now, Swami Vivekananda claimed that the so-called reality is also like a dream. It does not have reality per se. It is a sense deception, in a similar way, as at dusk a rope is mistaken to be a snake, even though in reality there is only a rope.

Truly true, he claimed, is our own inner being that permeates everything and makes all appearances miraculously shine forth. It is infinite. It is unimaginable, because it cannot be looked at. It is not an object. It is however possible to *be* it. Rather, we *are* it already. All is this oneness.

Vivekananda Memorial at Kanyakumari in 1980 where I bought Jnana Yoga.

Vivekananda told his American audience frankly, what he thought about their society. He considered it hypocritical. 'What is the use of your proud talk about your society, if truth has no place in it?' he asked. 'What you call progress is according to me nothing more than the multiplication of desires. And if one thing is clear to me, it is this: desires bring misery,' was his analysis.

He also was critical of religion. He admitted that it may be helpful for weak people, but he also asked, 'Are not all prevalent religious practises weakening and therefore wrong?' He considered religion as kindergarten. Consequently, he considered it meaningful to be born in a religion, but advised, not to die in it. He wanted strong human beings who worship the spirit by the spirit. His ideal he expressed in a few words: 'to preach unto humanity their divinity and how to make it manifest in every movement of life.'

What bold thoughts and what clarity! What power and energy! He started the Ramakrishna Mission, which runs schools, hospitals, bookstalls and ashrams all over India. This mission is very much alive today and probably will remain so for a long time.

Vivekananda's health had suffered during his early wanderings through the Indian countryside, and he died in 1902, nine years after his spectacular triumph in Chicago. He was only 39.

I liked Vivekananda's second book 'Raja Yoga', the royal yoga, as well, but it discouraged me somewhat. It demanded too much: 'Whoever wants to be a yogi, must practise hard, must take care of his diet, live alone if possible, not talk much, and fully concentrate on the goal…' I would have liked to become a yogi, I would have to change my life completely and that seemed impossible.

However, his books sowed a seed. Vivekananda introduced me to the Indian wisdom, for which I am immensely grateful to him. Over time, it became clear, that I wanted to live in tune with this wisdom. Soon, circumstances arose, and I encountered persons who helped me—without any drastic change in my life.

CHAPTER 3

Encounter with a 300-year-old Sadhu: Devaraha Baba

Juergen and I went to Delhi. It was April and hot. Juergen got ready to return to Germany and I wanted to catch a glimpse of the eternal snow in the Himalayas before moving on to Australia.

"Go to Haridwar on the Ganges. A big festival is being celebrated there right now", Rajesh Bedi, a photographer, suggested to me. We had visited him and his brother Naresh in their house on the outskirts of Delhi. They lived in a joint family and both had already made a name for themselves in wildlife photography and documentary filmmaking. "Haridwar is only five bus hours away from Delhi and from there you can travel to the higher ranges of the Himalayas."

Haridwar (also called Hardwar) is one of the very sacred places in India. No meat is sold there, and ascetics, sadhus (wandering monks) and pilgrims dominate the scene. Haridwar means 'door to god' and is the starting point for the popular pilgrimages to the temples in Badrinath, Kedarnath, Gangotri and Yamunotri, which are situated above 3000 meters altitude in the Himalayas.

Rajesh did not mention this. He knew Haridwar and was familiar with the circumstances there. He also did not mention that the big festival was a religious festival. That, too, was obvious to him, because in India almost all festivals have a religious background and he didn't consider it necessary to enlighten me about facts that everyone knew. He sent me to spiritual India, which is so different from Western countries and where he still had his roots, in spite of his professional success, his youth and a certain Western orientation.

Yet I didn't know this. I also didn't know that in Haridwar a long pilgrimage—inwardly and outwardly—would start and keep me in India for over 38 years and maybe until I die. His advice on leaving his home therefore perplexed me greatly: "Don't forget about god", he said while shaking hands Western style. He said it in a way, as if it was proven that god existed. It sounded natural and not at all artificial. I wondered why completely normal, young, not at all pious looking Indians talk so freely about god and believe in him so matter-of-factly. At Hamburg University, we would have rather bitten our tongue than admit that we believed in god.

I went to Haridwar. The bus headed north on the narrow, dusty road. In spite of the draught of air, it was painfully hot, and my clothes stuck to the plastic seat. Shortly before reaching our destination, the bus was waved down. Men in uniform boarded it. They wanted to see vaccination certificates against cholera. I did not have one and thank god, nobody insisted on giving me an injection. "It is a precautionary measure, because millions of pilgrims are expected", an officer kindly explained to me. It dawned on me that it was indeed a huge festival, where I was heading. It was the ardha (half) Kumbh Mela, which is celebrated in between the purna (full) Kumbh Melas which take place every 12 years. The full Kumbh Mela is the biggest religious festival on earth according to the Guinness book of records, yet the half Kumb Mela, 6 years after the full Kumbh Mela, also attracts enormous crowds.

In Haridwar, I went by rickshaw from hotel to hotel. No rooms available anywhere! Finally, I got a room in the tourist bungalow under the condition that I move to the roof terrace during the main festival days, because all rooms were booked. I agreed and then only noticed that I had landed up at one of the best places in Haridwar: in front of the building the channelled Ganges shoots past with tremendous speed, and behind the building the rest of the Ganges gets used to the plains after the exciting journey through deep gorges in the Himalayas and flows leisurely in a broad riverbed. There was even a spacious garden for the afternoon tea, and an old, friendly gardener almost daily gave me flowers. "Offer them to Ganga Ma", he said, and I threw them obediently into the holy water.

Some foreigners stayed there, as well—Americans, Australians and Italians. We got in touch with each other. They were without exception on the spiritual path and waited for their guru—a woman, who was soon to arrive. Her name was Anandamayi Ma. She was already old, above eighty, and an American assured me that god was clearly shining through her person.

I determined to find out what 'god' means, because this concept came my way more frequently in a few days here in India than in ten years in Germany. But how to find out about god? I postponed the investigation. It was too hot anyway.

A few days later, I met an impressive man.

I sat on the bank of the Ganges and saw on the other side of the broad riverbed a wooden hut on poles right on the sandy beach. An American, whom I knew from the tourist bungalow, waded through the Ganges straight towards me. "Would you like to see an extraordinary man? If so, I help you cross the Ganges", he made me curious. "Over there, in that hut, Devaraha Baba is presently living. He is supposed to be more than 300 years old and enlightened. He is one of those who know what life is all about. And it is always worthwhile to meet such people."

Of course, I was interested; we crossed the Ganges together. The river had appeared so peaceful and calm from the bank, yet the current was amazingly strong and the stones on the ground were slippery. I was glad that my companion was over two-meter tall, and gave the impression that there was nothing to fear.

Devaraha Baba had obviously watched us coming, because he scolded us, when we reached him. It was far too dangerous to cross the river. We should take the bridge, which was about two kilometres up the river. A sadhu, a sort of monk with matted hair piled high up on his head, translated this for us.

Devaraha Baba, the ancient yogi who was said to be at least 250 years old.

Baba waved us closer and asked me where I came from. He benignly nodded his head a few times. He murmured a mantra in Sanskrit and asked us to repeat it line by line.

Then he instructed the sadhu to give us sugar candies, so many, as we just managed to hold with both our hands. With difficulty, we wrapped them into a shawl, including those, who had landed in the sand. Baba gave us his blessing and sent us abruptly away. He turned to others, who had come by car via the bridge and carried a basket full of fruits to him.

Back in my room in the tourist bungalow I noticed that I liked Baba. In fact I like him very much. My heart jumped with joy at the thought that I would see him again the next day—almost as if I was in love, which seemed inexplicable.

From then on, I went every morning to him. Sometimes I walked over the bridge, sometimes I waded through the river with the tall American and sometimes I got a lift by a car. On one of those lifts, an elderly gentleman told me that his grandfather took him to

Devaraha Baba ever since he was a small boy. And his grandfather had assured him that, when he himself was a small boy, Baba looked already like a very old man.

Baba usually sat on the narrow wooden balcony that was supported by poles. One could only see his head with the unkempt, long hair and the aged bluish eyes. His arms were hanging down from the balustrade and he often raised his hands to give generously his blessing.

Occasionally he was not there. Then he either was in the small room behind the balcony or took a bath in the Ganga, and all of us, who had come for his darshan, were sitting in the burning sand, from time to time dipping a handkerchief into the Ganges and placing it on our heads to cool down. Sometimes we waited for half an hour and not a single tree nearby to give us shade. The Indians quietly chanted "Siya Ram, Jay Siya Ram". They could chant those names hundred, thousand and probably even million times without feeling tired.

Why did we wait so meekly? I could not find an explanation. Yet I also didn't want to leave, even though at times my mind played up and resisted the waiting, when the discomfort became too evident. I asked myself, why I took upon myself the heat, the waiting, the hot sand, just to see an old man. I wondered whether the others also faced such rebellious thoughts. Nobody left.

Then, when all of a sudden the door opened and Baba appeared on the veranda, a whisper went through the crowd and it surged towards him. The atmosphere was suddenly charged and light. The heat and the waiting were forgotten. He radiated strength, confidence and above all kindness, when he, like a father figure, compassionately inquired about the problems of his devotees or brushed them aside, whatever he felt was more appropriate.

It was an odd picture:

On one side there were cultured, often rather wealthy people, the ladies in silk and with lots of jewellery, and their car parked nearby with a driver waiting. And yet they were the supplicants, who with folded hands and barefoot tripped from one foot to the other to avoid burning their delicate soles in the hot sand and imploringly looked up to Baba, hoping, that his blessing would make their difficulties vanish and fearing, that maybe they won't get what they wanted or that he would give them a short shrift and not spare time for them.

And on the other side up on the balcony there was the ancient Baba, naked, with unkempt hair, but free—free from fear, free from desires, free from the world and full of confidence and radiance.

No matter which problems his devotees had mentioned, his advice was basically always the same:

'Trust in god, think of him, repeat his name, hand over your worries to him, and don't be attached to the world, to family and money. Make god the centre in your life. Develop love for him and do not be afraid, because everything is in his hand. Understand that the world has nothing worthwhile to offer to you. Find out, who you really are. Realise that god and you cannot be separated.' And:

'Always tell the truth. Be righteous. Contribute to the welfare of society. Don't harm anyone and help, wherever you can. If you honour dharma (right way of living), dharma will protect you.' And so on.

His devotees probably had heard this umpteen times. Yet they rushed to him whenever they got a chance to hear it again. Baba was by far not the only one, who gave this advice. During the festival, I heard it being broadcasted via loudspeakers to the crowd from many platforms. Often those sermons sounded like obtrusive advertisement. I realised that all depended on who gave the sermon. Was it someone who wanted to show off or who wanted to be helpful? Did he know what he talked about when he spoke about truth, trust in god and having no fear and desires or did he not know it and he himself was still full of desires and fear, didn't quite trust god and knew about truth only by hearsay? Regarding Devaraha Baba, I was sure that he was genuine. I could sense that he wished us well and that he couldn't quite understand why we take our problems so seriously and why we don't just shake them off and laugh about them.

One morning, Baba had disappeared. I saw it from my window already before breakfast and did not want to believe it. The few sadhus, who stayed around him, had dismantled the hut before dawn and moved with him to Varanasi. The sandy beach on the other side of the Ganges looked now very deserted—painfully deserted.

Some ten years later, in 1991, I stood in the queue in the dining hall of the Aurobindo Ashram in Puducherry. A friend joined the young man in front of me and they started talking in English. Suddenly I listened to them intently. "Really? Devaraha Baba has died?" I butted in. They nodded their head. "Yes. Devaraha Baba has left his body."

A film passed before my inner eyes. I saw him sitting on his balcony in bright sunlight with long, unkempt hair, murmuring mantras and his hand raised for blessings. I was grateful to him that he had been here with us. And personally, I was especially grateful to him for a small episode:

It was in Haridwar, shortly before he disappeared: It was the first and only time that I took courage and talked to him. I told Baba that I would like to stay longer in India—longer than the tourist visa allows. The sadhu with the pile of matted hair on his head translated that Baba gave me his blessing. Yet Baba didn't seem to agree with the translation. He spoke with a lot of gestures to the sadhu, who again turned to me and said: "Baba gives you his special blessing."

CHAPTER 4

Nobody there behind those eyes of Anandamayi Ma

The foreigners in the tourist bungalow had made the journey to Haridwar primarily because of Anandamayi Ma. They considered her as their guru.

"She is coming tomorrow morning!" Manfred from northern Italy called out to me over the balcony. "Come with us to the railway station to meet her." He didn't have to persuade me. I was curious about Ma, because I remembered seeing a photo of her in Paramahansa Yogananda's 'Autobiography of a Yogi': Yogananda, Anandamayi Ma in the middle, and her husband, who looked much older. The photo was taken in the 1930s and showed a beautiful, attractive woman. Almost fifty years had passed since then and I was surprised that she was still alive and anyone could meet her.

At dawn, we went by rickshaws to the railway station. Even at that early hour pilgrims flocked to the Ganges in a steady stream. They were mainly poor people, who carried their bundle of belongings on their head or over the shoulder. The railway station, too, was already full of people and activity: groups of travellers sat in between their luggage, the women in saris of the brightest colours and some of the men with similarly colourful turbans on their head. Children ran around—their mothers calling out for them or sitting quietly breastfeeding a baby. Boys offered 'Chai' with strong voices.

Dogs were sniffing around in search of something eatable. Sadhus sat in a pose of meditation with one elbow resting on a wooden crutch or inhaled, with hands cupped, from a chillum. And some figures wrapped up in sheets were soundly sleeping on the ground.

Here I was at that early hour, waiting for Anandamayi Ma. A group of Indians were conspicuous by their neat and well-groomed appearance. They were devotees of Ma.

Then, hooting, the train from Varanasi pulled in and screeched to a halt. Four young men in spotless white dhotis, the traditional substitute for trousers in northern India made of thin, starched cotton, entered the first-class compartment and carried Ma out on a chair, to which four handles were attached. Ma appeared delicate, was wrapped in white cotton cloth and her black, oiled hair fell over her shoulders. She looked at us with calm eyes. There was no reaction on her face, no sign of recognition of her devotees, many of whom she would have known for decades. She simply looked, and her eyes moved slowly around the group. It was pleasant, and I had the strange feeling, that nobody was there behind those eyes.

When I saw her like this, my reaction came as a surprise: tears were rolling down my cheeks. I was neither especially happy, nor sad. There was no reason for tears to well up and yet they kept flowing and didn't want to stop. "That's normal, when one is touched by a great soul", someone next to me, who had noticed it, reassured me. And indeed, I had the feeling that I had been touched by a very pure soul.

Anandamayi Ma went to her ashram in Kankhal and we followed her in taxis. Kankhal extends to the south of Haridwar and in 1980, it was still idyllic, quiet and laid-back. It mainly consists of large ashrams surrounded by boundary walls.

Ashrams are often compared to monasteries, and in a sense, this comparison is valid: its residents are ideally striving for god- or self-realisation (god and self are interchangeable in Indian philosophy). Yet there is a major difference: an ashram comes up around an extraordinary human being: an enlightened master or at least someone, who is spiritually above average. That person attracts attention, because s/he rests in the innermost being and does not

Anandamayi Ma as a young woman.

seek any benefits for her own person. People, who are interested in knowing the truth, want to stay near, because someone, who knows the truth, is said to be of invaluable help to someone, who wants to realise it. So they erect huts or build houses and an ashram is taking shape. It usually continues to exist, even when that personality dies without a designated successor. Henceforth the tomb, called samadhi, becomes the focus of veneration, as it is supposed to have power. Anandamayi Ma's samadhi in Kankhal is today such a focus, since her death on 27th August 1982.

The taxi stopped at the gate of Ma's ashram. Flower vendors eagerly awaited us. They offered garlands of jasmine, marigold or even roses, which shed a wonderful fragrance. Everyone entered the ashram with either flowers or fruits in his hands.

In the centre of the courtyard, a chair was placed for Ma. She sat down and we, about thirty people, were standing around her. Now she asked some of her devotees, how they were doing, whether everything was okay and so on. The questions were commonplace, and yet there was a sense of sublime sacredness in the air.

Then with a garland in his hands, somebody went up to her and kneeled down. He placed the garland at her feet and his forehead on the ground. Two women assistants, who sat on the floor left and right to Ma's chair, threw the garland over his head. Then he got up, slowly and with folded hands, his gaze fixed on Ma and probably hoping that she, too, would look at him, which was not always the case. One by one people went up to her like this, including my foreigner friends and it became plain to me, that the garland in my hands was waiting for a similar destiny.

I walked up to Ma, kneeled down and put my flower garland at her feet and my forehead on the ground. When I lifted my head again and looked up to Ma, she looked above my head towards the group. I went back to my place disappointed. "When you couldn't see, Ma looked down at you", someone next to me kindly whispered into my ear. I had noticed it already on the railway station, and now, in the courtyard, I noticed it again: her gaze was different. It touched the heart and widened it. And it was painful, when it was withheld. Because of her short, fleeting gaze and the feeling that it induced, I went from then on every evening by rickshaw to Kankhal.

Was Ma enlightened? I didn't know, but felt, it was possible. Melita Maschmann, a journalist, who has lived in India since 1963 and written several books, two of them about Anandamayi Ma, was the only other German in the courtyard and she explained to me what enlightenment meant:

'Ma sees in everything and everywhere only the one god, i.e. her own self. For her, 'others' don't exist. She herself has said that only because of convention she differentiates between herself and others. In truth, she doesn't see a difference and there is no difference.'

So, basically there is no difference between an enlightened being and us ordinary mortals. We differ only in one aspect: an enlightened being lives in that oneness, feels it, is at home in it, whereas we think that we are separate and even prefer to hold on to this illusion, though we, of course, are also at home in the oneness. Oddly, we *want* to be separate; we are fond of our person, our thoughts, feelings, relationships, memories, hopes and even our worries and pain. We are used to the illusion. It is familiar and almost everyone shares it. So far, we were okay. Why should we give it up? Just because of the truth?

Few are ready for it in spite of the assurance that truth is heaven and illusion is hell in comparison. All our suffering originates from our imaginary isolation and is completely unnecessary, claim the sages. We don't need to be afraid of the truth. In fact, truth is the fulfilment, for which we unconsciously long for.

I tried to imagine what Anandamayi Ma perceived, while she looked at us. Did she see our bodies and her own among them as fleeting, transitory waves on the one ocean, while she felt immersed in its immense depth and vastness?

Concepts like truth and god, which had hardly figured in my vocabulary in recent years, seemed in the Indian context important, relevant and natural.

"Life is meant to realise the truth. Truth has to come first. Everything else is secondary", Anandamayi Ma claimed and did not compromise on that. It seemed logical, if we are indeed taken for a ride by our senses and take falsely an illusion for the truth. And doesn't science, too, maintain, that the perceived, manifested multiplicity in this universe is a deceptive appearance and that in truth everything is one, a whole?

For the majority of Indians it does not matter, whether the one is called God, Brahman or Allah. "There is only one supreme being.

Sages call it by many names", is stated in their Vedas, the oldest scriptures of humankind. This view is probably one of the reasons, why Hindus, compared to Christians and Muslims, are more generous regarding differing worldviews. I have not yet met a Hindu, who depicted Jesus Christ in poor light, on the contrary, most hold him in high regard. On the other hand, most Christians tend to depict Krishna, whom Hindus revere as an incarnation of god, in poor light and sometimes even as a devil.

Ma talked about god as if he was naturally the dearest friend we had in this world. She saw that it was true and did her best that we also could see it. When scholars put questions to her, she argued highly philosophically and gave inadvertently proof that she, who had attended a village school in today's Bangladesh for only two years, not only knew the scriptures but knew them from direct experience. Scholars were impressed by her. Many came.

On the other hand, she formulated the essence of Advaita Vedanta, the highest wisdom, in clear and simple terms:

"Behind all the different, perpetually changing names and forms in this universe there is only 'one thing'—Bhagawan, god or however you like to call it. *That* alone is eternal, ever the same. This god plays with himself as it were. All appearances are contained in him, like in a mirror. He is the I of our I. Life is meant to realise this—to realise who we really are and drop the wrong identification with our person."

Her words had power, probably because she was genuine and said only, what she definitely knew was true.

For example, when her mother had died and was laying out in the ashram, Ma was cheerful and laughed her hearty laugh as usual. Her devotees felt that her behaviour was not quite appropriate for the situation. Ma reacted surprised: "Why? Nothing has happened!" For her dying was like changing a dress. Who would be sad over losing an old dress, when one is still fresh and alive?

In May, when the temperature shot above 40 degrees Celsius in Haridwar, Ma moved to Dehradun in the foothills of the Himalayas. Dehradun is some 800 meters above sea level and the temperature a few degrees lower. During the following years, this city became the place in India, where I felt most at home.

Anandamayi Ma towards the end of her life as I knew her.

A wealthy couple had built a cottage for Ma in their spacious compound on the outskirts of the town on Rajpur Road. Towards evening, around sunset, Ma would give darshan there. She sat on a cot on the veranda, behind her the outline of the first range of the mountains against the evening sky that changed into ever new shades of colour. The atmosphere was uplifting and pure.

While waiting for Ma, we were singing the Hanuman Chalisa and other devotional songs, and the repertoire of such songs seemed infinite. Once, a girl of about ten sat next to me. She sang full throatily, yet a little out of tune. Her clapping of hands was also slightly out of rhythm. When I heard her singing like this and felt her presence next to me, I liked her more and more. My heart went out to her and was overflowing with love.

Then the veranda door opened and Anandamayi Ma appeared, supported by two women. Even before she reached the cot, she briefly stopped, half turned and looked sort of irritated into my direction. When she finally sat down on the cot, her glance settled on me for a long time—so long, that the three women sitting behind me afterwards whispered about it to each other. Yet this time, Ma's glance did not strike me or induce any feeling. It seemed as if there was no centre that could have got struck and affected. I simply looked back at her.

Probably Ma's glance was attracted by the love that I felt for that girl and probably she really did not perceive us as separate persons. After all, she often declared that it is a mistake to consider oneself as separate from others. But certainly all of us, as we were sitting there on the veranda during her daily darshan, wished that she appreciated us *personally*. And if we were honest, we most likely even wished that she appreciated our own person a little more than the others.

But Ma didn't oblige. She was not consistent in her attention and affection, as Devaraha Baba had also not been consistent. Sometimes he had suddenly and abruptly turned to someone else and left one abandoned and ignored standing in the sand. A genuine guru can see, even if his disciple cannot see it, that the ego is the culprit who makes life difficult. Naturally, he is not interested in flattering the ego and strengthening it—on the contrary.

"The association with an enlightened being consists in getting blows for the ego", Anandamayi Ma once remarked. My ego felt sometimes the blows, for example, when she did not look at me for long and it reacted with heavy, resentful thoughts. On the other hand, I felt attracted to Ma, because I learnt around her almost effortlessly a new way of life—for example that everything is right as it is.

"Trust in Bhagawan. He certainly will look after you and all your affairs, if you really put full trust in him and if you dedicate all your energy to realise your self. You then can feel completely light and free", Ma claimed, and it sounded convincing. By 'Bhagawan' she meant the formless essence in everything. However, this essence is not something abstract and cold. It is love and can be experienced as the beloved. She also said, "You are always in his loving embrace."

No doubt, there had to be something far greater and far more intelligent inside me than this Maria who I think I know. I, as Maria, cannot even manage the functioning of my liver. And what about coordinating all those billion cells in my body? An impossible task. It also made sense to me that that great being is the source of love. Where else would love come from? Anandamayi Ma drew my attention to that Great Spirit in me, in whom it is possible to feel fully safe and protected.

CHAPTER 5

Atmananda—a woman from Austria

I had noticed Atmananda right in the beginning in the surrounding of Anandamayi Ma in Dehradun. She was already above 70, had her head shaven and wore a simple, orange coloured cotton sari—the orange colour symbolising the fire of knowledge that has ideally burnt up all worldly desires. Yet she was not the type who wanted to show off her stand. Once she disclosed to me the reason why she wore orange. "You know, in India one gets invited to so many functions—first of all of course to weddings, but then, when a baby is born to the naming ceremony, then again to the first haircut and so on. If I wear orange I don't have to explain why I don't come."

A tiny cottage on Rajpur Road was her domicile. As I found a place on the same road a few hundred meters away, where I used to stay frequently during the early 1980s, we became good friends and had long, for me very inspiring talks. In spite of her age, Atmananda was amazingly aware, interested, open minded and knew for each topic an appropriate comment by Anandamayi Ma or other saints like Ramakrishna Paramahansa, Swami Vivekananda, Ramana Maharshi and others.

Atmananda was twenty-nine and called Blanca, when she started on her journey to India from Vienna. That was in 1935 and she never went back to the West—soon had no family left where she could have gone back to. Atmananda was Jewish, and she sometimes wondered, whether her grandmother, who was 90 when she was taken to the Nazi concentration camp, could die before being forced into the gas chamber. Her father had managed to escape to the United States, yet survived only for a few months after his arrival there. However, there was no bitterness, when she recounted this to me, a German.

I asked her, how she came to Anandamayi Ma. Originally, she had come to India because of Jiddu Krishnamurthy. Already as a teenager, she had admired him and finally taught English for full 18 years in his school in Varanasi. In addition, she gave piano concerts for All India Radio.

Occasionally she heard the name of Anandamayi Ma. Yet she was not particularly interested. She was more interested in meeting Ramana Maharshi, the great sage from Tiruvannamalai. However, during the Second World War, she was classified as a national from an enemy country and restricted in her movements.

Then an Englishman, Lewis Thompson, came to her school in Varanasi. She, as the only other foreigner, was asked to look after him. The newcomer was seriously in search of the truth. When he had not found spiritual guidance in England and France, he came to Sri Lanka, at the age of 23. Thereafter he spent seven years near Ramana Maharshi in Tiruvannamalai. Otherwise, too, he had met many great spiritual personalities of that time, even those who were not easily accessible and known only to insiders.

Atmananda stressed that he had a sharp intellect, was very analytical and radically pushed aside everything that he felt was not genuine. When Atmananda talked about him, I could sense that she liked him. Yet only when I read her diaries, which were published after her death, I realised how much she had liked him. Thompson was a poet, overly sensitive, had often not a single paisa in his pocket, did not look after his health because of financial constraints and died early—in 1949, four years after he had landed up in Benares. He was forty. It was painful for Atmananda.

Thompson had come to Varanasi because of Anandamayi Ma. She happened to stay at Sarnath at that time, where Buddha gave his first sermon after his enlightenment. Thompson started off and wanted to be back in the evening—and did not show up for three days. He had not taken any change of cloth and in the school opposite his room, there had been a case of cholera. Atmananda concluded that he must be sick. She bought medicine and went by rickshaw to Sarnath. There she found Thompson hale and hearty and completely enraptured by Ma. "She surpasses my highest expectations. It is incredible, how profound her answers are", he gushed.

Anandamyi Ma sat on the veranda of a pilgrims' shelter, surrounded by Buddhist monks. Atmananda, too, felt that something fascinating emanated from her. From then on, she walked every evening to Sarnath and before sunrise back to Varanasi to reach in time for her English class.

Once, late at night, she had a talk with Ma. "What she said was so simple and convincing that I wondered why I had not discovered it myself. She said only a few sentences, actually nothing new, and yet—the effect was out of proportion. It was as if someone had switched on light and I suddenly clearly saw the path. I was confident that I would always see the next step before me. My thoughts had not stopped to wander, but worries had stopped", she recollected.

"For everything there is a right time. Nobody can come to me if the time is not right", Ma used to say. The time was right for Atmananda to come in close contact with Ma. It was the year 1945—when she was completely alone in this world.

Atmananda was proficient in languages. Her mother had died at the birth of her sister, who was two years younger and the father employed ayahs in his upper middle-class home in Vienna—one after the other from Italy, France and England, so that his daughters would learn languages. In India, Atmananda further learnt Hindi and Bengali and often translated for foreigners or South Indians, when they talked to Ma. She kept a diary about those talks and published them in the monthly magazine of the ashram. Occasionally I helped her with typing or proof reading and thereby came to know from close quarters how Ma responded to each one and to human problems in general.

Ma stressed that a guru was necessary on the spiritual path. In the same way, as one needs a guru for maths or physics, one needs a guru on the spiritual path, she claimed.

On one hand, I could see her point, yet on the other hand, I did not want a guru. Atmananda knew how I felt. She herself had gone through a similar struggle, because Jiddu Krishnamurti was vehemently against any kind of guru, and she used to value his opinion highly.

I soon had several occasions to meet Krishnamurti—in his public talks, in discussions with teachers of his school in Rishi Valley and at a reception in a private garden in Delhi. Krishnamurti talked in a low voice and repeatedly asked his listeners to 'see what is'. "*How* can I see what is?" This question popped up without fail. "There is no 'how'!" he answered firmly. "Just see. The truth *is*."

Thousands came to listen to him, and he doubtless looked like a guru, even though he claimed not to be one. During one of his last talks in Chennai (then Madras) in 1985, he suddenly interrupted his talk and sternly addressed a young man in the first row, "Don't stare at me like this. Go to the back!" The young foreigner had probably come early, because it was not easy to get a place in the first row. He obediently got up and went to the back, as told. When I observed him, a sentence of Anandamayi Ma came to my mind: "The association with an enlightened being consists in getting blows for the ego." But how can one know that it is not the ego of the guru which enjoys having power over his disciples?

Atmananda was certain that she had done the right thing when she changed over to Ma and took her as her guru. Yet it was not always easy. She talked of 'operations' which Ma quietly conducted. "They are painful, very painful, these operations and if one would not be certain about Ma's great love, one could take her to be cruel", she told me. Her diaries of her first years with Ma give a good picture what a devotee goes through once he got caught in the net of a guru. More of pain than of joy seems to be the rule.

Atmananda told me that earlier in life she used to flare up at the smallest cause. I could not notice any quick temper anymore. Atmananda was a beautiful human being in spite of her age and the shaven head. Everyone enjoyed her company. She was non-judgemental and accepted each one as he or she was. The time with Ma had obviously benefited her.

Atmananda had given her diaries to Ram Alexander. Ram had come from the US to India as a young man in the early 1970s. Anandamayi Ma offered him to live in her ashram in Kankhal, a privilege that was rarely granted to a foreigner. He stayed in Ma's ashram for about ten years. Thereafter he married and settled in Assisi.

Atmananda felt that Ram was Lewis Thompson reborn. That was the reason why she wanted him to have her diaries and publish them if he thought them to be helpful for others. Ram got them published under the title "Death Must Die". His foreword shows literary flair, yet he does not live in penury in this life. Atmananda's diaries have become a sort of underground bestseller among foreigners. It fascinates, because it is so authentic.

Anandamayi Ma left her body on 27th August 1982 in Dehradun. She barely ate for several months prior to her death. We could see her in her room where she lay on her bed. There was never an expression of pain or revulsion on her face. Once, she vomited when I stood before her. An assistant held a bowl in front of her mouth. She retched and brought up bile, yet her facial expression was completely indifferent. She seemed untouched by what the body went through.

Three years later Atmananda celebrated her 50-years anniversary in India. She was full of energy as usual. Soon after, she fell sick. For two days she lay in her room, looked after by friends, who took her to Kankhal for better medical care. "You will be back soon", a friend said to her when she was sitting in the taxi to Kankhal. "No", Atmananda said firmly. "I go now and won't come back.' It took only three days and she was dead and her body was immersed in the Ganga—a privilege reserved for Sanyasis.

Atmananda had occasionally worried as to who would look after her in case she needed care. Ma had claimed, "Bhagawan looks after you". He has looked after her.

Would He look also after me? Anandamayi Ma maintained that he looks after everybody. In India, it was easier to take her view seriously. I worried amazingly little about my future. Maybe because of the general atmosphere in the country, where most people do not have financial security. In the 1980s, insurance companies had not yet discovered India as a huge potential market—which they meanwhile did. "Trust in God and let him do. He will look wonderfully after you." This German proverb was my motto. From retrospective, it has been the right attitude.

Nevertheless, I needed to become clear about my options. There I was in the middle of India, all alone, with not too much money in my pocket, which steadily decreased, and did not know how I should live my life. Inwardly, things had become clear: my true essence has to take centre stage. Regarding my outer circumstances, I wanted to stay on in India for longer. However, to be able to do this I needed a visa and an income.

An idea crystallised soon in my mind: writing about the Indian view of life. Not everybody has so much time to become familiar with it, and I felt that this view is not only the highest philosophy but also very helpful in practical life. A few months later, I wrote my first article and sent it to a German magazine.

I had hardly dared to hope—the article was published und even reprinted twice.

CHAPTER 6

Rishikesh and Yamunotri in Himalaya

Thanks to my friends from Haridwar, who had introduced me to Anandamayi Ma, Devaraha Baba and several more gurus from that time like Mastaram Baba, I now felt confident to visit other saints as well on my travels around the country. Spiritual India felt like home. I went to reclusive hermits and to famous spiritual teachers, even though I did not quite know, what I wanted from them.

In Rishikesh, half an hour up the river from Haridwar, I heard of a sadhu (hermit), who lived in a cave in the jungle on the left side of the Ganges. I asked for directions on how to reach him and started off. The path disappeared in the thick jungle and I felt apprehensive to move further. A group of monkeys played and chased each other nearby. I sat down on the trunk of a tree and watched them. Suddenly a young man appeared. The white cloth, which he had wrapped around himself, indicated that he was a Brahmachari. A Brahmachari is a kind of novice in an ashram. He wants to experience Brahman and has some rules to follow, for example sexual abstinence.

The young man came towards me. He lived in the ashram of Maharishi Mahesh Yogi which had become famous due to the

Beatles staying there in 1968 for several weeks, learning TM. Incidentally, it was also their most creative phase. Meanwhile, this ashram in Rishikesh has been taken over again by the forest, but then, in the early eighties, it was still functional.

I asked the Brahmachari, whether he knew, where the sadhu lived. He did and offered to guide me. We trekked through the hilly forest and landed at his cave. The Brahmachari called out loudly to him. He appeared, smiled and invited us in. It was a tiny cave and the Brahmachari stayed outside. I sat silently near the sadhu, not only because I did not know what to say, but also, because of language problems. The silence did not embarrass me. My reasoning went like this: if he is enlightened, he accepts me as I am, because he sees that his own self is basically the same as mine. And if he is not enlightened, then it is not my problem.

I liked the hermit and his lifestyle fascinated me. I asked him, how he sustained himself. He showed me a spring nearby. He also knew what was edible in the forest, and locals brought him provisions. Some cooking utensils were lying in front of his cave. I felt sorry that I had not brought anything for him. Day in and day out, he lived alone in this cave in the thick jungle of the Himalayan foothills, where snakes, leopards and elephants roam and where occasionally a visitor like me shows up.

On our way back, the young Brahmachari asked out of the blue, "May I enjoy your company?" I wondered why, because he was already in my company all this while. However, he meant something else. He pointed towards bushes. "Behind these bushes we will be completely undisturbed." I was slightly shocked and reminded him of his vow of celibacy. "You only have a prejudice against Indians", he became unfair. "An American didn't have such prejudice", he continued to complain. "She took a friend of mine, who was a Brahmachari in Sivananda Ashram, with her to America."

Apparently he, like many others, believed, that Western women are 'loose' and easy to get. And actually, his impression may not have been so wrong at that time and maybe even now. “Make love, not war” was the slogan of the hippies, and sadly, many Western girls had set their eyes even on sadhus. A few years ago, I met a German who came from Tibet via Nepal. She told me that many young travellers see it almost as a sport to “break monks”. I wondered what it meant. It meant to make them break their vow of celibacy. She also had seduced a sadhu, with whom she was madly in love. It was no secret. She wrote a book about it, titled “Meeting Shiva”.

My Brahmachari companion was sulking a little, but he led me safely back to Rishikesh.

America may be a dream for many Indians, yet for me, the Himalayas were a dream. I wanted to go up to the temples above 3000 metres—to Badrinath, Kedarnath, Yamunotri and Gangotri. Every year a few hundred thousand pilgrims from all over India go up to them. In the course of years, I visited those temples several times and each time it was an unforgettable experience.

For Indians it probably was strange seeing a lone woman go up to those heights. Some men, mostly heads of families, spontaneously took on the role of a guardian—unobtrusively and for me very comforting. I felt a lot of warmth, from fellow pilgrims, with hardly any talking involved.

The hardship on the journey is even today considerable, but compared to earlier times much less, since busses reach close to the temples. Some decades ago young and old trekked from Haridwar on foot for about 400 km—through difficult, but majestically beautiful terrain. During the nights, they huddled together in simple, open shelters, hoping that no leopard or tiger would attack them, which happened repeatedly.

Today, mainly sadhus, a bundle on their head or over the shoulder and often barefoot, can still be seen occasionally wandering on the roads and are overtaken by crowded, sturdy busses or jeeps which keep moving till the road ends or till a landslide stops them.

Many pilgrims are already old, when they are finally able to fulfil their dream to go up to those heights near the eternal snow, where god's presence is supposed to be felt in a special way. They start on the journey late in life, when their families do not need them anymore urgently. It was touching to watch old, bent women in white saris—a sign that they were widows—braving inclement weather and progressing slowly step-by-step with the help of a walking stick and with tremendous perseverance and determination to reach the goal on a muddy, uneven path.

On my first trip to Yamunotri, the source of the Yamuna river, I took advance permission from the District Forest Officer in Barkot to stay overnight in the Forest Rest House in Hanumanchatti, which was earlier the starting point for the 13 km trek to Yamunotri. (Nowadays one needs to trek only 6 km as the road has been extended up to Jankichatti). Hanumanchatti is a tiny hamlet deep in the Himalayas and I wondered where all those pilgrims who descended from busses in droves would find a place for the night. Thanks to the letter from the District Forest Officer, I got a small single room. The Forest Rest House and all other overnight shelters were overflowing with people. Someone looked into my room and remarked to a friend, "Only one person and so much space!"

Jankichatti is nowadays the road head for the 6 km trek to Yamunotri. Earlier one had to walk 14 km from Hanumanchatti.

This news apparently spread. Soon after, the head of a big family came to me declaring what he probably assumed to be a fact, "Two of my daughters will sleep with you tonight."

I objected, "There is only one bed and no space."

That's how I saw it and I don't think that he understood me. Our Western need for privacy seems odd and incomprehensible for most Indians, and in retrospective I felt bad about it. If I came into a similar situation today, in all likelihood I would take the two girls into my room for the night.

Next morning everybody took breakfast in one of the teashops, and then started on the trek. On foot those who could and wanted to walk. Others, belonging to the middle class, opted for being carried by four men in a wooden chair and again others, thin, old people or children, were placed in a woven reed basket and carried up by one local man on his back. Many took a mule. The price was written on a board and a clause was added: 'for fat people it costs 10 Rupees extra.' The definition was also given, 'Fat is who weighs more than 50 kilos'. Many years later, however, on another trip in 2011, the definition for motiwallahs had changed. "Normal" weight was now up to 60 kg, and the categories "heavy" (between 60 and 90kg) and "very heavy" (above 90 kg) were added.

There was a lot of noise in the bazaar while bargaining for the mode of transport. Yet on the trek it became suddenly very still. The majestic scenery contributed to a quiet, inward looking mood.

"Siya Ram, Siya Ram", a plump woman in her forties, who was carried past me by four strong men, kept murmuring, almost, as if she wanted to make up for the easy way of getting to the top by repeating her mantra with great diligence. Those, who were sitting on mules, also had enough strength to murmur their mantra or even sing it aloud. The pedestrians, however, limited themselves to some encouraging shouts. "Prem se chalo! (Go with love)" the patriarch of a big family for example called over to me. It was the first time that somebody advised me to go with love. Over the years, I heard it several times. To go with love means—being aware of god's presence.

Walking at that high altitude was strenuous and already after two kilometres, the first teashop invited for a break. An old man with a long white beard and turban sat at a little distance trembling—surely not because of cold, for we all were already sweating due to the exertion and the sun was shining. I asked him whether he would like to have a cup of tea. He did not answer, took the two Rupee note that I offered, but didn't order tea.

I continued walking, alone. Part of the path was cut in the slopes of the mountains and followed the bends of the river below. After each bend, a new, fantastic view of the incomparable Himalayas presented itself. The snow peaks came closer. Dark, menacing clouds also came closer, which—according to the locals in the Forest Rest house—would release their heavy load late in the afternoon. Yet the clouds did not stick to the timetable. At noon, it started pouring heavily.

Only those who were very fast were already at the temple. I still had full five kilometres and a difference in altitude of about a thousand metres ahead of me. There was no other way: if I ever wanted to reach up there, I had to walk the way, step by step. This fact was never as clear as during that exhausting, laborious slogging in pouring rain, which higher up changed into snow. The ground quickly turned slushy and my feet in the plastic shoes were wet and ice-cold.

After three hours, I finally reached Yamunotri. The sight was spectacular. The temple was perched high up on an almost perpendicular rock with steps leading up to it. Lower down, water from hot springs was dammed in a pool, and my freezing toes as well as the toes of many others got defrosted there. Then it was time to enter the temple.

It was small, and looked like a temporal structure, unlike the solid, strong buildings in Badrinath, Kedarnath and Gangotri. It was a makeshift. A snow avalanche had destroyed the temple and only the statue of the goddess had been saved.

Close by was a Hanuman temple that had survived the avalanche. I sat down in a corner and was pleasantly surprised: the floor was warm because of the hot springs. The temple priest and the few sadhus, who had made themselves comfortable inside the temple, seemed to understand why I kept sitting in that corner. The atmosphere was relaxed. In another corner of the temple, some sadhus were cutting vegetables for their next meal.

My place there was ideal: on one hand very close to the deity and on the other hand, I could without being noticed observe the pilgrims, who appeared one after the other, fresh after their hot bath and in their hands a tray with a coconut and other items for worship. The hard shell of the coconut symbolises the ego, which, when broken, reveals the sweet milk inside (the god in man). All types of people came—simple villagers and modern city youth in jeans.

Towards evening, when it was already getting dark, he suddenly appeared in the doorframe: the old man with the long white beard from the first teashop. He had made it, yet he was breathless and trembled now even more. In his hands, he held the tray with a coconut. Slowly he came closer, his eyes fixed on the murti of Hanuman. With one hand, he fingered in his shirt pocket and pulled out a two-Rupee note. He put it on the tray and handed the whole to the temple priest.

The priest, a likeable young man with several kilos of matted hair on his head, took a lot of time for him and gave him more prasad (blessed offerings) than what he usually gave. The sadhus, too, were still and watched the old man, who with folded hands and still trembling, gave his full attention as the priest performed arati with his right hand slowly circling a camphor-fed, bright flame leaping up from a shallow messing bowl and with his left hand steadily ringing a small bell. Arati symbolises a respectful greeting of the divine. It shakes all Hindu temples from north to south in the mornings and evenings, because in most cases it is not only that little bell which tingles, but a conch is blown and those present often beat drums, big bells and all kinds of percussion instruments and sing loudly a meaningful and elevating Arati song.

When the priest had finished the Arati, the old man lay down flat on the ground as a sign of full surrender and then walked slowly backwards out of the door.

For some time it was still in the temple. Then a sadhu broke the silence, "What devotion!" and added, "How straining it must have been for him to climb up."

Tapas—this word was heard often during the pilgrimage. It means: to accept difficult circumstances without complaining "for god's sake" literally. There are plenty of occasions for tapas on these treks. The following night, which I spent in a tiny storage room full of provisions at an altitude of 3500 metres, surely also counted as tapas.

For some the hardship proved too much. A well to do and well-fed man of around fifty years did not conduct himself as an ideal pilgrim when a local porter, who was carrying a person in a basket on his back, requested him to make room for him near a teashop. The man kept sitting on the raised platform with a stony face. The local, who was sweating from his heavy load, managed with the help of others to get rid of his basket from his back on the flat ground.

Some pilgrims took the man to task for his unkind behaviour. However, he reacted rudely. Someone showed understanding for his stressed temper. "Shanti, shanti (peace)", he mediated. "It is over. Let us forget it."

Descending the mountain was faster than climbing up. But when I reached Hanumanchatti in the afternoon, the last bus had already left. Only a few private busses were still around, waiting for their groups of pilgrims. I asked one of the drivers, whether he would take me to Uttarkashi. He consented. It took a while until all the members of his group had reached and we started.

At dusk, in a small village, a police officer stopped us. A loud argument flew between the driver, behind whom I sat, and the officer. Finally, we were told to get down. It was forbidden to drive in the dark—no doubt a sensible order, but here, in this village, there would certainly be no places to stay. Indeed there was no hotel or guesthouse. Yet a solution was found. We were altogether 13 women in the bus and a small, bare room was shown to us, in which we were to spend the night. For the men a similar room was found. None of the women complained. They rolled out their blankets and then went outdoors to cook.

I was terrified of the night. We would lie next to each other packed like sardines. Yet luckily, a local lad saw a chance to make some money. "Do you want to rent my bed for 20 Rupees?" he asked. I immediately accepted the offer. Around his bed, there was even a small room. The young man got into the bed of his friend, which stood on a wooden veranda in front of the room. My joy, however, was short-lived. The bedding was full of bugs and sleeping impossible. I complained to the young men on the veranda. They immediately offered me their bedding and took mine in exchange. I fell asleep and both men obviously, too. In the next morning, nobody gave the impression of not having slept well.

I used to think that I can adapt even to difficult circumstances. Yet when I saw how calmly the Indian women accepted the unexpected interruption in their travel programme and how cheerfully the young men welcomed the bugged bedding, my self-image clearly took a beating.

CHAPTER 7

God—who is that?

Ever since Rajesh, the photographer in Delhi, had told me "not to forget about god", I wanted to find out for myself what 'god' means, without referring to books. By now, I had come to realise that, what in English is called god, generally plays a big role in the daily life of Hindus, who form the majority of Indians. In contrast, god seems rather dead in the West. Many people still go to church there on Sundays, but in daily life, god is almost non-existent.

Several months later, when I was again around Anandamayi Ma in Dehradun, I took time out for it. I sat on the roof terrace at night under the stars, and asked pointed questions. My thoughts often took me astray to other topics, but when I noticed it, I brought them back to the question. I simply waited, until answers came. Of course, I had already read about Indian wisdom, yet the answers were my own nevertheless. I was not surprised that they were in tune with Indian wisdom:

"What do I mean by God?"

"That which really exists, the basis of everything, eternal, independent, formless, conscious and mighty.

"God must definitely be here. Why don't I see him?"

"Because he is not separate from me. That is why I cannot see him with my eyes. He rather is that which makes looking out from my eyes possible.

"How can I get close to him?"

"I am close, so close, that closer is not possible."

"But I don't feel it. Why?"

"Because thoughts and feelings fully absorb my awareness and these conceal That which makes thoughts and feelings possible in the first place."

"What can I do that thoughts and feeling go out of the way?"

"Be conscious that they are just thoughts and feelings, simply observe them non-judgementally, do not take them so seriously, and do not identify with them."

"Who am I actually?"

"Deep inside one with God."

"What does it mean`"

"I am not an object, am essentially without form—am conscious with infinity as circumference. The fact that 'I am and know that I am' is stupendous."

"What will happen to my life, if I focus on god?"

"I don't need to worry about it, if indeed I focus fully and sincerely on god who is my inner Self."

I was grateful to Indian wisdom. The concept 'god' refers here not to a transcendent being, separate from humans. The concept refers to the whole, to the oneness, to the base of everything, to our very own being, to That, which really is, though it cannot be touched or looked at and ultimately not even thought of. It refers as it were to a scientific god, to an analysis of truth—and therefore it is acceptable for everyone with an open mind.

However, that does not mean that a Hindu does not think of a personal god, when he calls out "Hey Bhagavan!" He may turn to Rama, Krishna, Shiva, Ganesh, Devi, depending on who is his Ishta Devata, i.e. his most beloved deity. But basically he knows that all those deities are aspects of the One.

I devoured books and read not only about philosophy, but also about the life stories of those great sages of ancient and modern India and their lives touched me. It became clearer what it means to live a meaningful life: If there is one essence responsible for all appearances of this world (and it made sense to me), then I wanted to make this essence the focus of my life. I prayed deeply: Please help me. Let me see the truth; let me see that You are always present.

One day, family friends of my landlord invited me for tea. The head of the family was a protestant priest. I soon discovered the reason for the invitation. They had observed me going to Anandamayi Ma and wanted to bring me back to the 'right path'.

"What benefit do you get from going to this woman? What can she offer you? Jesus is your saviour. He died for you on the cross. Don't you know that you were born into the best of all religions? Hinduism is no equal for Christianity. God has revealed himself in Christianity. Hinduism is only a nature religion. They worship all kinds of things", he started.

It was a strange situation: an Indian missionary trying to make a Westerner a faithful Christian again. I replied that only in India I found back to god—a god who is alive, here and now—and asked him, whether he is not happy about it. I told him that I cannot accept that the Church portrays god as eternally separated from us and regards man as a sinner. I also do not believe in eternal hell. It makes more sense that everyone is permeated by god and finally will consciously merge with him. I also told him that I felt it was very wrong to try to convert Hindus to Christianity, as Indian wisdom comes much closer to truth and the Hindu concept of god is far more solid and won't crumble if one intelligently enquires into it.

I had earlier met Christian missionaries. "Even sadhus come to our talks in Rishikesh", a young Canadian missionary who had a whole box of small pocket Bibles to distribute and gave me one, once proudly told me. "Do you offer anything to eat?" I asked. "Only tea and biscuits", he answered.

Even though I have no sympathy for Christian missionaries, the pocket Bible was welcome. Now I could compare it with Indian wisdom and discovered several quotes in the gospel, which were in tune with it. For example: "The kingdom of god is within you". Or "I and my father are one." "First look for the kingdom of god.

Everything else will be given unto you." "Don't worry about the morrow", and so on.

Unfortunately, those sayings do not have much weight in official Christianity, because the Church stresses on other aspects. The opinion of Saint Paul, which he propounded in his letters, carries crucial weight in the doctrine. He claimed that Jesus was the only indigenous son of god and that through his death and resurrection he saved humankind from the original sin. Paul even said that "your faith is in vain, if Jesus has not been resurrected from the dead".

It is all about belief, for it is impossible to know whether Paul is right. In fact, common sense says that he is not right. How could possibly an alleged event 2000 years ago determine the fate of all future human beings? Yet whoever does not believe those dogmas is eternally damned according to the Church. A genuine enquiry into truth is not welcome.

There are exceptions, but generally, Christian theologians do not look for the truth, as Hindu sages did since time immemorial. They are not concerned with the welfare of all people, but foremost with the welfare of the Church and then, maybe, with the welfare of Christians.

One's own, direct experience of truth is not accepted as touchstone and mystics who experienced truth and openly talked about it, were excommunicated, like the German Meister Eckhart or were burnt to death during the Inquisition. Even today, in the 21st century, the Pope can order members of the Church not to speak out. It happened to the German monk Willigis Jaeger.

The Christian theologians justify dogmas in hair-splitting ways and jealously guard the boundaries to other religions. The Church lives on boundaries, in contrast to the Indian tradition, which reveres not only Ram and Krishna, but also Buddha as an avatar and might incorporate Jesus, as well. Yet the Church will not allow it.

On the other hand, the Church does not hesitate to incorporate Hindu concepts and present them as originally Christian, like meditation and even Advaita philosophy to make Christianity more attractive, and at the same time, it brazenly denigrates Hinduism.

Several years ago, in Shantivanam, a small Christian ashram in south India, I met the head of all Benedictine mission monasteries worldwide, who was based in the Vatican. He had just come from Japan. After dinner we had some small talk under palm trees in Bavarian dialect, since he was from my home state.

I knew it would spoil the atmosphere, but I nevertheless asked him, "Do you think that one day the Church will agree that Hinduism is a valid path?" "But this would go against the self-esteem of the church", he immediately shot back. I was not surprised.

The Church obviously suffers from a superiority complex, which she also injects into her members which she gains or—as is claimed with substantial evidence—buys' in India. In the West, the superiority complex is not so obvious, because Christianity was the main religion since ages and nobody questions its status. But here, in India, the claim that Christianity is better seems preposterous. Indians, however, rarely get into an argument. They are too generous for that.

I asked a young village teacher, himself a Christian, how Christians and Hindus get along in his village in Tamil Nadu state. "Good", he said. And added after some reflection, "The Christians think they have the better god and the Hindus let them think so."

In Christianity, as well as in Islam, the concept of god means the one 'true', personal god, who has clear preferences and dislikes, and who is male. He sends those who do not believe in him for ever into hell, and rewards the believers with heaven or paradise. Everyone should believe in him, and so he sends his followers out to convert. The Christian god has one begotten son and the path to god leads exclusively via his son Jesus Christ. The Islamic god has a last prophet and what he said is valid for all humans for all times.

This type of god is a matter of belief. And belief cannot be the ultimate truth. Truth is that what is, independent of thoughts. The god with form is as it were a symbol for the formless, highest truth. Yet the representatives of the Christian and Muslim god do not seem to realise that the symbol stands for the one, invisible basis of everything; that god permeates Christians, Muslims and Hindus all the same, even animals and so-called dead matter, and nothing would exist without That. They do not realise that 'He' is the one essence in everything in creation.

It is rather incomprehensible that such truth has not yet taken root in the Occident, which considers itself highly intellectual. The reason may be that the intellectual elite is neither interested in god nor in Church, because not very long ago the Church threatened scientists with death when they did not submit to her view, for example that the earth was the flat centre of the universe. The Church finally had to admit that the earth is round—a fact, which the Rig and Yajur Veda stated thousands of years ago.

The Church still insists that only Christianity has the *full* truth and everyone has to join it to be saved— such attitude, which Islam also endorses for itself, is the best recipe for discord in humanity.

CHAPTER 8

Love in India

After my reflections on god, another basic question was about love. I wanted to gain clarity about what love truly is. I had come from Germany not even two years ago, yet my worldview was already badly shaken.

I withdrew deep into the Himalayas—to Nepal, because my Indian visa had expired. A little outside of Pokhara, on the slope of a hill, I rented an isolated mud hut. It looked like a barn—there was only one room with a place to cook on open fire and a wooden bedstead. The door could not be locked. The walls had big holes, which were filled with loose stones. At night, rats were roaming freely outside the mosquito net. On my way to the spring, I would meet only cows and buffaloes. I wanted to be alone and was alone there. I had to change my attitude, if I wanted to be true to my conviction: I had to give less importance to falling in love, which in the West is regarded as highly attractive. And I had to find out more about what the Indian sages mean by 'true' and 'genuine' love.

"True love is not possible between individuals", Anandamayi Ma had claimed. And, "Genuine, true and permanently fulfilling is only the love for god." God here means Brahman, the One that is our Self. I had heard this view right from the beginning of my stay in India. Our 'human loves' don't quite merit the word love, the sages say. They suggest expressions like attraction, dearness, fondness, infatuation, friendship, even delusion for our love-feelings, because there are always egoistic intentions involved. True love however has no hidden agenda and one's ego does not come into the picture. In true love, boundaries disappear.

The following analogy illustrates it:

The wave (individual) is one with the ocean (the whole, god). If the wave fixes its gaze only at other waves, chooses some to give its love to and to receive their love, then this love is limited, small-minded and definitely not as eternal as the wave may dream it is. Eternal is only its oneness with the ocean. The ocean is also much more attractive as a lover, because it is always present, never forsakes one and is mighty and invulnerable. It encompasses all the waves, and the wave is anyway forever one with it. The ocean is its great love, even if the wave does not know it. Incomprehensively and even foolishly, the wave considers itself simply a wave, unconnected with the ocean, and does not even see the ocean because of all those other waves. So naturally, it suffers from the illusion, that it is lacking in love and that it has to look for it among the other waves.

"Don't get caught up in the illusion," the sages advise in one voice. The senses are deceiving you. There is only the One behind all names and forms, whether they are beautiful or ugly. "Think of the projection of a film", says Ramana Maharshi, the sage from Arunachala in South India. "The different persons and their actions are fascinating, but they don't have any substance in themselves. Substance has only the screen, on which they appear. This screen stands for the one consciousness."

I knew not only intellectually that a whole is behind the multiplicity—a fact that nobody can question anymore thanks to the findings of modern science. Therefore, I also knew that the Indians are right when they claim that only love for the Supreme really and permanently fulfils, because it alone truly exists.

However, it was one thing to understand this, and another to live accordingly. I sat on the little mud porch in front of my house, to my right the impressive Annapurna massif, down in the valley the glittering lake and in my head thoughts which almost hurt. On one hand, I could not justify anymore that I like a small bit of the screen more, that my eyes search only for this particular small bit, yet on the other hand the whole screen just did not, in spite of my understanding, appear equally beautiful and lovable. I felt like somebody who knows that the earth moves around the sun, but only sees the sun moving around the earth...

There was another difficulty. When I was honest, my love for God was not very great. I certainly would not have called it 'true love'. Moreover, I could not imagine how I could deeply love the One that is encompassing everything and that is not accessibly to the senses. I felt that at least eyes into which I could look were needed. "Let me learn to love you", I prayed. The second prayer, which had to follow, was more difficult: "Let me not fall in love again, but let me love all equally."

I tried to resign myself to the fact that I would have to manage now with a kind of 'medium' love for everyone for the rest of my life without the occasional highlights that so far had made life worthwhile. I did not quite believe that the 'whole screen' could become my 'great love', compensating me for my renunciation. The One was so incomprehensible, without any substance, like space. However, if I wanted to live with integrity, I had to develop love for it.

By thinking such thoughts I had moved far from normal Western thinking, however in India it is considered normal and important, to develop love for god. After all, life's goal is to realise the truth and there are essentially two methods.

- Jnana, knowledge or wisdom. In jnana the main point is to be aware of the one limitless being, to identify with it and to deny the reality of the manifold appearances continually. This path is more difficult, says Sri Krishna in the Bhagavad-Gita.

- Bhakti, devotion. The main point here is to develop love for god, for one's true self and to dissolve in it. In both cases, the goal is the disappearance of the ego. The bhakti path is easier, says Sri Krishna. And as he knows that the human being needs something tangible to love, he suggests to Arjuna, "Love me". Or love Rama, Shiva, the divine Mother. One has the choice of many personalities with the noblest qualities—as a close companion as it were in one's life.

In contrast to their contemporaries in the West, Indians usually don't expect heaven on earth from the romantic love between a man and a woman. Therefore, they do not give so much importance to falling in love in spite of Bollywood projecting romantic love as true love in tune with Western mores.

Another difference—one usually does not try out, whether a relationship works. Often the parents are searching for a partner, and the ancient scriptures list criteria, which should be considered—a similar family background for example, physical and mental health for the benefit of the offspring. Often horoscopes are compared. However, no consideration is given whether the two young people are in love with each other.

I was surprised that even today, for many young people 'love marriage' is not a priority. They seem not to mind that their parents make the choice.

"The parents have more experience, they know their children and are in a better position to judge who matches them", Sunita, a 23-year-old computer programmer from Bengaluru tried to make me see her point. "I feel it is very risky to bind oneself lifelong to another person just because of bodily attraction. But then, you in the West don't bind yourself lifelong. You get a divorce right at the first quarrel, don't you? I don't like this. I could never feel secure", she added.

"Here in India, love develops after marriage and in the West, it ends with marriage", a young man summed it up half in jest. How long the love lasts has a question mark now also in India. Divorce is not anymore the great exception.

Sunita saw one more disadvantage of the Western model of love marriage: "I would be constantly stressed that someone should fall in love with me. I would always have to show my best side. What terrible stress!"

A friend from South India suffered from this stress. She was pretty and always neatly dressed. Her family was Christian, and her father had told her: "Find yourself a husband, like your sister has done." My friend was not at all happy about his 'modern' attitude. She felt, her father was shirking his responsibility and wanted to save the dowry money. She was already 26 and had a degree in medicine. She had had a boyfriend once. When she, however, brought up the topic of marriage, he disclosed that he had left it to his parents to search for a bride.

Then a German came along. He fell in love with her and asked her to come to Germany and marry him. He went ahead, and she was to follow him. I met her on the evening before she took the flight. She was excited, and proudly showed me a photo of him. "He is interested in spirituality and lived in a Zen monastery in Japan", she shared with me, happy, that he seemed a decent guy. When she reached Germany, she was painfully introduced to the Western life style: the young man whom she considered her fiancée had just fallen in love with another woman. Marriage was out of question.

Was it really love that he had felt for her in India? Probably he would have given it on oath when he wanted to marry her. I am not so sure, whether she would have called her feeling for him love. She wanted a husband and children, and she liked him. She was ready to build a family with him.

I asked myself in my little mud house in Nepal, whether our Western attitude towards love is really the pinnacle of wisdom—an attitude, where the love between man and woman is considered the highest of all possible feelings, 'love for the neighbour' is delegated to charity organisations and love for God doesn't even count as love. I did not doubt that we sincerely search for love and sincerely want to give love. But I felt that we are lacking in wisdom. In India, people have not yet completely thrown out their ancient tradition and the wisdom contained in it, even though many, especially in the cities, are eagerly doing it. Yet many Indians still know where they have to look for happiness and love—in themselves...

Here it was again—the central theme of Indian wisdom: only in myself can I find what I really long for. I have all the love of the world inside me, but—I do not feel it as long as I look for it 'outside'. Unfortunately, this eager 'outside search' is the natural tendency of the mind, which keeps one trapped in the illusion to be a separate, independent wave, and which blocks the realisation of one's union with the ocean.

In India, I learnt that the dream of eternal love is not unrealistic. I was convinced that it is not outside, but deep inside, intimately connected with my own being. I just needed to be quiet, at least sometimes. Must not put all my stakes into thinking but give <u>Being</u> a chance. Then love certainly will be felt, ever more strongly.

CHAPTER 9

Abdullah

Back in India, I travelled to Nainital, which is situated 2000-metre-high on the first mountain range of the Himalayas and is a popular hill resort. It was August and the monsoon clouds were heavy. Together with a porter, I walked for about an hour towards Ban Niwas, a branch of Aurobindo Ashram, on top of a hill.

Abdullah had reached by night bus from Delhi some hours before me. I saw him sitting by the window trimming his beard, when I put my laundry on the washing line and liked him at first sight.

Abdullah was from Jordan. He was the eldest of ten siblings and had worked in Saudi Arabia to contribute more effectively to the family budget. One day he came across a small book by Sri Aurobindo titled "The basis of Yoga". Aurobindo's thoughts touched him so deeply that he started saving for a journey to India. He was 27 when he flew to India in October 1979 and straight away headed for the Aurobindo Ashram in Pondicherry. There he integrated himself into the community and worked on the ashram farm. Soon, however, he felt stagnation.

"People liked me. I was popular. But I was disappointed, in fact really depressed. Even in Saudi Arabia, I had been popular with co-workers. But if this is all in life, I don't want to live, I thought at that time", he later confided to me.

Abdullah

He changed the place and went to the Delhi Branch of the ashram. There, too, he was welcome. Among other tasks, he guided the visitors around the ashram. Surendranath Jauhar, the grand old man, who had built up the Delhi ashram on his huge, private property and regularly spent the summers in Nainital, told me over lunch, "Since Abdullah shows the guests around the ashram, everyone is very impressed. In fact they are extremely impressed." And after a dramatic pause he added, "Not by the ashram, but by Abdullah!"

It did not take me long to realise that Abdullah was not average. We spent a lot of time together and soon almost the whole day.

Every morning Abdullah asked the cook whether he needed anything from the bazar in town. Something or other was always needed and Abdullah offered to get it. Then he asked me, if I would come with him and I always said yes.

We also wandered into the surrounding villages. The peasants invited us into their houses and urged us to have tea and snacks. Abdullah accepted their hospitality without any hesitation, whereas I, with my German mind-set, started calculating. I calculated that those farmers were poor, and I did not want to deprive them of the little they had, like their hard-earned biscuits. Yet I also could feel that they genuinely enjoyed our company and happily offered whatever they had.

Abdullah sometimes sang one of the songs of Kabir, a saint who lived 600 years ago, when India suffered under Muslim rule and who worked in his life for a reconciliation between Hindus and Muslims. When Abdullah sang, everyone was quiet. He touched the simple folk with his sincerity.

Abdullah was intuitive, calm and loving and I could learn a lot from him. For example, when he took the soiled hand of a beggar child into his, looked into his eyes and asked what his name was. Then that little, grimy face lit up with joy.

The monsoon was almost over. Abdullah suggested visiting the temples in Badrinath and Kedarnath at a height of over 3000 metres. When we silently walked down to the bus stand at five o'clock in the morning, I briefly glanced over to him. In the same moment, he looked at me, earnestly—and I realised that I had fallen in love with him. Not with the god in him who is also in me and in everyone, but with Abdullah with the curly black hair and calm brown eyes. And I knew that I was disloyal to my insights about true love only a few months earlier in Nepal. Yet I could not help it.

Yet it probably was my good luck that I fell in love with Abdullah, because he had not fallen in love with me. Maybe he did not even know that state. He simply loved. Only years later I got a notion what the difference is. And after I could feel that difference in myself and not discern it merely intellectually, being in love with somebody automatically lost its attraction. I am in love when I *need* the other person to be happy, when life seems grey and dull without him or her. I love, however, when out of my own fullness I flow out to the other in love. When I love, I am free; when I have fallen in love with somebody, I am bound to that person. Yet when our eyes met on that morning, I did not make these distinctions.

It was a dream to climb together almost 4000 metre high. Everywhere we got in contact with locals and pilgrims, who had come from all corners of India. The atmosphere on the treks and in the busses was full of joy and excitement.

Three times landslides stopped our bus. Once we even had to stay overnight. We found a place on top of a large mud stove in a teashop side by side with other pilgrims. Once, the road had completely given way. It would take days to repair it. So we all passed over to the other side with our luggage. Soldiers had taken position on the steep slope with their boots planted on whatever firm ground they could find. They reached out to us helping us to move from one soldier to the next until we reached the road again. The busses had to turn on the narrow road. There was sweat in the neck of the driver, while he inched the back wheels towards the edge, again and again, stopping only a few centimetres short of the drop into the abyss.

Our co-travellers enjoyed Abdullah's company and during tea breaks, some passengers inevitably called us to join them. They wrote down mantras for us, taught us the Arati song "Om Jaya Jagadish Hare" and kept singing the tune till we had internalised it, gave us addresses of temples and saints whom we should not miss, told us stories about Ram and Krishna and discussed highest philosophy. It was interesting. Nevertheless, I would have sometimes preferred to be alone with Abdullah. He, however, did not have such preferences.

"When I came to India, I had consciously given myself to the One—to Him as the Absolute as well as immanent in His manifestation," he later wrote in a letter to me. "I try to be open for everyone whom I meet. It is not for me to judge or be selective, because He is looking out from all eyes."

Abdullah talked about god in the same way as Anandamayi Ma did—as if he was the only true beloved, ever close, intimate, present, and whom one meets in each human being. Therefore, there were only brothers and sisters for him. The path that he so consequently followed was theoretically the same that I also wanted to follow but kept forgetting in daily life. He reminded me of it through his behaviour. He seemed to have an inexhaustible store of love. It made it easy for him to give his time so freely to others and it made him so lovable.

"What is your work", somebody asked him once in the Aurobindo Ashram in Delhi. An ashram resident answered for him, "His work is to love". Once, an acquaintance asked us when we are going to marry. Abdullah said calmly and with a serious mien,

"Don't you know that I am married already?" "Really? With whom?" the questioner reacted in surprise. "With everyone", Abdullah replied, and it was typical for him.

We also attended several talks of Jiddu Krishnamurti in Delhi. After one of those talks, a friend took us back on his motorbike. He asked Abdullah to get down at a certain crossing, in case traffic police was there. "It is not allowed to be three on a bike", he explained. "No problem", Abdullah replied. "I will convince the policeman that we are not three, but one."

Abdullah felt closely connected with everyone. He was convinced that Indian wisdom was right: there is only one Brahman, Allah, God or Self (names don't matter). So his Self was also the Self in all others. For him it was clear that in every human being the one god strives to give expression to his beauty, love and fullness. The differences among human beings are only in the degree in which the potential is manifested. The potential itself is in everyone the same.

"On the physical level you are closest to me. But my love is for everyone the same", he told me once. It was not what I wanted to hear. I would have rather had him say that I was special, that he loved only me. However, Abdullah could not do me the favour, if he remained true to himself.

He tried his best to make me understand how he perceived the world. "Do you feel the beauty here?" he asked for example, when we admired the fiery evening sky at sunset from the top of a mountain near Tungnath. My attention had been directed outwards and I had not felt my heart. But when he pointed to it, I sensed what he meant.

There is an amazing potential of bliss in us, far more bliss than what sensual pleasures can give", he said out of the blue when we were on our 14 km trek to the Kedarnath temple. I knew he was right, because I had once experienced amazing bliss. I was 22 at that time and a trainee with Lufthansa. I was meditating with a mantra that a TM teacher had given. Fully unexpected, almost unbearable bliss spread out all over for a long time.

I knew that there was great bliss in me, though I had no idea how to access that state. It was helpful to be with Abdullah. He kept redirecting my attention back to my self.

Something had happened to Abdullah a few months after he had arrived in India. He felt deeply depressed and seriously thought of suicide. "In addition to my depression I had a bad flu with high fever and truly felt miserable. I don't quite know what happened. Something shifted, and I felt absolutely wonderful. There was not a trace of depression. I still had a bad flu, still had fever. Yet now I enjoyed it", he shared with me. "This shift stayed. It is not important whether I am healthy or sick."

On Diwali, the festival of lights, we visited a family in Delhi who were friends of Abdullah. They had two sons, 20 und 21 years old. Everyone was in high spirits and I enjoyed a talk with Karu, the elder one of the two brothers. He had dark, calm eyes, and like many youngsters in India, was very bright and cheerful.

Three days later, Abdullah got a message from the mother. "Please come. My son has died." It was a heart-breaking situation. The body of Karu was lying on the floor in their flat, covered with a white sheet, dead. His father sobbed uncontrollably. Abdullah did not have to fight back tears like me, though he had been close to Karu. He knew not only intellectually that everything is for the best and nothing is lost by dying. Karu's father put his head on Abdullah's shoulder and wept. Abdullah sang with a low voice a soothing song into his ear. He had calm shining eyes.

He also had calm, shining eyes when he dropped me at the airport some weeks later. I went to Germany to see my parents for Christmas. I held on to his parting words, "I am always with you". I knew he referred to the one 'real thing' in me and that indeed 'He' was always with me. Yet there were tears in my eyes because I could not *see* the truth of it.

CHAPTER 10

Sri Aurobindo and Auroville, the city of the future

How vast and warm India is! It became even more evident when I came back from Germany in January. Abdullah happened to be in Auroville, some 150 km south of Chennai. He considered Sri Aurobindo as his guru and therefore felt closely connected to Puducherry (former Pondicherry), where Sri Aurobindo and the Mother, his spiritual companion, have their Samadhi, as well as to Auroville, the 'city of the future' visualised by the Mother.

Sri Aurobindo was from an upper-class family in Kolkata. His father did not think much of the Indian tradition and wanted to give his sons a 'good' start in life. So he sent them as small boys to England for their education. Aurobindo was very intelligent. However, he did not become the high officer in the colonial government, as his father had wished. When Aurobindo came back to India as a young man, he rebelled against the colonial power and became a freedom fighter.

For the first time, he came now in contact with the ancient Indian tradition and was greatly impressed by it. He met a guru, Lele by name, who taught him meditation. Aurobindo locked himself up together with his guru in a room for several days and had deep spiritual experiences.

Sri Aurobindo.

His plotting against the British landed him in Alipore jail in Kolkata. There he continued his meditation and had a spiritual breakthrough. He suddenly saw everything as Krishna—even the jail warden. After being freed, he escaped from British dominion and settled in Pondicherry, a French colony. There, he lived in seclusion until his death, dedicating himself to yoga and philosophy. Around him, a big ashram developed, which the Mother, as Mira Alfassa was called, managed. She was a French woman of Turkish-Egyptian parentage, who lived by his side from 1920 onwards.

In his numerous writings, Sri Aurobindo propagated the integral yoga, i.e. he was not in favour of withdrawing into a cave, but recommended a 'divine life' right here in the world by perfecting one's abilities. He, as well as the Mother, expected a quantum leap in the evolution of humankind in the near future. A new, better human being was to come—a human being, who would be dominated by divine qualities and not animal tendencies. The time was ripe for a super consciousness and a super man on earth. This was Aurobindo's conviction.

After Aurobindo's death in December 1950, the Mother wanted to create a protected zone for people to live a divine life in this world and thereby accelerate the birth of the super man. Her dream: "There should be a place somewhere on earth, which no nation can claim as its property; a place, where all human beings of good will and sincere aspiration could live freely as citizens of this world and follow only one authority—the highest truth, a place of peace, of harmony."

That was a high goal, yet the Mother, who had grown up in Paris, had married twice, had lived in Japan and had a son and a daughter, was a strong woman. Since her childhood, she was clairvoyant and was convinced that dreams were meant to be manifested.

On February 29th, 1968—the Mother was 90—the first step was taken. About twelve kilometres north of Pondicherry near the Bay of Bengal, the 'international city of the future man' was founded in a colourful ceremony with guests from 124 countries. Auroville was seen as a great experiment and the world media took notice of it.

The area of some 20 square kilometres looked barren then: red earth under a merciless sun, ravines created by the monsoon and only the odd Mango, Banyan, Cashew or Palmyra tree far in between. There a city of 50.000 inhabitants was supposed to come up.

It started well. The first international settlers worked hard, donations came pouring in, trees were planted, buildings constructed, and the foundation was laid for the centre of Auroville, an orb shaped temple of the Divine Mother, called Matrimandir.

Then, in November 1973, the Mother passed away and everything got stuck. She had been the absolute authority concerning Auroville. After her death, the Sri Aurobindo Society in Pondicherry took charge of the administration and the funds. Soon, however, discord arose. The approximately 400 settlers on the ground, many from France, accused the Indian administrators with financial mismanagement, arrogance and unacceptable conditions for getting funds.

Later the Aurovillians split into two camps—a bigger one with mainly French settlers, who advocated a total break from the Sri Aurobindo Society and a smaller group with several Germans, who wanted to come to some agreement with the Society. The fight was fierce in the early 1980s, when I landed there. The population of Auroville was meanwhile around 800 and the two groups had so much hatred for each other that they even hired goons for the battle.

I met an American woman whose front teeth were missing. She had been beaten up by goons.

The French group finally won and the Sri Aurobindo Society lost its influence. The group had gone to court and had asked the Indian government to take over Auroville. That happened in 1988. Since then the tension has eased and Auroville is growing slowly. Optimism has returned and the barren landscape was turned into a lush paradise with some 3 million trees and shrubs. A hurricane in December 2011, however, caused tremendous damage. Now in 2018, over 2500 people are living there (still a far cry from the 50.000 originally envisaged) and the 50th anniversary of its foundation was celebrated grandly with the Indian Prime Minister Modi in attendance.

Life in Auroville is not easy, even though the houses are spacious and beautiful, in many cases servants look after their upkeep, the climate is sunny and the ocean just outside one's front door. People from all over the world are living in small communities in midst of a verdant paradise and have the chance to experiment with their ideas and find new ways to make a living. Seems like an ideal setting for a divine life.

On the other hand, friction may be necessary for the divine life to prove itself. And of friction there was enough in Auroville. Apart from the inevitable ego clashes between hundreds of people trying to work out a better way of life, there is tension between the locals and the Aurovillians, many of whom are foreigners. Several villages are located in the area of Auroville and the Mother had called those villagers the 'first Aurovillians'. After her death, however, they were ignored. Only a few villagers were accepted as Aurovillians, and the others rejected, as most of them wanted to join due to economic reasons. Naturally, the villagers and especially their youth, who are daily confronted with a luxurious and for their standard immoral lifestyle, became resentful and even hostile.

Thefts are endemic in Auroville and probably justified by the village youth as taking justice into their own hands. In the 1990s, when I stayed once more in Auroville, my camera disappeared from my hut in the Centre Guesthouse, while I was only some 50 metres away. I was told that in many communities, one cannot even leave the windows open without risking loosing things. Unfortunately, a murder, too, happened. On February 1st, 2004, a Dutch national was murdered. He had witnessed a theft in a neighbouring house and feared that the thieves might get back at him. He had pleaded to set up a security system for Auroville. His plea was not heeded in time. He died at the age of forty.

The house, where Abdullah and I stayed in1982, belonged to the smaller of the two warring factions. Abdullah and I were not affected by the hostilities, yet we had to carry our passport and money on us whenever we went out, as there was a danger that the rival group would take over 'our' house. In spite of reading several reports and asking questions on how the hostilities could have gone so much out of hand, I did not understand the reasons. It seemed that financial and political interests played a role. My impression was that even in Auroville there were already 'small' and 'big' Aurovillians. Maybe man has first to encounter the darkest depths of his being before he can soar to the lofty heights of the superman.

Abdullah and I cycled through the barren landscape on sandy roads in the hot sun, as the trees planted were still too small for shade, and visited people whom Abdullah knew. He had many friends and Abdullah was the same as on our trip in the Himalayas. He would give his time freely to whoever wanted it. Yet here, in the Westernised atmosphere, his attitude was a challenge for me. I could sense that two foreign women were in love with him. I could not blame them, but it brought out jealousy in me. When Abdullah once came back from a long walk with one of them, I sulked. Abdullah had calm, shining, eyes when he held my head in his hands and asked, "Did you ever think of being humble?"

A guru could not have aimed a better blow at my ego. I cried in my room, without really knowing why it hurt so much. Maybe, because I used to think that I was rather humble. Since childhood I have been extremely shy, a feeling of being unwanted and of not fitting in with others was always in the background. So I usually claimed very little space for myself, tried not to give trouble to anybody, not to put myself up in front, though I did not like it either when I was overlooked and felt easily dejected. I might have considered this attitude as humble, but Abdullah's remark showed me that being humble meant something else. It meant not wanting to be special. This seemed impossible. Wanting to be special seems to be ingrained in human nature. Maybe, those tears were some sort of an initial cleansing and the wish to be special has to fall off by itself. It cannot be 'done'.

In spite of my love for Abdullah, I could not see Sri Aurobindo as my spiritual guide. I saw him as an inspired, enlightened yogi, philosopher and politician who had a great vision for India. In fact I wished he had not withdrawn from the freedom struggle so early and had continued helping to shape the future of India. However his ideal of a divine life in the world, which also demanded bringing to perfection one's practical abilities apart from full surrender to the Divine, did not attract me, probably because I did not think much of my practical abilities. I rather would have liked to withdraw to a cave in the Himalayas or, with Abdullah, to a lonely island. Yet this was not to be. Instead, we went to an international conference in a five-star hotel in the mega city of Mumbai.

CHAPTER 11

A conference on modern science and India's wisdom

The German magazine, which had published my first article, asked me to cover the international conference on the "Convergence of Ancient Wisdom and Modern Science" in Bombay in February 1982. The editor had included Abdullah as my photographer in his accreditation letter which saved us over 400 dollars each. A devotee of Aurobindo had offered us to stay at his flat, which was just 5 minutes on foot from the Oberoi Sheraton Hotel, where the conference was held.

Abdullah did not feel intimidated by the roles the delegates played, whereas I did. "Everything is the one god. He shines from all eyes, everything moves because of 'Him'"—this ancient wisdom had seemed completely logical outside in the simple India of the ashrams. Yet here, in the conference atmosphere of the five-star hotel, where well-dressed scientists, psychologists and journalists hurried business-like from one talk to the next, this ancient wisdom seemed somewhat out of place—in spite of a lot of talk about the oneness of all. I had the impression that the oneness was here a mere intellectual, academic matter, which had no relevance for day-to-day life.

Though there were many well-known spiritual personalities present,—Indian swamis, Christian mystics, Sufis, Buddhists, a

Parsi priest—their exposition of ancient wisdom didn't inspire much. I had become familiar with this wisdom in a more authentic way in the 'real' India outside. Yet the exposition of modern science was fascinating.

Fritjof Capra, Rupert Sheldrake, Karl Pribram and other scientists explained that new research in physics, biology, neurology and other subjects pointed to a convergence between India's wisdom and modern science. Scientists claim now that our senses deceive us and that nothing that the senses perceive truly exists—completely in tune with the ancient Indian concept of Maya.

The old 'scientific' worldview, formulated in the 17th century and based on the findings of Descartes and Newton, compared the universe to a gigantic machine, which functioned according to specific laws. Space was three dimensional and full of solid objects. Time was linear and each cause had an effect. Matter was essentially without intelligence. This worldview was useful, and the immense scientific progress made by building on those laws seemed to endorse it as true, as well. Spirit had become obsolete. Our society had become 'modern and progressive'.

And how did this 'modern and progressive' society present itself in the 1980s? On one hand material comfort and on the other hand a growing discontent, moral degradation and mental depression among its members. Yet in this bleak situation, science itself provided now the means to change the underlying worldview, and proceed into a new direction.

Fritjof Capra, who was a physicist at the University of California in Berkeley at that time and later founded the centre for Ecoliteracy, presented the new paradigm resulting from Quantum physics and the theory of relativity in a comprehensible manner.

I shall try a short outline of his talk.

While searching for the substance of matter, no substance was found. The universe is not seen any more as a three-dimensional space full of things, but as a homogeneous web of happenings and relations. Matter and energy are interchangeable and the three dimensional space and the linear time have become the four dimensional space-time–continuum that is beyond human imagination. There are no separate objects or separate entities. Everything is related and is in perpetual movement.

The old paradigm is still useful for this reality of the senses, for our familiar, daily world. On this level, a chair and a table are still separate objects. Yet this is not really true. In truth, there is a gigantic, conscious, cosmic dance of energy happening right now, in the eternal now, in which you and I and everything else dissolves. Capra compared it to Shiva Nataraj, the dancing Shiva.

At the end, Fritjof Capra made an important statement, in tune with India's wisdom. He said that the one energy of science is probably conscious. However, today, almost four decades later, most of his scientist colleagues still do not subscribe to this view. They may eventually come around and acknowledge that the universe is alive with consciousness, as the Indian Rishis have so far never been proven wrong. To realise this, they need to literally turn around and look into their own consciousness instead of only observing the world outside.

Psychology also got a major facelift at the conference thanks to transpersonal psychology. This new branch is based on the Hindu concept of Atman—the transpersonal or transcendental essence in all human beings. The core of Vedanta proclaims that Atman (the individual consciousness) is one with Brahman (the universal consciousness), like in "Ayam Atman Brahman".

Finally Sanatana Dharma will get its due, I felt. India's knowledge would again become the guiding light for humanity. After all, according to Vedic tradition, the goal of life is to realise what we truly are—not a separate person but Sat-chit-ananda,—blissful awareness. This knowledge would surely influence the lives of the common people, when even psychologists see the value of it.

Yet I was wrong. Over 35 years have passed, and if anything, our societies have become even more divided, confused and less wise. Intriguingly, over those years, the connection to Indian wisdom has been erased.

In 1982, the pamphlet openly acknowledged that the conference was held in India, because the theories propounded were based on ancient Indian insights. Yet nowadays, there is not a word about

India or Hinduism in Wikipedia's longish piece on transpersonal psychology. Why? India should be mentioned first on the list of influences that "set the stage for transpersonal studies". Yet only Western thinkers are mentioned. The long Wikipedia piece ends with a revealing remark:

"... transpersonal psychology has been criticized by some Christian authors as being "a mishmash of 'New Age' ideas that offer an alternative faith system to vulnerable youths who turn their backs on organized religion (Adeney, 1988)".

Who fears that vulnerable youth turn their back on organised religion? Who threads this scenario? Obviously it is the Christian clergy. They are not interested in finding out whether the 'I'-feeling could indeed be transpersonal and the same in all. Whether the new theory could be closer to the truth is not an issue for them. Loyalty to the 'revealed truth' overrides it. The mind is stuck in a straitjacket. And in the process, humanity is missing out on truth.

The conference was my first assignment for a magazine and I had no idea how I could do justice to the huge flood of information that had been pouring on us. For a whole week, there were three to four parallel topics presented in separate rooms and I often did not know what I should attend.

On the last day of the conference, I suddenly had an idea how to structure the article. "It is simple", I said to Abdullah in the garden restaurant, where we had our dinner, and explained it to him. It really turned out to be simple. The text flowed—27 pages written into my diary by hand, as I had no typewriter yet. The magazine published it over two issues and another magazine reprinted it. However, before I started writing I had placed a chit next to my pillow: "Please, You write."

CHAPTER 12

The perfect missionary—Swami Chinmayananda

"Abdullah", I heard from all sides, when we came back to the Aurobindo Ashram in Delhi. Everyone seemed to be his best friend. And I felt almost a little proud that I was associated with him. Swami Chinmayananda happened to give a course on Vedanta philosophy in Delhi at that time and Abdullah and I attended the weeklong classes. The swami was a perfect teacher—humorous, clear and convincing. It was a joy to listen to him.

Originally, he was a journalist, who moved from his home state Kerala to the Himalaya to find out whether the Swamis and Sanyasis were genuine or simply impostors and parasites of society.

I do not know which conclusions he drew in general, but at least two of those holy men impressed him: Swami Sivananda of Rishikesh and Tapovan Maharaj of Uttarkashi deeper in the Himalaya. He stayed for nine summers with the latter as his disciple. Discipleship, however, was not easy and once he even packed his bags determined to leave. His guru had accused him of having torn his robe while washing it. Chinmayananda had denied it. It had not been him for sure. Yet from now onwards, Tapovan Maharaj called him a liar, often in front of other disciples. Chinmayananda felt hurt and decided to leave, never to come back. An elder ashram resident saw him packing and convinced him that the accusation was just one of the guru's ways to hit at his ego, in his (Chinmayananda's) best interest. Chinmayananda got the point. When he saw his guru the next time, the guru laughed, "Why are you so touchy when I call you a liar? Aren't we all liars as long as we don't know the truth? Do you know the truth?"

After nine years with his teacher, he wanted to share his insights—by now convinced that the happiness we all look for cannot be found outside, when it is hidden inside. In the early 1950s, he left the Himalaya for the dusty, hot plains and started teaching his fellow compatriots about the ancient, sacred scriptures—especially the Bhagavad-Gita and the Upanishads—as even after independence the education system ignored the Indian tradition under the pretext of being secular. Until his death in 1993, Swami Chinmayananda taught tirelessly and hardly took leave for a single day. The Chinmaya Mission that he founded still exists and the teaching goes on by his successors.

The Bhagavad-Gita is considered as the essence of the Vedas. It is a small part—the teaching of Lord Krishna to Arjuna on the battlefield—of the great ancient epic "Mahabharata". The Upanishads form the last part of the Vedas and deal with philosophy. He felt that the language of those scriptures is not understood nowadays, yet their message is evergreen and extremely beneficial. These scriptures not only offer the highest philosophy but also a systematic, scientific method to live a meaningful, happy life from a higher level of consciousness.

A big tent had been put up for the camp. Chants from the Bhagavad-Gita were played in the background. Over thousand people gathered at dusk, sitting on rugs on the floor. When Swami Chinmayananda entered the stage, people welcomed him with heartfelt clapping. He looked stately, was tall, had long hair and a long, white beard, sparkling eyes and a roaring laughter. He was completely at ease and made us enjoy the class with his great sense of humour.

"Do you know the essence of Vedanta?" he asked in a booming voice and himself gave the answer, "Undress and embrace" he thundered. People were nonplussed. He chuckled and explained, "Undress the body, mind and intellect. What remains is automatically in the embrace with OM, the pure awareness."

All our suffering stems from identifying with our body, thoughts and feelings, he claimed and gave an illustration: "You go and watch a film. The persons on the screen experience happiness and suffering. You also experience happiness and suffering. Why? Because you identify with those figures. You sit in the theatre and cry into your handkerchief. And you even pay for it!"

He kept asking us to analyse the human situation intelligently. "Man has body, mind and intellect. If he *has* body, mind and intellect, who *is* he? Certainly a good question! Usually a question that we have never asked. Amazing!

He took the example of electricity: "If you believe only what you see, then each light bulb surely shines all by itself, since some shine brightly and others dimly and some red and some green. Does it not follow that each light bulb has its own, independent light? Yet whoever inquires deeper, will laugh at such ignorance. He *knows* that the one electricity is solely responsible for the light in *all* bulbs (and even for the sound from loudspeakers). The different colours and forms of the bulbs count for the variety in the lights. Yet would there be lights without electricity? Similarly, one has to enquire: would I exist without awareness (Atman)?"

Of course, Swami Chinmayananda too, like all sages, advised to direct one's attention inwards to That what truly is. He himself must have done it for innumerable hours in those long years in the Himalayan ashram of his guru. A bulb might not be able to discover the electricity in itself, yet the human being can discover pure awareness. He only needs to drop the *content* of his awareness to discover *pure* awareness which is his real nature. He gave an example: if you shine a torch into a dark room, you see all kinds of objects in the room, but you don't notice the light. Forget about the objects, focus on the light.

The more we become aware of our real nature, the less we will be attached to the world. Desires will reduce automatically. They simply drop off. The world does not bind anymore. Love and joy are not sought outside anymore. They are right here, inside.

Swami Chinmayananda gave again an example how a drastic change in attitude comes about naturally: One day, the elder brother calls his younger brother, shows him all his toys and tells him, 'it is all yours. If you don't want it, throw it away.' The younger one is now convinced that unfortunately his elder brother has gone mad. Yet the elder one is not bothered. He has discovered better toys, and *knows* that they are better. The little brother cannot see it yet as long as he is so small. One day he will understand…

On the last evening, it became obvious that the Swami had done a great service to the audience. Long queues formed and slowly and silently moved to the carton boxes that had been put up for envelopes with donations. We were simply grateful to him for the many insights that he had prompted us to have.

Abdullah's birthday was coming up. He felt that 30 was an important year for him and he wanted to start it in Pondicherry. I, however, dreaded the humid climate near the sea in the heat of summer. It was a difficult decision, but in the last moment, I cancelled my train ticket. He left at six in the morning from New Delhi railway station. Until 3 a.m. we had talked—had so much to share. Well, he would come back to the north, we would meet again…

Meanwhile I could test whether I was still able to travel alone.

CHAPTER 13

A beautiful youth—Babaji of Haidakhan

Ever since I had the connection through the initiation into Kriya Yoga in Pune, I dreamt of encountering Babaji, the great, eternally young Babaji, who occasionally appears to his disciples in the Himalaya. Who never ever forsakes his disciples. Who can manifest himself at will wherever he likes, and who even can bring the dead back to life—as Yogananda had claimed in his 'Autobiography of a Yogi'. I wished that someone like Babaji really existed.

I heard from a German woman that Babaji has appeared in the Himalaya, not as an ephemeral apparition, but as a young man in flesh and blood. He lived in a small village called Haidakhan, a few hours on foot from Haldwani, and everybody, who wished, could visit him there. She even showed me a paperback with the title 'Babadschi', published in Germany. The photo on the cover depicted a young man with curly hair falling up to his shoulder, a beautiful face and an extremely peaceful countenance. The photo fascinated me. The youth had been found in a cave in 1970 by a villager, who was told in a dream to go to that cave. The handsome lad himself claimed that he was the Babaji of Yogananda, so it was said.

Soon I heard other stories, too: He had to appear in a court case in Lucknow, because he had occupied the ashram in Haidakhan. He

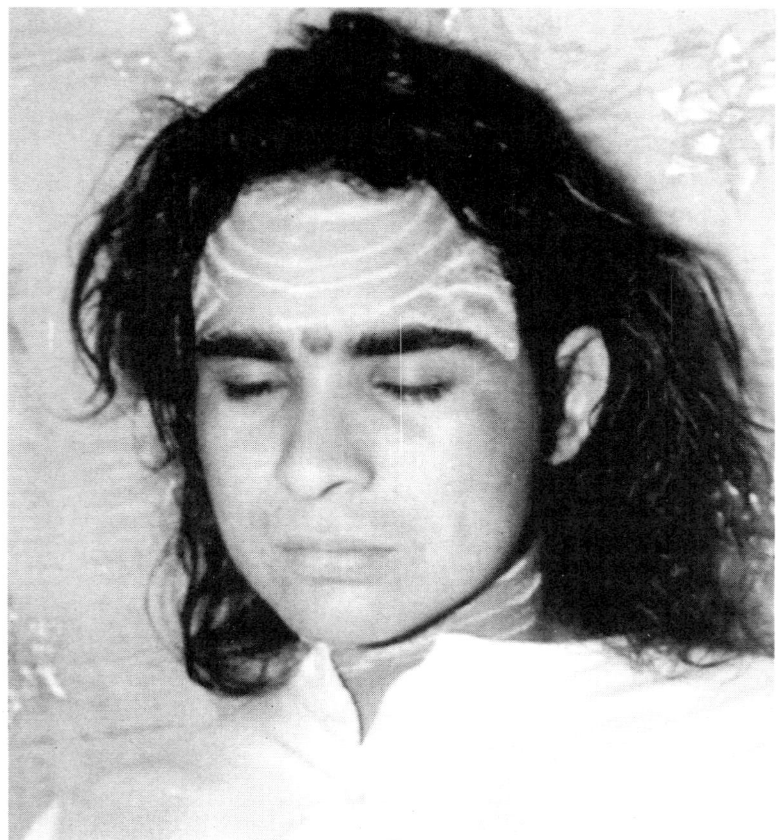

Was this beautiful youth the real Babaji mentioned by Swami Yogananda?

has become very fat, somebody else knew. And the owner of a teashop divulged to me that the most beautiful girls from among his followers would give him milk baths in a golden bathtub.

In spite of the rumours, I went to Haidakhan soon after Abdullah had left. I stayed overnight in Haldwani in the Kailash View Hotel. This hotel, as well as the shop 'Hind Traders', whose owner Muniraj became the successor after Babaji's completely unexpected death, were the meeting points for people who wanted to go to Babaji.

On the way to the hotel I had for the first time a frightening experience. I had taken a rickshaw from the train station to the hotel and it went through a deserted lane. Two men stopped the rickshaw, said something to the driver and then turned to me. I had everything, passport, money, in a bag on my lap and I saw it already gone in my imagination, when I suddenly screamed. The men disappeared as quickly as they had come—without my bag.

On the next day, some Italians and I hitched a ride into the valley of the Gautam-Ganga-river up to Haidakhan in an empty truck, which went to collect timber. The riverbed was about one kilometre broad and had only a few rivulets running along, which we occasionally had to cross during our bumpy ride. We made ourselves as comfortable as possible on the loading area under a tarpaulin.

I prayed that I would not fall for a false guru, because in spite of my doubts I wanted to believe that this Babaji was the genuine Babaji. The truck stopped. We had reached. I jumped down from the truck and got a shock: I had landed right in front of Babaji, who was going for a walk in the riverbed with a group of his followers. He had indeed become rather big and only vaguely resembled that beautiful youth from the photo. But his gaze was powerful.

Babaji had to give permission for staying in the ashram. I had heard that he sometimes sent followers—without giving any reason—with a vehement "Go!" out of the ashram and sometimes did not allow new arrivals to settle into a room in the first place. I was afraid that he would send me back straight away, but to my relief he nodded a "yes" when I asked him, whether I could stay.

The ashram was in the midst of nature, far away from the noise of the cities. The ashram buildings were located on a slope above the river. 108 steps led up to them. But I soon realised that life there was hard and food was bad. We got only one meal a day. In the evening, the leftovers from lunch were served cold—if there were leftovers. Luckily, there were some teashops nearby, which we visitors frequented.

The few bathrooms in the ashram were reserved for the sick and those above 60. I had to walk down the 108 steps to the riverbed at

108 steps leading up to Haidakhan ashram from the riverbed.

4 o'clock in the morning for a wash in the ice-cold water of the mountain stream. According to Babaji's order, I should have fully submerged myself three times. However I obeyed this instruction rarely, and the few times when I did, my heart almost stopped, yet afterwards I literally felt newly come alive. Most mornings I balanced barefoot on the cold stones near one of the rivulets in my attempt to

get as little wet as possible during my bath. A 'real' bath I postponed until the afternoon.

Regarding the loo, the instruction was to go far away from the river. Day had already broken, when I walked into the forested hills with a tin of water in my hand.

There were mainly foreigners in the ashram and some aspects I found difficult to digest. Almost all of them—women as well as men—had shaven heads; the women wore saris and the men dhotis and they gave the impression of being members of some club who confirmed each other in their conviction that they were chosen for something great. The Italians wore black. Babaji had recommended it. A Swiss and an American walked around only in a loincloth.

When Babaji came down the steps to the riverbed or into the temple for worship in the evening, he was accompanied by some of his faithful who shouted strange slogans, like, "Mahaprabhuji ki jay!" It was a huge drama, and no doubt over-the-top with its theatrical effect. The Arati, the waving of light in front of the deity, was also the loudest, I had ever experienced. A conch was blown, small and big bells were beaten, rattles, drums and everything that produced sound was made use of. Babaji took his seat in front higher up on a couch. We sat down on the floor—men on one side and women on the other—and, supported by drums and harmonium sang loudly for a whole hour simple, rhythmic songs from a booklet mainly in praise of Shiva. The singing was a good opportunity to unwind und certainly did not harm us Westerners. In fact, I fondly remember the joyful, boisterous atmosphere during those gatherings and the tunes of those devotional songs still keep coming to my mind after 35 years.

Babaji's strong presence impressed. He, however, took it quite easy, when it came to teaching. He simply advised: truth, simplicity and love. He could not go wrong on that. And he put the greatest importance on Karma Yoga, the yoga of action. Besides Jnana Yoga, the yoga of wisdom and Bhakti Yoga, the yoga of devotion, Karma Yoga belongs to the three main yogas, which Krishna recommends in the Bhagavad-Gita. Karma Yoga requires giving one's best without having an eye on the result. "Do your best in whatever you do, but don't be concerned about the outcome", is the advice. The advice is worthwhile and even business schools propound it. The logic behind it is: if one gives one's best now, the result in the future will automatically be as good as it can get. If however one is concerned about the result while doing the work, the work will suffer and the outcome will not be as good.

We were about 60 people in the ashram. Between 9 and 12 o'clock in the morning and 3 and 5 o'clock in the afternoon Karma Yoga was to be practised. Three hours were a long time, during which, in scorching sun, we built a wall in the riverbed to gain some land for a vegetable garden. When we were thirsty, someone filled a bucket with water from the river, and went around with a big ladle and poured water straight into our throats. We piled up stones in a row. Some of the men selected big, heavy stones and hauled them to the wall. Most of the others, including me, picked two small, easily portable stones and added them to the teamwork. In the previous year, too, a wall had been built—and got washed away in the monsoon. Our wall was likely to meet the same fate. Having the probable result in mind, we did not do our best—with few exceptions.

Sometimes we had to peel peanuts during our work-shifts, for hours, and my fingers became sore. I suspected that the Karma Yoga which was allegedly imposed to benefit *us*, actually benefited the ashram and rebellious thoughts took hold of me. I almost waited for a "Go!" from Babaji. The "Go!" did not come, not even, when I skipped work and accidentally met Babaji on the steps leading to the ashram. He gave me a penetrating look, did not say a word and moved on.

One day, however, he told me to wear a sari, and "No sari you go!" Defiance got the upper hand. "I leave after lunch", I told some roommates in the dormitory, who offered to lend me a sari. "Don't be silly", they advised. "Give in and wear a sari."

After lunch, I happened to meet Babaji in a tea shack in the middle of the riverbed. He sat there, surrounded by some of his followers. I suddenly felt sad that I was to leave. The atmosphere was good. There were some nice people in the ashram and the place was beautiful. And who knows, maybe Babaji was enlightened and his presence was beneficial.

"Babaji, if I wear sari, can I stay? I suddenly heard myself asking. He slowly moved his head from side to side, Indian style. "Yes", he smiled. "Sari and Mundan." Mundan meant shaving the head.

'Shaving the head' clinched the issue. In the afternoon, I hitched a ride to Haldwani in the driver's cabin of a truck carrying timber.

I could not make up my mind whether Babaji was enlightened or not, even though I spent more time in Haidakhan in the following year and met Babaji also in other places like Delhi and Vrindavan. The photo of the amazingly handsome young Babaji had doubtless pulled me, as well as many others, to him like a magnet. If I had only seen that photo and not the man in flesh and blood, it would have been easy to take him to be genuine, because the photo glowed with beauty and calm. Even today, this photo draws Westerners to Haidakhan. Most of them have never met Babaji and bowed to Muniraj, the owner of 'Hind Traders', who took over the role of the guru after Babaji's death and who meanwhile also has died.

But I am proceeding too fast. Babaji was young and nobody expected him to die. He was in the early 1980s only in his 30s. Among his followers, there were some VIPs, as well. Shammi Kapoor, a famous Bollywood star would routinely visit and find space for his huge physical and social weight right in front of Babaji. Leonard Orr, a well-known rebirther, also had VIP status.

Then, on 14th February 1984, Babaji died, completely unexpected. Somebody who was there at that time told me later that he thought that Babaji was joking and would soon sit up again, laughing. Babaji did not sit up again. He was dead.

Why Babaji died so suddenly will probably remain a mystery. There were rumours that he was poisoned. Yet wouldn't he have realised—provided he was a great yogi—that someone wanted to kill him?

In June 2005, after more than 20 years, I was once again in Haidakhan. Only a handful of young foreigners stayed there. None of them had met Babaji. "Really, you have met Babaji? You have

Babaji and Muniraj, who became his successor, in the riverbed of Gautama Ganga.

been here when he was still alive?" they asked astonished. Most of them were only born in the early 1980s. They dutifully did several hours of Karma Yoga and performed Arati in the mornings and evenings, yet the zest was missing.

I went to the shop in the ashram, where photos were for sale. Strangely, the photo of the young Babaji, which had attracted me so much at that time, didn't fascinate me any longer. I still saw a beautiful youth, but nothing else. During the long time interval, the projection that he might be the great, powerful yogi had disappeared. In the ashram shop, photos of Muniraj were now for sale, as well. However, I could not possibly see a guru in him.

A couple of years after Babaji's death, Muniraj's newfound guru-status was contested: a beautiful, about 16-year old youth appeared in Haidakhan and claimed to be Babaji. Many locals in the area believed him. Some of the Indian devotees of Babaji, too, were in favour of this lad. Muniraj and his assistants, however, doubted him. They asserted themselves and refused him entry to the ashram in Haidakhan.

After my last visit to Haidakhan, I hired one of Muniraj's jeeps back to Haldwani and gave a lift to some villagers on the rough ride on a newly constructed road. The villagers were surprised that I spoke Hindi and an animated conversation ensued.

"What do the villagers think about the foreign devotees of Babaji?" I asked.

"The foreigners have great faith and are fully devoted to Babaji and Muniraj", they said early on during the ride. We needed almost 3 hours for the 31 km on the narrow road high up over the riverbed. Later, during a tea break, my co-passengers became more open and explicit: "The villagers think that most of the foreigners are mad. They take things far too seriously and always think that they know better."

CHAPTER 14

Abdullah's death

After the simple life in Haidakhan, I longed for a little comfort and rented a cottage on an estate in Mussoorie, a hill station 2000 m high near Dehradun. At that time, I was writing a series for my German magazine, titled "Indian wisdom from A to Z". I had reached the letter 'T', and chose to write on Tod (German for death) and Trauer (German for mourning). The place was beautiful, deodar forests all around and, as the monsoon had arrived, plenty of rain and mist. However, the atmosphere felt a bit heavy, but I could have never imagined that Abdullah had died already. I copy here what I had written on mourning, as I soon would need to practise what I had written.

"Anandamayi Ma once told a true story: A mother was inconsolable over the death of her 12-year old daughter for years. One night her husband had a dream. He saw his daughter—with flowers in her hair in a beautiful surrounding—coming towards him and saying, "I cannot bear any longer Mama's pain. I'll come back to you." Several months later his wife gave birth to a girl…

Whether we believe this story or not, the Indian sages claim that too much mourning is a hindrance for the person who died and they request us to have the courage to let go. The reason is that mourning is a sign how much we were attached to that person, not how much we loved him—and we tend to mix up these two. Yet in Western societies, mourning is seen as a virtue and somebody who does not mourn looks rather suspect. This encourages staying immersed in mourning. Of course, as long as we are attached to someone (and this is probably the case for all of us), it is only natural to suffer at a loss. This suffering can even become an irresistible force which cannot be controlled. Yet when we are honest, even in the deepest sadness there are moments, when we have the chance to be bold and let go. These moments we need to make use of, the sages advise—in our own interest as well."

Abdullah would come back soon—that's what I thought. Later I heard that he had already booked the train. He used to write long letters from Pondicherry and shared his thoughts and daily life in detail. He had also mentioned that he and Mahmud, a Syrian friend, took swimming lessons from an Australian. His last letter had been posted on 19. July and now it was already early August. I became restless. Finally, a letter came. Yet it was from one of his friends in the Ashram. Confused, I hastily opened it: "Dear Maria, I don't know whether you know already. On Tuesday, July 20th, he (the 'he' was crossed out and Abdullah written over it) drowned in the sea in Pondicherry."

NO!!! was all I could think and feel.

I felt so alone, deserted. He had left without saying good-bye, without leaving an address. Every night I dreamt of Abdullah and every morning I had to get used to the somehow unbelievable thought that he really had died. It was for the first time that I lost someone close.

Mahmud, his Syrian friend, also could not believe he had died. For many hours, he had wandered along the beach in Pondicherry on that 20th July, expecting him to come out of the sea, alive and smiling as usual. "Abdullah had put the key of our flat into the pocket of his swimwear, he simply had to come back", Mahmud cried when I met him a few weeks later. He was inconsolable. "It is my fault. I had asked him to come for a swim. Abdullah felt we should not go, as the swimming teacher was not there that day, but I suggested that we only splash in shallow water near the beach," he deplored. They had learnt floating and were practising it when Mahmud heard Abdullah call for help. Maybe he wanted to stand and found no ground underneath.

The wife of the swimming teacher was in the water, not far from Abdullah. She said she could have saved him, but suddenly and inexplicably the fear overpowered her that if she did so, her small daughter who was playing on the beach might walk into the sea. So she rushed out and pleaded with some Westerners to go in. Mahmud also shouted to them for help. Nobody came, not even a man, who swam a big round far out in the ocean every evening. Meanwhile people gathered; Abdullah was still visible not far away. Then the kids of fishermen, who played some distance away, realised that something was amiss and came running. They immediately went into the sea, yet by then a wave had sucked Abdullah underneath the surface. The young, skinny boys fearlessly kept on diving. They swam far out, further than where he had been seen earlier, but they could not trace him anymore. His body landed up two days later near Auroville.

"Ma, I just cannot believe that something has happened," a man once told Anandamayi Ma, after his wife had died. "That's right. Nothing has happened," she had affirmed.

Already on that Saturday, when the letter reached me, I heard occasionally very clearly: "Be bold, Maria! Be bold! You know that I am not dead." This came again and again to my mind, in spite of the dark, overpowering pain and emptiness in my heart. It sounded like Abdullah: 'you know that what I am has not died. Hold fast to the truth. I am here. We are one.'

There were small, beautiful incidents. For example a couple of weeks later in Haridwar, I had brought a friend to the night train to Delhi. It was late, when I came back to the Tourist Bungalow and sat for meditation. It was more a kind of dozing, yet suddenly I jerked awake: "Happy birthday, Maria! Happy birthday, Maria!" I clearly heard. "This is Abdullah", I knew, and wondered why he wished me a happy birthday. Then I remembered that 'tomorrow' was my birthday. "Maybe it is tomorrow already?" I switched on the light. It was midnight sharp.

Another time I asked the I Ching for advice and got "modesty". I smiled, as I never forgot Abdullah's admonition to be humble when I had been jealous. "What would *you* advise me now, as I got already your advice?" I asked him teasingly and threw the I Ching again. He teased me back: The result was exactly the same, including the moving and unmoving lines.

Abdullah had written in his letter of 10. July: "Our love is true, great and eternal." I knew that he had again mixed me up with the divine essence in me. He did not mean 'Maria' with whom I automatically identified. Now I was determined to genuinely also consider the essence of Abdullah as present and real; to connect with That and forget the memories of the perishable form with the brown eyes and black, curly hair. It helped that Abdullah had often told me that behind all forms there is only one Self. It wears masks—the Abdullah mask, the Maria mask, etc.

I wrote letters to this Self in Abdullah who, until recently, wore a body that I could touch. Now it seemed as if he had gone through a curtain. Not visible anymore but still there. 'He' reacted. I felt his presence and the curtain seemed at times a little transparent.

"Maria, let me write", I once scribbled while writing in my diary. And further: "I love you. I am always with you. We are not separate from each other. Never cry again. Have a smile for everything. Don't be afraid of pain. You will have enough strength to bear it. Don't be afraid of dying. I will be with you. We are not only of this world. We are from a different world. You just don't see it yet. Forget every sense of guilt. Forget all memories. Be aware that NOW we are together—I, your own self, that loves you infinitely, much more than what was expressed through Abdullah. There I had to stick to my leela (play) that you also influenced. But this is not important. True is that we are one in love. Stay open for me. Try to feel me in your heart. Be patient."

Another time I wrote: "Every form has the same essence. Identify with this essence, with the true thing in you and not with the impermanent form and fleeting thoughts and feelings. You have place for everyone and for everything. Be gentle, yield. This unreal 'Maria-ego' rules over your Self. This ego has to be given up, consciously. Give me all your desires and be always aware of my presence. Always—that means you have always something to do, isn't it? I help you. Eternity is now. Exactly now and always now.

Time is cheating you. Time has its role in the world of change, in the world of Abdullah and Maria, but not in the true Being. God *is*. He does not get old. Time is not for him—and therefore also not for what you and Abdullah really are. Hold tight to me."

I tried. "Om namah Shivay" kept automatically repeating inside me. I often reminded myself that all is Bhagawan and that he is here right now. Nevertheless, the joy for life had disappeared. I looked at the snow covered mountain peaks and did not see beauty anymore. Earlier they had looked so beautiful.

Once, however, I saw beauty. It was a face, a human being, a villager, who had a towel wrapped around his head. He climbed up the slope on a zigzag track. He reached the trail where I was walking some 10 metres ahead of me. "How beautiful he is!" shot through my mind. He had hardly reached the path when he gestured me to stop. I stopped, but wondered why. He put his right elbow into his left hand and formed with the right hand the head of a cobra. Then only I saw it. Between us, some 5 metres away, a snake slid across the path and down the slope.

I sometimes had day-dreamt that I would not mind also leaving this world and had thought of two possibilities. 'Maybe I get bitten by a snake', was one and the other, "Maybe I slip on a steep slope."

Soon after that, —averted, —chance of snakebite, I almost slipped, however in a different way than I had imagined: I took the last bus from Mussoorie down to Dehradun, which leaves before dark and as dusk does not last long, drives into the night. Everything went well. Yet when I reached, I felt sick and vomited repeatedly. I blamed the serpentine bus ride. But when it did not stop even the next day, a doctor came. He held a mirror to my face. I had never been so yellow. It was hepatitis and the doctor prescribed three weeks of strict bed rest.

Friends who visited me then gave me the news: the same 'last bus' on the following day had gone off the road and tumbled down the slope. Thirteen people died. Many were seriously injured and had to wait for hours in the dark and cold until help reached them.

I had narrowly missed the slip.

After a three-week long bed rest, I felt again joy for life and I could see beauty again. At night, I went to the roof terrace. The lights of Mussoorie glistened on top of the dark silhouette of the mountains and the stars sparkled in the clear sky. It was breathtakingly beautiful.

Now I travelled again; still felt tender and it helped to be more sensitive to the feelings of others. Earlier I had assumed that everyone was just fine, had not even tried to sense how the other person felt. Now I was not so sure anymore. Who knows, maybe the man in the teashop or the boy who rolls out chapattis has just lost somebody who was dear to him? After all, it is not so rare and the pain of it I knew now first hand.

CHAPTER 15

Born again and again

"Whatever has a beginning must have an end", the Tripura Rahasya states. The body had a beginning, so it has to have an end. There is no point in grieving over what is natural. Yet the body, though a superb instrument, is not the essential thing of what we are. Essential is consciousness. This essence is one and eternal. "Water cannot wet it, wind cannot dry it, fire cannot burn it", Krishna says in the Bhagavad-Gita.

This ancient knowledge seems to make dying easier in India compared to the West. Yet there is another, major reason why it is easier: the belief in rebirth. This belief is in the blood of Hindus and it is not blind belief. There are many good arguments in favour of it. The law of karma—that one reaps what one sows—for example, makes much more sense when it is not valid to only one life. The differences between human beings appear in a different light. Why is someone born in a palace and another in a hut? Why does one baby have loving parents and another does not? Why is one man healthy and another sick? Why is one person bright and intelligent, and another mentally retarded?

Such questions cannot be answered and lead many people to despair about a just god. Yet rebirth gives a reasonable explanation. Everything is always in a flux. Who cries today, may laugh tomorrow, and who laughs today may cry tomorrow—in a continuous circle of life and death.

Though I had studied psychology at Hamburg University, I discovered only in India that there exists a vast body of research on rebirth. Some 3000 cases have been systematically studied and are filed in the archive of the Division of Perceptual Studies of the University of Virginia, USA. Ian Stevenson who died in 2007 at the age of 88 was the initiator and main authority of the studies. Untiringly, he worked together with psychologists around the globe.

Their research came to the conclusion that rebirth is the most plausible and most rational interpretation of their findings. Nothing new for Indians, yet in the West this theory got a mixed response. Many Western scientists still refuse to consider the possibility of rebirth. They cannot get over their brainwashing in childhood that there is only one life and based on it god decides whether one ends up in heaven or hell.

Ian Stevenson's greatest frustration was not that people dismissed his theories, but that in his opinion most did so without even reading the evidence he had gathered. "Either he (Stevenson) is making a colossal mistake, or he will be known ... as 'the Galileo of the 20th century'," a Western psychiatrist wrote about him. It shows that academics in the West are either like frogs in a well or extremely arrogant. A great part of humanity takes rebirth for granted. Yet this academic feels that Stevenson will be credited with inventing this theory if it turns out to be confirmed.

In India, Professor N.K. Chadha of Delhi University worked together with Ian Stevenson. I met him in 1990 and though he had given me an half an hour appointment, it turned into two hours as the time just flew.

Here is how he proceeds with his research:

It happens occasionally that a child, around 3 or 4 years old, claims with all conviction he is capable of to be a certain grown up person whose name is such and such, who lived and died in such and such a way. Once the professor's team gets to know about it, they visit the child, gather the info, try to identify the person who had died, and if identified, crosscheck all insider information. It is a lot of work. Some 30 visits to a far-flung village might be necessary to rule out any other possible explanations, why the child has amazing insider knowledge about some person who died before his birth.

A case is considered solved, when the person, who the child claims to have been, is identified, all insider knowledge of the child crosschecked and no discrepancies found. Then it can be safely assumed that the child 'remembers' what he knows about that person and it is considered a case of rebirth.

Prof. Chadha has examined 25 cases out of which 11 were solved so far. The stories of those cases are fascinating—for example, the case of Titu Singh:

Titu was born in December 1983 in a village near Agra of Taj Mahal fame. As soon as he could speak, he started to claim that his name was Suresh Verma and that he owned a radio shop in Agra. One evening, when he came home, he was shot dead. Further, he said, he has two sons and a wife named Uma. He spoke in detail how he died: he had driven home in his Fiat car and honked so that his wife would open the gate. Suddenly, two men came running and fired at him. One bullet hit his head.

Titu was aggressive towards his 'new' parents, kept nagging them, for example claimed that his real mother did not wear such old saris, and occasionally even threw plates around. He did not believe they were his parents. His 'real' parents, he stubbornly maintained, lived in Agra. Titu's elder brother finally went to Agra and was shocked to find, indeed, a "Suresh Radio Shop" in the bazaar. He gathered information: the owner—a certain Suresh Verma—had died in August 1983, exactly in the way Titu had described. Uma, the widow of Suresh, was curious to see the boy who claimed to be her husband. She went together with her parents in law and Suresh's three brothers to the village of Titu.

Titu immediately ran towards 'his parents' and embraced them. He shyly glanced at Uma and then turned disappointed to his brothers. "Why did you come with this car and not with my Fiat?" he deplored. They had sold the Fiat after Suresh's death.

Titu was taken to Agra. The brothers, all adults, intended to drive past the radio shop to test him. However, the four year old pounced on the driver, "Stop! Here is my shop", he shouted. Inside, he commented on some changes that had been made after Suresh's death.

Prof. Chadha and Dr. Antonia Mills of Virginia University examined the case over almost 4 years. They were very systematic, to discover possible discrepancies and to rule out that Titu got his information through normal communication. They watched him and his reactions closely.

Once, when Prof. Chadha asked the little Titu to greet Maheash, the 35-year-old younger brother of Suresh, he refused. „He is my younger brother", the kid claimed. The researchers came to know that the relationship between Mahesh and Suresh had been tense. This explained why Titu usually ignored Mahesh. Significantly, Mahesh was the only member of the Verma family who had doubts: since Suresh was known in Agra and everyone knew about the murder, the parents of Titu could have fed this information to their son, maybe to get financial benefits from the Vermas who were wealthier than the Singhs, Mahesh speculated. But not for long. He changed his stand after he tested Titu himself. He grabbed Titu's wrist, Prof. Chadha narrated, and did not let go of it. "Tell me, what happened during my wedding?" he demanded to know. The boy reacted annoyed. "Why, nothing happened. I threw plates." Now, Mahesh was also convinced. It was true. Suresh spoilt the atmosphere at his wedding when he angrily threw with plates.

Professor Chadha discovered something else intriguing: Titu has a strange dent on his right temple. They studied the autopsy record and found that the bullet had entered Suresh's head at exactly that place. And where the bullet had exited, there was a mole.

Strangely, or not strangely, in about four out of ten rebirth cases, the child remembered a sudden, violent death, through either accident or murder. This happened at an average age of only 34 years. The interval between death and rebirth was also significantly shorter than if the remembered person had died peacefully. In Titu's case, it was only 5 months and on average below two years. There may be an explanation: if one suddenly and unexpectedly is pulled out from life, there may be the feeling that one is not yet finished with it and wants to come back as soon as possible to 'continue' living. The great interest in the previous life and the short span between death and birth may be responsible that the memory is easier accessible and that the identification with the earlier person dominates.

"Do you personally believe in rebirth?" I asked Prof Chadha. His answer was a clear "Yes". Hindus do not need 'scientific' proof. It is logical, the best possible explanation for all the differences between humans.

The belief in rebirth is ancient—probably as ancient as mankind. It was there also in ancient Greece and in early Christianity. Jesus for example hints that John the Baptist was prophet Elias reborn (Matthew 17. 12-13). Yet at the second council of Constantinople some 500 years after Jesus' death, Christianity did away with this belief and from that time onwards indoctrinated their flock into believing that only one life decides whether one goes to heaven or hell. 'So better don't experiment and believe what we tell you!' the Church officials might have wanted to convey. Yet today—with the whip of inquisition gone—not all Christians conform to the Church. Belief in rebirth is taking root in the West. 25 per cent of Americans believe in rebirth, a poll quoted by Newsweek magazine of 31.Aug 2009 suggested.

Tibetan society not only believes in rebirth, it has institutionalised it. When high Lamas die, their reincarnation is systematically searched for. The present Dalai Lama, the 14th in the line of Dalai Lamas und born in 1935, is considered the reincarnation of the 13th Dalai Lama who had died in 1933. In his autobiography "My life and my people", he describes in detail how the search party of high Lamas found him in the remote village that he was born in and why they became convinced that he was the 13th Dalai Lama reborn.

Yet in spite of all the evidence for rebirth, there is no rebirth on another, higher level of truth. "Find out, whether you have been born in this life," the sage Ramana Maharshi exhorted a visitor who wanted to know about his previous births. And when once asked, whether there is rebirth, Ramana replied, "There is rebirth and there is no rebirth." He probably meant that on the personal appearance level it is there. In absolute truth, where only One exists, there is no place for different persons to be born and reborn. In absolute truth, you and I are not separate. Our essence is the same.

CHAPTER 16

The Dalai Lama's home in India

In the spring of 1985, I received a letter from Inka Jochum, who used to run the health centre of the Holiday Inn in Munich. We had met at the conference on 'Ancient Wisdom and Modern Science' in Bombay three years ago. She wrote that she and her friend Erika would soon come to Dharmsala. They would have an audience with the Dalai Lama. "Would you like to join us?" she asked. "Yes, with great pleasure".

Inka had booked a taxi all the way from Delhi to Dharmsala. The drive took the whole day and we could stop whenever we wanted. My travel companions carried a big supply of sweets and made children from villages happy.

Dharmsala is located at an altitude of around 2000 meter. It is called 'mini-Tibet' and attracts tourist from all over the world. Many of them may not even know why there are so many Tibetans in India.

A lot of time has passed—several generations of Tibetans who have been born in India—since, in 1959, the Chinese shelled Lhasa and the summer residence of the Dalai Lama and suppressed with brutal force the uprising of the Tibetans against the Chinese invaders. The Dalai Lama had sneaked out of the palace shortly before the attack, dressed in a soldier's uniform and without wearing his glasses, and fled to India over high, snow-covered passes with a small group of confidants, including his mother, sister and youngest brother. He was only 24 years old, sick, exhausted and unhappy, when he finally crossed the border to India—"far more unhappy than I can express", he wrote in his autobiography soon after his arrival in India.

But in the next sentence he continued, "Nobody—including me—could remain fully unhappy due to the compassion with which we were received even in the first villages and towns of India."

Around 100,000 of his compatriots followed him to India, mostly under dramatic circumstances. Only a few thousand of them moved on to other countries. The majority settled in the 'noble land', as they call India, because Buddha has lived and taught there.

The Indian people were kind to the refugees and the government generous. They provided land in moderate climate zones across the country, so that the Tibetans could preserve their culture and religion and do farming. Dharmsala became the seat of the Tibetan government in exile with the Dalai Lama as the spiritual and temporal head. Over the years, the Dalai Lama made the functioning of the government more democratic, and relinquished his political powers. But he still carries a lot of weight, politically as well. His people hold him in highest esteem.

Inka had founded a Tibet Aid in Munich, which focusses on preserving Tibetan medicine. At a conference in Austria, she had met by chance Dalai Lama's sister in law and felt immediately at home among Tibetans. She asked her friends not to bring any gifts for her 40th birthday, but to bring money for Tibet. She promised that the money would reach the right place, because she would ask the Dalai Lama personally, how it should be used and she herself would carry it to Dharmsala once a year at her own expense. On that first evening already some 4000 Mark were collected.

Inka had therefore a certain VIP status in Dharmsala and Erika and I benefited from it. We stayed in Kashmir Cottage, a small guesthouse, which belonged to the youngest brother of the Dalai Lama

With H.H. the Dalai Lama on the veranda of his bungalow in Dharmsala (to the left Erika, to the right, Inka and I).

We also visited Namlha, the sister in law of Dalai Lama, and her husband. It was a happy, friendly atmosphere. Her husband was charming and full of humour. At that time, none of us could have imagined that a few months later, at the age of only 52, he would die of hepatitis.

The highlight of our stay was no doubt the hour-long audience with the Dalai Lama.

„Like family, isn't it? Like family", the Dalai Lama beamed, when we three were sitting with him and his secretary in his bungalow. It truly felt like family. His joy was infectious and his strong presence inspiring.

I told him that I genuinely wanted to be aware of the oneness of all or, in other words, the presence of god during the whole day, but it just didn't work. "This doesn't matter. It happens to me also," he laughed.

When he noticed that I was more familiar with the Indian tradition, he surprised me with a question.

"Do you think that the concept of Atman in Hinduism is the main difference between Hinduism and Buddhism?"

"No", I said, because in the Upanishads it is clearly stated that Atman is Brahman.

However, I was not sure whether the official Buddhism held this view, too, and made a test. When I visited Sakya Trizin, the head of the Sakya sect, who lives in Dehradun, I asked him, "What is the difference between Buddhism and Hinduism?"

"The concept of Atman", he promptly replied.

Buddhists generally believe that the concept of Atman, which is usually translated as self, refers to an independent, separate self and that only Buddhism does not postulate an independent, separate self. There are philosophical schools in India who indeed claim that Atman stands for an independent self, but Advaita Vedanta leaves no doubt that 'Atman is Brahman', i.e. that, which alone is and which is called by different names, but which ultimately has no name.

After this encounter in Dharmsala, I met the Dalai Lama on several other occasions—during the inauguration of monasteries, press conferences and teachings, which he gave for his countrymen.

I was there in Bodh Gaya in December 1985, when he gave the highly valued Kalachakra initiation to some 250,000 people. This meditation requires a talent for imagination, because it is stipulated in minute detail, what one has to imagine—for example, that one is a pure deity in a palace that symbolises the universe. In the end, one dissolves all this imagination into emptiness. The purpose is to expand far beyond the small ego, and to get closer to the truth that we are formless, infinite and empty.

Some 8000 Tibetan monks and—so it seemed—all lay Tibetans had gathered in Bodh Gaya from all corners of India, as well as from Nepal and Bhutan. They all converged at the place, where over 2500 years ago Buddha got enlightened. Yet the greatest surprise was that the Chinese had temporarily loosened their grip on Tibet and allowed Tibetans from Tibet to take part in the function.

Some 10,000 people had travelled to India from Tibet. They looked different from the Tibetans in exile and were easily recognisable, not only because of their dark, heavy coats which indicated that they had come from a harsher climate into the North Indian plains. They had a different expression on their face and appeared calmer, slower, and radiated a dignified pride.

The Tibetans from Tibet had not seen the Dalai Lama for 26 years and the younger ones among them saw him for the first time—and many cried. The adoration and love they expressed for him was overwhelming.

Once, an evidently poor man carefully unfolded a cloth from which a ring with a turquoise emerged. Then he unfolded another piece of cloth and took a hundred rupee note out of it. He placed the note through the ring and held it up, waiting for the Dalai Lama who would soon pass by. Yet before the Dalai Lama appeared, a security officer discovered the man in the crowd. He obviously explained to him that he could not hand over his gift to the Dalai Lama personally, because the man then entrusted his gift to the officer. I hoped that it would reach the Dalai Lama.

When the Dalai Lama finally walked past, surrounded by an entourage, a young girl near me started crying. I could have cried, too, about the fate of Tibet.

I remembered scenes from the 1970s at Hamburg University—congregations in the auditorium or pamphlets on the tables in the canteen, wherein the different communist groups praised China's policies up to the skies. Mao Tse-tung was a hero for us students. Even I bought the red booklet with Mao's sayings. At that time I had no idea, how brutally the Chinese had dealt with the Tibetans, that they had massacred several hundred thousands of them and had destroyed thousands of their monasteries. "Cultural revolution" sounded progressive for us students at Hamburg University. We were very immature that we had applauded the fiery speeches by student leaders about Mao's great revolution. Yet I realised this only, when I got to know Tibetans in India.

The Tibetans are strong and have a noble pride. There are faces among them which I will probably never forget.

One evening for example I went with Susan, a photo assistant of Geo magazine, to one of the food tents for the daily noodle soup. A Tibetan sat down opposite to us. He wore a heavy, dark coat and had his long plaits tied around his head with a red ribbon. We both were speechless with wonder—so beautiful he was. Susan later even claimed that he was an apparition, because such beautiful human beings just do not exist.

For dessert, I had a bar of chocolate in my bag. I took it out, put it on the table, broke it into pieces and offered it to our table companion. He took one piece, turned it in his hand and looked at it closely from all sides. We put our fingers to our mouth to give him a clue. He understood and ate it. And he seemed to like it, for he took one piece after another and finished the whole bar, and we were happy. Then he said something and of course, we wanted to know what he had said. We requested one of the exile Tibetans to ask him. "Nowadays there are also people from your tribe in Lhasa", he had said.

He disappeared into the darkness as beautiful, noble and proud as he had come.

CHAPTER 17

In favour of the wandering monk: Kumbh Mela

Luckily, I do not feel claustrophobic, when I am stuck in a huge crowd, otherwise India would be the wrong country for me. I actually enjoy the atmosphere, so incredibly colourful and diverse, a wave of human beings that carries everyone along, innumerable pair of eyes meeting my eyes, fleetingly, friendly—for a short while thrown together at the same place.

So when I heard in Bodh Gaya that the full Kumbh Mela will be celebrated in Haridwar in April 1986, I wanted to be there, for surely, there must be a reason, when millions of pilgrims from all corners of India undergo a lot of hardship to reach this festival on the Ganges. In fact, there are even two reasons.

Number one, a bath in the Ganges at the auspicious time of the Mela is a big attraction, because it is supposed to be very powerful, purifying and giving a boost to one's spiritual development.

And number two, there is the prospect of benefitting from the presence of great Rishis, the successors of the ancient wise men and women from Vedic times.

Traditionally, the Kumbh Mela is the meeting place for those pillars of Indian spirituality, who have dedicated their life to the search for truth. Even today, the hermits who are usually hidden in caves in the Himalayas and the Sadhus (renunciates) who wander all over the country with a begging bowl and a staff in hand stand for an ideal. They embody the dream of freedom and independence for those who feel tied down in the world.

The reason why during the time of the mela bathing in the Ganges is especially helpful for spiritual growth is given in a story, which since ancient times is connected with specific locations in northern India.

Long, long ago, at the beginning of our present world cycle, gods and demons tried to release the lost nectar of immortality by vigorously churning the milk ocean. When the jar (kumbh) filled to the brim with the nectar finally emerged, a wild chase started. The son of a god had seized the vessel with the precious content and the demons followed at his heels in hot pursuit. Sun, Moon and Jupiter played the role of protectors for the gods and influenced the outcome in their favour from certain positions. The chase lasted for 12 days, until the jar was finally safe with the gods.

According to the ancient story, a few drops of the nectar spilled over at four places in northern India, which thereby became especially sanctified and celebrate the Kumbh Mela once in twelve years: Haridwar, Allahabad (originally named Prayag), Nasik und Ujjain. When the drops fell into the Ganges in Haridwar during the chase, the Sun protected it from the position of Aries and Jupiter from Aquarius. This constellation repeats itself once in 12 years, because according to Indian tradition one year in the life of human beings corresponds to one day in the life of gods. Each time, when this constellation repeats itself, the influence of the celestial bodies is again supposed to be highly beneficial at the place, and millions of pilgrims converge to celebrate the Kumbh Mela.

So much about the background. It explains why many pious Hindus dream of bathing in the holy river during the Kumbh Mela. The explanation however may not convince a European. When I walked along the banks of the Ganges, and watched the pilgrims, who stood up to their waist in the water, held their nose with their fingers, and submerged themselves again and again, I would not have guessed that this kind of gymnastic is helpful in getting to know the truth.

But can I be sure? Whether the astrological constellation in question charges the atmosphere and the Ganges water in some subtle way, can so far neither be verified nor falsified. And after seven years in India, I was broad minded enough to consider the Indian view as possible, never mind that most Westerners would regards such belief 'from a scientific angle' as nonsense. Hindus trust that their sages and their tradition know a lot about the subtle interdependence between man and cosmos. They have a point, as science keeps validating more and more insights of the ancient wisdom. To be fair, Westerners should have at least the same level of acceptance towards the Indian belief, as they have towards baptism in the Church. Rather even a higher level, as no Indian threatens anyone with eternal hellfire, if he does *not* bathe in the Ganges.

I personally did not consider the bath as important. Nevertheless, it so happened that at 2 o'clock at night, at the supposedly most auspicious hour and day, I took a bath in the Ganges. A group of people around a tiny, fragile woman, Rani Ma by name, took charge of me. I had landed up in this group the previous evening by chance.

I liked Rani Ma. Not much was known about her past. She was from Bengal. It seems she had lost her parents early and when her foster parents wanted to marry her off, she simply left her home and wandered to the Himalaya as so many before her. Nine years ago, she had reached Haridwar and stayed on there in an ashram. On her veranda a group of visitors assembled every evening. She did not talk much. Her guru was Babaji and I was happy when I saw his picture on a locket around her neck. Her devotees from Kolkata considered her enlightened.

There was no doubt that this group would take a bath in the Ganges in the night and Rani Ma insisted on taking me along. I did not object. We slept for a couple of hours on reed mats on her veranda and then joined the steady, unending stream of human beings winding their way through the town to the Ganges. The stream was so dense that I hardly managed to take off my slippers when we reached the ghat. The others had wisely walked barefoot from the start. There was real danger that the stream of people would run over one, if one bends to the ground.

It actually happened. Fifty people died in that night. The continuous stream of pilgrims had been blocked for a while to make way for some VIP politician and then was waved on. Many, who had squatted on the ground and had dozed off while waiting, could not get up fast enough, when the crowd suddenly surged forward. They were trampled to death.

Nevertheless, I was glad about that amazing experience and would have regretted, if I had slept through the night in the press camp.

About half a million sadhus, swamis, sanyasis, as the potentially holy men and women are called, had come to Haridwar—a good representation of spiritual India. Anandamayi Ma and Babaji had already passed away, but Devaraha Baba was there. The Mela imparted a colourful, fascinating picture.

Many sadhus were naked, just smeared with ash from head to toe. Yet most of them had wrapped around their hips a saffron coloured, sometimes also white or black cotton cloth. On their foreheads, they had painted mysterious marks. Their hairstyle was eccentric. If their heads were not shaven, their hair was matted and piled up in several layers or reached down to the waist or even to the toes.

If I had not noticed it already earlier, I would have noticed it during the Kumbh Mela—not all of them were close to sainthood. Only because someone is naked or dressed in saffron, does not mean that he is a pure, calm, great being who is a well-wisher for all of humanity. As is the case everywhere, there are good and not so good individuals. Therefore, there were also the genuine ones who had dedicated their life to the search for the truth—fully and sincerely—and among them, there might have been some who had come to an end of their search and 'knew' what they truly were in their essence.

Once for example, I was sitting on a small wooden bench in front of a teashop on the roadside. An elderly man with a towel wrapped around his head sat down next to me. I automatically moved a bit away from him, because his clothes looked dirty. The dhoti and wide shirt must have been white a long time ago. He carried a sack over his shoulder, which had the same dirty colour. A skinny bitch, whose puppies were tumbling over each other under her belly, positioned herself behind our bench and looked at us with eyes full of hope and expectation. We both turned towards her and I was surprised, how much compassion shone from the eyes of this man. From then on, I liked him a lot, sitting quietly next to him, I wondered whether it was appropriate to pay for his tea. He looked poor. Yet just then, Melita Maschmann passed by on the road and we had a chat. Meanwhile the man paid and left. We also left and Melita pointed at him, "Look at this man in front of us. People here claim that he is enlightened. He is always calm, kind, unperturbed, even though he is poor and earns his livelihood by collecting mud for soaps."

Melita and I participated in the morning Arati at Anandamayi Ma's Samadhi. Afterwards we went off in different directions. I was walking on the road, when the man from the teashop came to my mind. I would have liked to see him again. Somebody walked in front of me, but he did not have a towel around his head, only a short crop of white hair, so I did not take further notice of him. Suddenly I became aware of the prominent varicose veins on his legs and realised that it was he. At the same moment, he turned and smiled at me.

Some other time I sat with a group of people around Rani Ma on her veranda, when a sadhu from Uttarkashi in the Himalayas joined us. Rani Ma greeted him warmly. He seemed to be an old friend of hers and a pleasant, likeable person. Both of them conversed with each other for a while. Then he sank into stillness. We all were still and it felt very peaceful. After he had left, Rani Ma claimed, that he was enlightened.

Probably I have walked past a number of people without recognising that he or she felt the oneness of all.

I suppose that there were some in those huge tents, which the government had put up for the very poor. There, people kept non-stop chanting one of the many names of the Divine. Among them were emaciated, old men with hollow cheeks and eyes sunken deep in their sockets, who accompanied their chanting with cymbals—and had time to look up and invite me with a smile and nodding of the head to join in.

They were devotees of Vishnu, who is the preserver of the universe. Vishnu is said to incarnate in human form on earth, whenever the evil gets the upper hand, to show again the right path to human beings. Ram and Krishna are Vishnu's most loved avataras. The life story of Ram is narrated in the Ramayana and Krishna's in the Mahabharata, which consist of 100.000 shlokas. Krishna lived according to the tradition some 5000 years ago and Ram many thousand years earlier. The devotees of Vishnu are generally milder compared to those of Shiva. They want to be constantly and lovingly aware of his presence and merge with him or rather merge with that form of him, which they love most.

When I got up to leave, an old man advised me to travel to Ayodhya and even enquired whether I have enough money for the train ticket to get there. He genuinely wanted me to visit the birthplace of his beloved Ram, who was for him god in human form.

I enjoyed moving from camp to camp and observing today's successors of the ancient rishis.

In front of a photo shop, an about 20-year-old sadhu approached me and asked in fluent English where I came from. He was a naga sadhu, wearing only a loincloth—"since yesterday", he told me already in his second sentence. The previous day I had witnessed, as a few thousand young men sat on the banks of the Ganges, their heads freshly shaven and wearing only a loin cloth. They "took sanyas", that means, they vowed to renounce the pleasures of the world and not to dream anymore of wealth, family and fame, but instead to dedicate their life completely to the search for the truth.

Shiva is seen as the destroyer in the trinity besides Brahma, the creator and Vishnu, the preserver. But Shiva is also seen as the Highest, the One above the trinity.

One of those young men stood now before me, handsome, likeable, who, only day before yesterday, would have looked completely normal, with shirt and trousers on his body and hair on his head. I asked him why he chose to become a naga sadhu. "I want to meditate in a cave in the Himalaya to become one with Shiva", he answered, as if this kind of desire was the most natural thing in the world for a young man of his age. I used the opportunity to ask him whether he could introduce me to his guru. He readily agreed.

The naga sadhus consider themselves as the warriors of Shiva. Shiva is on one hand the destroyer in the trinity besides Brahma, the creator and Vishnu, the preserver. On the other hand, Shiva is considered to be the Highest, the one above the trinity. In the 8th century (some place him earlier), the great philosopher Adi Shankara had grouped the individual sadhus into ten orders, as per their main spiritual practice. Adi Shankara also asked them to visit the Kumbh Melas, to keep in touch with each other and to exhort the common people to live a righteous life.

The naga sadhus fought against the Muslim invaders, who between the 8th and 18th century, made life very difficult for Hindus. They were not only discriminated against, but millions were killed if they refused to convert to Islam.

I dared to take a photo of the naked nagas, even though the press officer had asked us not to do so, as they may get angry. I did it quickly with my small camera and was sure that nobody had seen it—until the film was developed. Three nagas looked directly into the lens.

The manager of the tourist bungalow in Haridwar had warned me about the naga sadhus and advised me against going to their camp. In case they do not like something about me, it could have disastrous consequences, because most of those sadhus have occult powers, he claimed. Yet my young companion seemed extremely peaceful and his guru, too, was surprisingly friendly, almost gentle and rather stout. He not only allowed, but seemed happy that I took photos, because he called the whole company of his sadhu disciples to his tent. He offered me tea. Conversing however was difficult, as my Hindi was poor.

He dictated the shopping list to the young man who had become a sadhu only the previous day, who carefully noted down all the items needed. I wished him the best for his path, wished that he may realise the truth and keep up his enthusiasm. For the vow to renounce the world by itself is no guarantee that worldly desires do not get again the upper hand. I have respect—not only for those who have achieved the ideal of an even-minded, serene personality, but also for those who strive for it.

It is easy to ridicule those strange looking figures because of their appearance or to put them down as parasites of society. There is no doubt that many of them wear saffron only because it is easier to beg in this colour, and possibly there are even some criminals hiding in that garb. But, can I really know how much courage many sadhus muster to let go of the dream of a happy family life and success in a career—in favour of an inward journey, where they have to walk alone, without health insurance and without being certain that the next meal will indeed find its way into their begging bowl?

They demonstrate a life style, which is diametrically opposite to the modern life style. They are not interested in increasing and fulfilling desires, but in relinquishing them. They do not want to create needs, but to reduce them. In this way, they act like a barrier against the mighty trend towards the consumer society.

'If in doubt, be in favour of the sadhu' is the motto in India. Even critics of the spiritual scene in the country do not doubt that there are enlightened beings among them, somewhere high up in the inaccessible Himalaya—who leave their cave only for the Kumbh Mela.

CHAPTER 18

Ramlila in Varanasi

A journalist in the press camp of the Kumbh Mela suggested writing about the colourful, grand Ramlila in Varanasi. I still enjoyed travelling and even more so if it served a purpose.

The Ramlila is a play (leela) about Ram, the prince of Ayodhya. He lived many thousand years ago, long before Krishna. Yet even today, every Hindu child knows in detail his eventful life story, which the Ramayana depicts. The Ramayana is one of the great epics, in which the poet Valmiki, supposedly a contemporary of Ram, vividly narrates the life story of the prince, who later becomes the king of Ayodhya. This story was narrated orally over millennia before it was written down in Sanskrit. In the 17th century, Tulsidas wrote Ramcharitmanas, the story of Ram, in the vernacular Avadhi language and made it even more popular. Ram has greatly influenced the art and literature as far as in Nepal, Burma, Laos, Thailand and Indonesia. If there is one great epic for the whole of Asia, it is the Ramayana.

In India, however, the Ramayana is not just a great epic. It is a holy scripture. India without Ram would not be India. His name is everywhere. "Ram, Ram", is a common form of greeting among Hindus in northern India. There are hundreds, if not thousands of songs extolling Ram and many people know at least some of them.

Ram is considered as an avatar—God incarnate in human form.

He showed how to live a dignified life and how to conduct oneself in an ideal way in the different human relationships. Ram is an outstanding example for others—noble, just, brave, ever protecting the weak, ready rather to die than to break his word and prepared to wage war to rescue his wife Sita who had been kidnapped by a demon king.

Sita, on the other hand, possesses all the virtues, which a woman is supposed to have according to the ancient Rishis. She is modest, chaste, always intent on the well-being of her husband, warm hearted, full of trust in Bhagawan, considerate, graceful—and exquisitely beautiful. Some women's liberation groups, which also exist in India, find fault with Sita, yet the majority of Indian women do not care. They revere Sita as their ideal even today.

For Ram to be a model for others, he has to have a difficult life. And he indeed faces countless, unexpected complications and hardship. For example on the very day, when the handsome, much loved prince is to ascend the throne, his father Dasaratha, caused by an intrigue in the palace, has to send him into exile for 14 long years. It breaks his father's heart. Ram calmly takes off the festive robes and dresses in the simple gown of an ascetic. Sita and his brother Lakshman insist on joining him. So the three walk out of the town into the forest—and the whole of Ayodhya weeps.

Indians do not get tired to listen to the story of Ram in ashrams or to watch it in village plays. When in the 1980s the Ramayana was shown on TV every Sunday morning over a couple of years, the streets were as empty as otherwise only during curfew or a world cup cricket match between India and Pakistan. Even the flights on Sunday morning had fewer passengers as usual.

Once I was sitting high up in the mountains near a small temple. I could hear the crackling of loudspeakers coming from a village below. Some boys traced me. "Do people in your country also know about Ram?" they asked me. "No, they don't know about Ram", I replied. "How sad!" was their spontaneous reaction. Then only I realised that the crackling of the loudspeaker indicated that preparations for the Ramlila were going on in the village.

In Varanasi, the Ramlila stretches over 30 evenings in October/ November and is traditionally held under the patronage of the Maharaja. The play is staged opposite the town on the other side of the Ganges in Ramnagar and culminates on Diwali festival, when Ram returns to Ayodhya after his exile and takes over as king.

Before the play, a pooja (worship) is performed for the actors and thereafter they are considered true embodiments of their roles. Many spectators touched respectfully the feet of the 12-year old boy who played Ram, when there was an occasion during breaks. The actors were right in the midst of the crowd in some of the scenes. Nearby, a group of men dressed in white cotton cloth with yellow turbans sat in a circle on the ground and chanted the whole Tulsidas Ramayana of 24,000 shlokas. The Maharaja paid a pension to those men. In return, they had to promise to live a pure life without drinking, smoking or eating meat.

There was a festive atmosphere with plenty of food carts and stalls selling trinkets. When Ram went into exile, several thousand spectators walked with him around two kilometres to the place, where the next episode would unfold. An amazing experience in itself.

The Maharaja was present and moved high up on a fabulously decorated elephant through the crowd. His son, the prince, was sitting on another splendidly decorated elephant.

I have particularly fond memories of the journeys back across the Ganges in the middle of the night after the play. Mainly men crossed over to the town on the other side on countless, crowded boats in the stillness of the night—once it was even four in the morning. They excitedly narrated to each other how admirably Ram had conducted himself today and how exemplarily Sita had reacted –as if it just happened and they had the good fortune of being present. When the talking stopped, they started singing "Siya Ram, jay Siya Ram"—everyone in his own tune and rhythm. Towards the end of the boat ride, while gliding past a Shiva temple on the ghats in Varanasi, they interrupted "Siya Ram" and full throatily shouted a salutation to Shiva: "Hara Hara Mahadev!"

I was not afraid of riding alone in a cycle rickshaw at that late hour from the Ganges to the tourist bungalow near the railway station through unusually empty streets. My trust was never disappointed. Varanasi is a fascinating, intense city, where life and death are present side by side, and this world and the beyond merge into each other. Kashi (light) was the name of the city in ancient times. In all likelihood, it is the most ancient of all towns on earth and has its origin in an age, when the world was still more transparent for its luminous essence and less dense in the material sense.

Maybe the special, spiritual atmosphere of the town contributed to an amazing coincidence that happened on the side-lines: Georg, a college mate from Hamburg, had planned a trip to India. He sent a letter to my address in South India asking if we could meet. "Write to American Express in Delhi. I will be soon in Delhi" he wrote. Yet I knew nothing of that, as I was in the North and his letter was lying in the South. Those were the times before email and mobile phone. Georg went daily to the American Express and was daily disappointed. As he could not spend his vacation waiting for a letter, he decided to go on the usual tourist route—Agra, Khajaraho and Varanasi. One morning, as I had breakfast in the tourist bungalow, the door of the restaurant opened and in came Georg. For a while, we both stared at each other, completely stunned, unable to believe what we saw. Then we both came back to life, overjoyed at this incredible coincidence.

CHAPTER 19

Ayodhya—the birthplace of Ram

Ayodhya, Ram's birthplace, is three hours by train from Varanasi. I remembered the old men in the big tents at the Kumbh Mela in Haridwar, who had invited me to join in their singing and who had urged me to visit Ayodhya, where their beloved Ram was born. It is a very ancient, holy place.

Ayodhya was a quiet town in 1986 when I reached there. While wandering through the streets in the evenings, devotional songs praising Ram accompanied by cymbals could be heard from almost every house. The sacred Saryu river that originates near Mount Kailash flows by serenely. People bathed or washed their cloth at the ghats. The town itself is full of temples and ashrams. One could even visit Ram's palace and for 50 paisa extra enter his private chambers, which looked ancient and had such low ceiling that I could not stand upright. The pilgrims from the villages probably had no doubt that Ram rested or still rests on those very same cushions, which were draped on the bed. They tenderly touched the objects in the rooms and then respectfully placed their fingers on their eyes. They also put letters for Ram on the table in his room. Once, it was said, Ram had replied—in form of a love letter.

At that time I had no idea that six years later Ayodhya would become 'famous' in the media all over the world. Even today, there is mention of the destruction of an unused mosque, the Babri Mosque, on the outskirts of Ayodhya.

Babar, an invader of Turkish-Mongolian origin and descendant of Genghis Khan, had built this mosque in the early 16th century, after he had defeated the Sultan of Delhi and had established himself as the ruler and founder of the Mogul dynasty. I visited this mosque, because on its compound stood a small, makeshift shelter for Ram, which seemed to have great importance for Hindu pilgrims. At that time, I did not know that the Hindus claim that Babar had destroyed a temple on Ram's birthplace and built the mosque on it.

Under the Muslim invaders, who ruled with a brutal, iron hand over big parts of the Indian subcontinent from the 11th century onwards, countless temples had been destroyed and mosques built on top (a Hindu organisation put the number at 30 000). Yet the temple at Ram's birthplace was especially dear to the Hindus. Therefore, they had appealed already under British rule that the place, where the mosque stood, should be given back to them, so they could again build a temple for Ram. The building had since long been called a 'disputed structure' and since 1949 no Islamic prayers had been conducted there and it wasn't in use as a mosque.

Shortly before I reached Ayodhya in 1986, the government had given permission for Hindus to worship Ram in that small tent-like temple. The movement, which wanted to build a big Ram Mandir there, gained in strength. Many Hindus saw the Babri mosque as a symbol of their enslavement under the oppressive Muslim rule that needed to be removed in a free India.

In 1992, when the public sentiment was greatly in favour of a Ram Mandir, the government allowed a symbolic foundation stone laying for a temple at a safe distance from the mosque and extracted from the organisers the promise that the mosque will not be touched.

The events on 6th December, however, took a different turn. When young people broke through the barriers towards the 'disputed structure', the huge crowd could not be controlled. Activists climbed up the domes of the building and started pounding them—until the old structure finally crumpled. There was no doubt a certain satisfaction among the common Hindus.

In the domestic and international media, however, a tremendous storm followed. It was considered a national shame, a great tragedy. It was envisioned that Hindu fundamentalists were taking over in India.

It did not happen. From my experience, Hindus are exceptionally tolerant, even though they have suffered a lot under Muslim and afterwards under British rule. The philosophy of the Hindus is "to live and let live". It is thanks to them, who comprise close to 80 per cent of the population that over one billion of extremely diverse human beings are able to live side by side relatively peacefully. It evokes astonishment in other countries. The liberality of Hindus is obvious even in the top jobs of the government. Nobody is excluded—Hindus, Muslims, Sikhs, Christians, Parsis, Jains held high positions. Even an Italian born Christian, Sonia Gandhi, was for 10 long years, from 2004 till 2014, the de-facto head of the government.

Archaeologists found a temple under the mosque in Ayodhya. I felt that the Muslims, whose ancestors had also revered Ram not so long ago, could allow the construction of a temple, since this place is holy for Hindus, but not for Islam, and the mosque had anyway been built on a temple which had been destroyed less than 500 years ago. It would be an easy gesture of good will, which would go a long way to improve the relations between Hindus and Muslims.

Yet when I expressed my view to some of my leftist Indian friends, it caused their blood pressure to shoot up. My view was, as I quickly realised, politically incorrect and 'Hindu fundamentalist'. Politically correct is to support the demands and views of the religious minorities, never mind what they demand or what views they have. Naturally, this is a dangerous path. It seems to be slowly changing, mainly because the West is nowadays also getting a taste of Islamic terror and the narrative that Muslims are always the victims and never the aggressors is losing credibility.

Some years later, I travelled by train again through Ayodhya. It was early afternoon and hot. A young couple boarded the train and stood in the corridor. Sita and Ram came to my mind. Both of them were very beautiful. She wore a red sari and had her head covered.

The henna decorations on her hands and the numerous bangles on her forearms indicated that they were newly married. He was dressed in white. The train was full. We were already six sitting on the two wooden benches, yet I automatically moved to make space. He indicated to her to sit down next to me. Now there was movement on the other bench, as well, and he sat down opposite to her. The atmosphere in the compartment had all of a sudden changed. One of the passengers asked the newcomer some questions to which he replied. Then they were left in peace. The attraction between the two was palpable. The compartment was narrow and their knees were close to each other, but they did not touch.

She looked down at her hands most of the time. He often looked at her. Three hours they sat like this in full silence. Only once he bent forward and asked her, "Are you feeling hot?" she briefly looked up, smiled and shook her head. Only this one sentence "Are you feeling hot?" in three hours! They left as quietly as they had come.

CHAPTER 20

Ramana Maharshi and the most important question

Meanwhile I had written numerous of articles for German magazines—about Indian philosophy and about events like Kumbh Mela or Ramlila. My sister could follow what was on my mind and where I spent my time and it seems, she considered it risky.

"Make sure that you don't get hooked to one of those gurus", she warned me.

"Don't worry", I assured her. After all, I had already spent several years in the surroundings of gurus and still did not have one.

A guru signifies somebody who removes ignorance. In the spiritual realm ignorance stands for the strong conviction, that I am my body with its thoughts and feelings, which means, I am a separate person unconnected to others. The guru, if he is genuine, shakes this conviction and shows the disciple that everything is a unified whole, that, as it were, one single ocean miraculously produces all the waves. In other words, everything is made from essentially the same stuff.

Insofar I had no objection against having a guru. In fact, I would have actually needed a guru, because I definitely had not overcome the 'obvious' outlook that I am a separate, individual person. However, I was not sure whether great gurus still existed. Furthermore, I was weary of the absolute obedience, which was required in the relationship between disciple and guru. I therefore preferred to hold on to my inner guru and to take help from spiritual masters, who had already left their body.

Ramana Maharshi (1879—1950) was a kind of guru for me. He had lived in Tiruvannamalai in Tamil Nadu at the foot of Arunachala Mountain and was one of the great spiritual masters. Ramana Maharshi had mesmerised me, when I saw his photo in a book at the beginning of my stay in India. At that time, I did not know who he was, but his eyes radiated so much compassion and wisdom that I bought the book. I did not regret it. It contained conversations with him in the 1930s and 1940s. I could not stop reading, and the more I read, the more I appreciated his wisdom.

Ramana or Venkataramana, as he was named, had been a normal boy, tall and strong, a good football player and swimmer. In studies, too, he was good thanks to his phenomenal memory.

Ramana Maharshi

When he was 16, however, he had an intense spiritual experience: one afternoon, he suddenly felt a terrible fear that he was going to die 'right now'. He was healthy and the fear inexplicable, yet extremely real for him. On that afternoon, while lying stiff in his room, he realised that in him there was an eternal I or self that can never die. It was truly present. It drew his attention. It was incredibly attractive and fascinating. It was dearly beloved. From that time onwards, even playing football had lost its charm for him. He preferred to sit in meditation.

Six weeks later, he secretly left his home and went to the holy Arunachala mountain. He reached there on September 1st, 1896, threw away his clothes except for the loincloth, had his head shaven and went into deep, trance-like meditation for weeks together in a dark dungeon beneath the temple in Tiruvannamalai.

Sheshadri Swami, a well-known saint in town, noticed him, carried him out and looked after him. Ramana had festering wounds from the vermin in that cellar and from stones, which boys had thrown at him to find out whether he was real or a statue, as one of them later explained.

Ramana stayed about four years at the foot of Arunachala and then moved higher up to the Virupaksha cave. Wherever he went now, people followed him. They simply sat with him in silence; even children ran up the hill and sat with him quietly. His glance was luminous and full of peace. He seemed absorbed in the pure being that is the basic reality of all appearances. But a change was noticed now. He remained conscious of his environment. The trance states became less frequent. Yet he still did not talk.

The news went around town that there was an extraordinary, young swami up on the hill and people came to see him—including people who had been on the spiritual path for years, and yet had not found that inner peace. Among them, some had already followers themselves, like Ganapathy Muni, a famous and brilliant scholar and poet.

Ganapathy Muni was one year elder to Ramana and not yet 30, when he climbed up the hill in the midday sun. He knew the scriptures and had practised almost all possible methods but had reached a dead end. "What is the right striving for self-realisation?" he asked Ramana who sat alone on his veranda. His written answer: "observe from where the I-feeling emerges. Go to its source. If you go to this source, you will dissolve in it. That is the right striving for self-realisation."

This was one of the first instructions of Ramana Maharshi.

Ramana stayed for 17 years in the Virupaksha cave and five

more years in a cave further up, called Skandashram. By now, several people lived with him, among them his mother and younger brother.

In September 1896, his mother had not resigned herself to the fact that her son had disappeared. She did everything to find him and four years later, she stood before him. Yet her pleas to come home with her did not meet with success. Ramana wrote for her on a chit:

"….what is destined not to happen, will not happen even if one does everything to make it happen and what is destined to happen, will happen even if one does everything to prevent it. That is certain…."

Several years later, after her eldest son had died, she came to Ramana and stayed with him until her death in 1922.

There are many stories from that time on the mountain, which V. Ganesan, one of the grandnephews of Ramana Maharshi, shared with visitors to the ashram:

Dogs, monkeys, squirrels and also snakes, tigers and leopards had free access to Ramana. He was fearless. He did not move when once a snake glided over his foot or when his followers rushed into the cave and closed its door hurriedly, because a tiger came up the hill. In the safety of the cave, the people became courageous. They shouted that the tiger would harm them. "They are afraid. Why don't you go away", Ramana reportedly said to the tiger who turned and left.

He also did not interfere with people. Once for example a follower of Chilli Swami came. That Swami lived from chillies and rubbed his body with a paste made from chillies. His follower was disappointed that nothing of this sort happened around Ramana. He came back the next day with a bag full of green chillies, grinded a paste out of them and rubbed it over the body of Ramana who let it happen. Palaniswami passed by and chased the man away.

After the death of his mother in 1922, Ramana moved to the foot of Arunachala on the southern side, where an ashram came up, because people wanted to stay near him. Some years earlier, he had started to talk and now he became more and more the great spiritual teacher as whom the world knows him.

Paul Brunton, an Englishman who had travelled in India in search of miracles and spirituality in the thirties of the last century, had contributed to make him known in the West through his books.

"Find out who you are", Ramana Maharshi demanded from everyone who came to him. He considered this query as most important, because it will become obvious on enquiry that one is indeed neither a separate, individual person, nor anything else that can be pointed at or can be given a name. If we believe that we are small persons in a big world, we are wrong, he claimed. "Ask yourself, who you are", he advised. "Don't expect a verbal answer, but feel your I, keep your attention on it. It will become clear that you are not what you thought you are."

I had an inkling what he meant by "feeling the I". Once, in the night train between Cologne and Paris, I stood in the corridor near the open window. It was dark and I looked up to the stars in the sky. Suddenly it hit me with full force, what I had until then taken for granted and regarded as normal and rather unimportant: "I am and know that I am! What a wonder!" Bliss and amazement filled my body. I was 20 at that time. Ramana Maharshi reminded me again that the fact that "I am" outshines all other experiences. Everything else is in the truest sense 'secondary', because the basis for everything is this formless, conscious being—I or self or Atman.

I visited Tiruvannamalai, the place where Ramana Maharshi had lived for over 50 years. I sat in the old meditation hall for a long time and tried to discover who I am. The sofa, where he had sat for almost 30 years and answered the questions of visitors is still there.

In the canteen, too, I felt transported back in time. We all, maybe hundred visitors, sat in long rows on the floor, in front of each of us a banana leaf, on which we sprinkled water from a mug and cleaned it with the back of our hand. Then Brahmins entered from the kitchen. They looked like coming straight from a book on ancient history: the long hair pulled into a knot at the back of the head, the strong chest naked, the white or saffron coloured cotton cloth around their lower body folded up, so that it reached only to

Vedic chanting at the Samadhi of Ramana Maharshi.

the knees and of course barefoot, like all of us. Each one carried a bucket and with impressive speed spooned out on the rows of banana leafs whatever was its content: rice, vegetable, dal, pickles, rasam (spicy water) buttermilk and sweet dish. The food was good and there was even a non-spicy variation for the Westerners.

Near the flower decorated Samadhi of Ramana Maharshi in a new, sparkling clean hall the Vedas were chanted in the mornings and evenings—by young boys with clear, high-pitched voices under the supervision of their teachers, like thousands of years ago. Possibly, at that distant time the boys had even looked similar—with slim bodies, long hair, confident chests, a white cotton cloth tied around their hips and fresh, alert faces. And after the chanting, they possibly had rushed off as rapidly and turned into mischievous, playful boys like their successors of today.

From the back gate of the ashram, a stone path winds up the mountain towards the two caves, where Ramana Maharshi had stayed in the early part of the last century for altogether 22 years. During most of that time, he had kept silence. The climb through a lot of greenery—thanks to a reforestation programme—takes about half an hour. Armed with a water bottle I went up several times and sat in one of the caves.

The Virupaksha cave has a low ceiling and is dark inside. A pile of ash, covered with an orange cloth, is lying on a shrine. The story of this ash is strange:

Some 300 years ago, a yogi lived in this cave. He chose the time for his death, which is not uncommon among yogis. Yet he did not want to be buried, but remain inside the cave. He informed his disciples about his wish and asked them, not to enter the cave for some days. When they finally entered, they found instead of his body only its ash. This ash is still in the cave.

Ramana Maharshi passed away in 1950 and yet, in the winter season, when the climate is pleasant, he still draws people from all over the world to his samadhi. Along with visitors, gurus also gather in the town of Tiruvannamalai, genuine and not so genuine ones, because the Arunachala Mountain is supposed to be an exceptionally powerful place. The not so genuine gurus and their 'managers' take occasionally advantage of the fact that especially Westerners are quick to assume that someone is spiritually highly advanced, if only his or her appearance matches the stereotype of a yogi.

New arrivals to the ashram waiting for the office to open.

During one of my visits to Tiruvannamalai, every afternoon a long line of Westerners went across some wasteland towards a solitary house on the outskirts of the town and I joined in a couple of times. We respectfully and silently waited in the garden, until the yogi was willing to receive us in a big room on the first floor. Many visitors had brought cookies or fruit and offered their gifts at his feet.

The yogi was completely naked and sat in front on a podium. He looked around into the adulating faces turned towards him and occasionally made some remark, which always provoked laughter—it was the sort of laughter, which showed a lot of goodwill, because it arose even then, when he made very commonplace comments. At the end, he was kind enough to personally distribute cookies and fruit to all of us. He slowly stepped through the rows of visitors who sat on the floor—his penis right in front of our eyes.

A few years later, I was again in Tiruvannamalai. The stream of visitors to that house had dried up and I asked why. "Oh, he has been chased away—by the very same people who had provided him with the house and had built him up", a friend who lived in the town told me.

But genuine gurus exist, as well. During my first visit in 1984, several people told me about one guru who was supposed to be genuine. His name was Ramsurat Kumar and he lived in a small house right next to the temple. Later, shortly before he died, wealthy followers built a big ashram for him on the outskirts of the town, which still exists. I rang the bell and a man wrapped in several layers of cloth and with a turban on his head opened the door. "Can I meet Ramsurat Kumar?" I asked. He indicated to me to come in and sat down on the floor. It was he.

"Does one need a guru?" I asked among other questions. He waited long and then reacted annoyed, "I am not a philosopher. Ask a philosopher such a philosophical question!"

I changed my question, "Do I need a guru?" Again he took a long time to answer, looked above my head and then said, "Go to Satya Sai Baba."

"But I don't want a guru", I reacted.

He burst into laughter, "If you don't want a guru then don't take a guru. But nevertheless it is good, if you go to Sai Baba."

I was open to his advice, because by then, I knew a lot about Indian wisdom and this knowledge also helped me to some extent in daily life, but I still could not *feel* that I am really connected with everybody and everything. It remained theory. I hoped that a guru could help me to realise it.

Soon after, I had a guru—and my sister was not happy about it.

CHAPTER 21

Miracles, faith and hope: with Satya Sai Baba in Puttaparthi

In the early 1980s, Satya Sai Baba was in all likelihood the best-known guru in India and had already a big following in the West. At that time, Sri Sri Ravi Shankar had just founded the Art of Living organisation near Bangalore, Mata Amritanandamayi had just registered an ashram at her father's hut in Kerala, both being still in their twenties, and Swami Ramdev, in his teens, was studying in a Gurukul. None of them probably guessed how big their organisations would become in future and that they would eclipse Satya Sai Baba's. In the 1980s, however, the Satya Sai Organisation was already present in over 100 countries. Millions considered themselves as his devotees and many still do.

I had heard of Satya Sai Baba in the very first weeks in the jungle in Kerala. A forest official had invited us for dinner. My photographer friend mentioned that I was fascinated by Babaji. "Oh, I am also a devotee of Babaji", the forest official beamed. "He has materialised this ring for me", he showed me briefly the golden ring with a green stone on his finger and then disappeared in the prayer room. With a photo in his hand, he came back. "No. Not this one! I mean another Babaji", I exclaimed a little too fast, when I saw the picture of a man with an Afro-look hairstyle and a broad, rather grim looking face. Besides, the fact that his guru materialised rings made me sceptical. Someone who showed off his supernatural powers could not be genuine, I thought.

Yet over time, my scepticism towards Sai Baba mellowed. I met several of his followers who had great admiration for him. "You must see him. I had a talk with him and he knew things about me, which he possibly could not know. He is absolutely phenomenal!" Lelio, an Italian, whom I met in South India, told me. Such praise made an impact. Moreover, Baba himself declared that his miracles were only meant to make people aware of him. They were a kind of visiting card. Much more important was his teaching, he said. And when in 1984 Ramsurat Kumar advised me to see Satya Sai Baba, I made up my mind and went to Prasanthi Nilayam, the "place of highest peace", as his ashram in the village Puttaparthi was named.

It was the biggest ashram I ever saw. It looked almost like a small town that had sprung up in the dry, rocky, hilly countryside of Andhra Pradesh, three hours north of Bangalore. Coming into Puttaparthi by bus, I first passed several schools and colleges, a planetarium and hospital, as well as an open-air stadium with a capacity for over 100.000 people. All buildings were painted in light pastel colours—pink, blue and yellow.

In the ashram proper, there were several apartment blocks, office buildings, a line of shops, five round houses, 30 big sheds (which have meanwhile made way for more apartment blocks), canteens, a huge auditorium and in the centre of it all, the temple with the darshan area around it. In the ashram, too, the dominating colours were pink, blue and yellow and all buildings looked freshly painted.

Already from the bus, I noticed many foreigners. They all looked surprisingly neat and clean. Generally, especially young Western travellers do not care much about their clothing, in contrast to Indians, who as a rule take great care. Even the poor seldom wear only shorts and the plain, white T-shirts that are considered as underwear.

I soon came to know why the foreigners looked so neat. In the Public Relation Office a stern looking man dressed in immaculate white handed me a leaflet with detailed instructions how to dress and behave. For example, I was to cover breast and shoulders additionally with a shawl and forthwith not to look at any man.

Further it said: You have come from so far to this place, you have left friends and family, because you want to develop spiritually. Therefore, use your time here well. Do not make new friends and do not waste your time with useless talk. Concentrate completely on your relationship with Satya Sai Baba.

In the beginning, I followed the rules religiously and did not make any contact with others, except for necessary enquiries. After moving into a room in one of the apartment blocks I asked for example a German in the room next door, whether the tap water in the bathroom was drinkable.

"If you don't have trust in Baba, I can't help you", was her unexpectedly curt answer. It made me realise that life was apparently not that easy in the ashram.

"I have hardly reached and already want to leave", I wrote on the first evening into my diary. I felt regimented and irritated that, like a good child, I did whatever was asked of me. Did my ego fear about its autonomy and therefore wanted to leave? Or was it a feeling that needed to be heeded? I did not know, but guessed it was my ego.

Then I saw Sai Baba or 'Swamy', as he was called, for the first time from close. About 2000 people had gathered on the place in

Satya Sai Baba on the temple veranda.

front of the temple, who all sat in straight lines and in neat clothing on the sandy ground. Sai Baba emerged from the temple, on whose upper floor he had his residence, talked to some of his college students on the veranda and then first walked along the rows on the women's side. Only 5 feet tall, he looked delicate in his long orange robe. Nobody talked. Everyone focussed on him. Some tried to hand him letters, others tried to touch his feet. His gaze fell only fleetingly on me.

The first impression was not spectacular, yet I had resolved to keep an open mind. I had met many gurus on my travels—over thirty until then—and the question whether he or she was enlightened was always at the back of my mind. I never dared to ask this question and nobody else did. Occasionally a guru would hint as much, yet I did not hold such hints in his favour.

Regarding Satya Sai Baba the situation, however, was different. He not only declared that he was enlightened, but openly claimed that he was the Highest possible: a full avatar, a conscious incarnation of the Divine, as it has not walked the earth since Sri Krishna 5000 years ago.

That, no doubt, was a big claim and difficult to accept, yet I slowly believed that he was 'at least' enlightened, because his life story read like a fairy tale and I could not imagine that all those stories were false: Changing water into petrol, multiplying food, healing the sick—such happenings were witnessed by respectable members of the society.

For example, the former scientific adviser to the defence ministry Sri Bhagatam had been a close devotee. Sai Baba had operated on the spine of his son in his living room with instruments that he simply took from thin air, I was told. Yet Bhagatam had left Sai Baba before my first visit. Why? I asked. "His ego could not take the tests", was the answer. I could imagine this was possible.

A few days after my arrival I heard Sai Baba giving a talk on one of the many festivals. His voice had a high pitch. After each sentence, he made a break for the translator. The translator held his head stiffly bent upwards and spoke through his nose. Listening was straining.

"It depends on your thoughts, which type of human being you are", Sai Baba said. "Good thoughts make a good human being, bad thoughts make a bad human being and thoughts of god make a divine human being. Whether god is far or near also depends on your thoughts."

"A strong character is very important", he stressed. "Good company is essential for building the character—a company which sees the divine in the human being. The divine is potentially present as pure love in every human heart. This love, this divinity, has to manifest in life."

Sai Baba was in tune with the ancient Indian wisdom and had a simple way to explain it. He took for example his handkerchief. "This is a handkerchief", he said. "I am not the handkerchief, it is separate from me, belongs to me. Similarly, this is my body. I am not the body. I live in it, inhabit it. Ask yourself: 'what is this I?'" And he himself gave the answer, "This I is god."

Then he took the tumbler from his lectern. "This is a tumbler. But seen from a different angle, this tumbler is nothing but silver. Name and form can be changed. A silversmith can make this tumbler into a bracelet. The silver is the essential thing. Without silver no tumbler and no bracelet!"

In tune with Indian wisdom he stressed that mental activity prevents us from seeing the truth, in a similar way as seeing the tumbler prevents us from seeing the silver. "This truth cannot be known by thoughts and therefore neither by the intellect. Whoever hopes for that is like somebody who hopes to see the theatre stage by closely analysing the curtain which veils the stage."

At the end of his talk, he started to sing and he sang well: "Hari bhajana bina sukha shanti nahin" (without worship of god no joy and peace). Thousands repeated each line. The whole hall vibrated. I felt completely immersed in the sound. Seldom had I experienced such massive and immediate devotion for god. "Without meditation no union with god", resounded around me with full force and finally with a crescendo that could not be surpassed: "Without god not a single one of us!"

Was this mass hypnosis? Or was it just an opportunity to express one's devotion? The people around me in the auditorium appeared completely normal. Many foreigners were among then and some looked elegant in their expensive silk saris, with huge earrings and stylish hair-do. They seemed to have come straight from one of the chic cafés in Rome or Paris. Even a group from Iran was present, and Sai Baba gave them a lot of attention.

Why did he attract such enormous crowds and why so many foreigners among them, though he had never visited America or Europe? I found an explanation: the incredible miracles had had a snowball effect. Vidya, an American, who had lived in the ashram for many years told me that in the 1970s Sai Baba cured an Italian from paralysis. "Some months later a whole busload of Italians came—all of them paralysed. It was terrible! And Baba sent them back as they had come," she remembered.

Yet do miracles prove that he is what he claims to be? Probably not. Somehow, I needed to find out whether he was really an avatar.

CHAPTER 22

No proof, yet fully convinced

I started to read and read almost everything what was available in the ashram bookshop, including Professor Kasturi's hagiography in four volumes.

A boy with little education from a non-descript village which did not even have a road leading to it, becomes one of the best known personalities in India and attracts admirers from around the world. How did this happen?

It seems that he was a normal child. Yet at the age of 14—that was in 1940—a decisive change happened. Raju, as Sai Baba was called, suddenly jumped up and held his toe. His family thought that a scorpion had bitten him. From then on, he was not the same anymore. He threw his school books into a corner, recited Sanskrit shlokas and claimed that he was the reincarnation of the popular saint Sai Baba of Shirdi in Maharashtra, who had died in 1918—eight years before Raju was born. He further stated that his devotees were calling him and he had a mission to fulfil. He materialised all kinds of objects, gave visions of Shirdi to those who did not believe him and acted like a guru. His father was furious and his mother took him to an exorcist who tortured the boy so much that she could no longer bear it and brought him back home.

Raju called himself now Satya Sai Baba (Satya means truth) and soon people gathered around him. They were impressed by the many miracles he wrought. He wanted people to take notice of him, he said, and they did. There are amazing stories in his biography about this early time. An example:

Sai Baba was only 16 when one day a driver dressed in livery came wading through the river into Puttaparthi. An English officer had gone hunting, had shot a tigress and was now on his way home. His jeep had broken down just opposite the village on the other side of the river and in spite of all efforts refused to move. The driver had heard of a miracle boy in the village and asked his master whether he should fetch him. 'Main thing, the jeep gets all right and we can leave this god forsaken place', was the attitude of the Englishman.

When Raju alias Satya Sai Baba reached there, he gave the officer unexpectedly a lecture: This tigress, which you have shot, has four cubs, which are dying now without their mother in the jungle. It was I who stopped the jeep here, because I want you to turn back, trace the cubs and give them to a zoo. And in future don't shoot with a gun! If you can't do without shooting, shoot with a camera!

The British officer agreed to turn back and the jeep moved without any repair. He found the cubs and gave them to a zoo. Later he returned to Puttaparthi and gifted the skin of the tigress to Sai Baba.

I liked the story. Yet more impressive than miracles from books were miracles, which I heard directly from those who had experienced them, even if they were less spectacular.

For example, I got to know Mister Mc Dowell, a farmer from Kentucky in USA and his wife. He was already around 70 and had been searching for 'a higher power', as he expressed it, his whole life. Finally, when meeting Satya Sai Baba, he was convinced that he had found the higher power he had looked for. His whole family became devotees and regularly visited the ashram. Once he told me the following occurrence:

"We were back on our farm in Kentucky after our visit to Sai Baba and wanted to be serious about spiritual life. So we fixed an hour for meditation every afternoon. During this time, we locked our Collie into the garage, so that he would not disturb us. One day another Collie landed up at our farm—a beautiful dog and exceptionally friendly. I was sure that his owner would soon enquire about him. When the time for meditation came, I locked both the dogs into the garage. We all, my wife, my son and I were meditating. After an hour, we went out to the veranda and who was waiting there with his tail wagging? The new dog! I could not fathom how he had managed to escape from the garage and became pensive. I had earlier read that Sai Baba of Shirdi had often identified with dogs. For example, when one of his followers had beaten a dog, Sai Baba showed him the wounds of the beating on his own body. So I leant on the balustrade of the veranda and remarked half to myself and half to my wife: 'This dog—that must be Baba.'

"After about three years my wife went again to India. I could not spare time and she went alone. Sai Baba soon called her for an interview, as the talks with him in small groups are called. He made some friendly remarks to everyone in the beginning. Of my wife he enquired whether I was fine. Then he turned to three Indian women who were sitting on the floor leaning against the wall. He glanced at my wife mischievously and then made a comment to those women in their native language and they laughed. My wife was certain that the comment was about her. Immediately after the interview, she asked those ladies, 'What did Sai Baba say about me?" He had said: 'Her husband thinks I am a dog'."

Very few in India will doubt that miracles are possible. Yet it is also known that someone who has the power to do miracles can easily get stuck on a lower level. 'Keep away from miracles, if you discover the power in yourself. It is tempting but dangerous to use it as it will impede your spiritual growth,' advise the sages. Sai Baba incidentally gives the same advice, but he confidently adds that this does not apply to him, because he is an avatar—a full incarnation of the Divine. In his case, the danger of falling is simply not there.

I tended to believe him and over time, I became convinced. My reasoning went like this: if Sai Baba did not live a life of integrity, if he told lies and was not an avatar, as he claimed, then a certain 'fall' in his reputation would certainly have happened. At least he would have lost his supernatural powers long ago. But obviously he enjoyed a steady increase in his popularity for over 50 years—a fact, which he had already prophesied in his youth. Miracles he also still performs.... that means, he must be genuine.

I personally, though, have not experienced any miracle, unless a dream counts as one: when I once was rather depressed about the fact that I had a mass guru as my guru, I thought, "He doesn't even know my name." In the same night, I dreamt of Sai Baba. He stood on the other side of a small bridge, his car parked behind him, and called out to me, "Maria, come here!" Still dreaming I was pleasantly surprised, "Oh, he *does* know my name!"

Friends whom I met in the ashram had more impressive stories to narrate. A German friend saw him in her flat at home. He reclined next to her on her bed and she was blissful with him as a tender lover.

A Dutchman, who was about 30 at that time, did not even know who this short, slim man with the Jimmy Hendrix hairstyle was who stood in a corner of his flat in Holland. "He was definitely there, but not in the normal way that you would just ask him who he is", he tried to explain to me the experience. Soon after he chanced upon Sai Baba's photo in a bookstore, came to know who he was and landed in Puttaparthi. Sai Baba called him straight away for an interview. He welcomed him like a dear, close friend, for whom he had been waiting, hugging him affectionately. From then on, he called him very frequently for an interview. He gave him not only his loving attention, but also a ring, a locket and a Shiva lingam and promised to cure him from a pancreas ailment from which he had suffered since his youth and which had made him unfit for work. Everyone envied the extremely good-looking young man for his VIP status with Sai Baba.

He was not healed and Sai Baba ignored him more and more. After some five years, he did not call him anymore for interviews.

Some 10 years later, around 1996, I was on a bus stand in a small town near Mysore. Our driver had stopped for lunch when I heard my name being called from the window of another bus. It was the Dutchman and he told me his story: he had left Sai Baba soon after I had left in 1993; he had lost his faith and had even returned the gifts to Sai Baba. He was by now around forty, extremely thin, and still had his health problems. He lost faith not only in gurus but also in god and spirituality. He seemed disappointed by life, almost cynical and lonely. He looked very different from the man I had met for the first time around 1987, and who lit up the atmosphere in the ashram. He was one of those everyone enjoyed to meet. I knew several women who kept a tab on his routine so that they could plan to 'accidentally' meet him on the way if only fleetingly, as contact between the sexes was monitored.

In 1987, another handsome young man was much sought after, though he was more elusive and came only a few times for short visits. His name was Nalin. He was only 19 at that time and from Sri Lanka. Sai Baba told him that he had been Swami Vivekananda in his previous life. Of course I believed Sai Baba and was awed to have the former Swami Vivekananda almost as my neighbour in the same building.

Some Indians went to his room to touch his feet, until word got round that Sai Baba wanted him to be left in peace. Later, he would assist in his mission and take care of the ashram after he (Sai Baba) left his body in 2021, and before his next incarnation, Prema Sai, would appear, Sai Baba predicted. That seemed far off, yet we did not doubt his statement to come true and were looking forward to have such a charming man running the ashram.

In the late 1980s, Sai Baba was only in his early sixties and drew people from all over the globe to his native village in southern India. There were many nice people in the ashram and the fact that they considered Sai Baba as their guru was one more factor that convinced me about his genuineness. An ex NASA scientist, was one of them. Twice a week he gave lectures for foreigners and one had to come early to find a place in the hall. He was extremely popular. He stayed in the ashram on Sai Baba's instruction and taught in his college.

Yet in 1992, Sai Baba dropped him and even forbade him to enter the ashram. He had married without his permission. Did Sai Baba give him the dreaded, yet ultimately beneficial, blow to the ego by outing him so openly or did he show off his power? A friend half-jokingly suggested that Baba might have been jealous of his popularity among women.

Apart from popular people there were the rich and famous. They got VIP treatment, for example an American actress from the 'Dallas' TV serial. Her daughter was married in Sai Baba's presence.

Isaac Tigrett who as a young man had founded the Hard Rock Café chain in England and the USA, also came regularly. For many years, hardly anybody guessed how wealthy he was, until he made a huge donation of millions of dollars. Sai Baba built a super speciality hospital where open heart surgery was conducted free for the poor. Apart from the hospital, Sai Baba initiated many other social service projects and asked his followers to engage themselves for the welfare of society. They did so gladly and this was yet another aspect in favour of Sai Baba.

The topmost elite of Indian society were also endorsing him. The Indian President, the Prime Minister, the highest judge of the county, governors, chief ministers, members of parliament, vice chancellors of universities, super rich businessmen from Hongkong or America, scientists from all over the world—they all came to see Sai Baba during the seven years I lived in the ashram. He was, as it were, a publicly certified saint. Can so many people go wrong in their judgment regarding his genuineness? I did not think so. I was by now 100 per cent sure that Sai Baba was what he claimed to be—a full avatar—and was glad that I had the good fortune to have him as my guru. To share my guru with millions of others was not what I had dreamt of but, since Sai Baba was extraordinary special, I felt it was great that so many people recognised him as an avatar. We were lucky, because it was not easy, said Sai Baba himself, to entrust oneself to somebody who was still alive. It is much easier, if someone has passed away already.

He had a point. Don't today about two billion people consider themselves as followers of Jesus Christ who in his lifetime was controversial and even killed by those who opposed him? Don't they base their faith entirely on stories? Prophet Mohammed, too, was known only to relatively few Arabs and had his share of enemies. Yet after death, both became greater than life and the founders of the two most powerful religions. Would the followers of those religions not wish to have met Jesus or Mohammed personally during their lifetime? How would they have reacted? Would they have turned away, finding them too human?

CHAPTER 23

Light and its shadow

Now, that I was convinced that Sai Baba could not possibly tell a lie and therefore was what he claimed, I believed everything else he said, for example, that he resides in the hearts of everyone and knows our thoughts and feelings. Instead of praying to an abstract god, I prayed now to his human form. There was a heart to heart connection. I felt protected, very close to god and under his gaze. I could always contact him and was sure he heard me. My trust in him was amazing. But compared to others I was lacking in love. Several women devotees confided to me that they were madly in love with Baba. They longed to come to Prasanthi Nilayam as one would long to meet one's lover.

Because the pull of love was missing, I was not desperate to stay in the ashram. Yet my reasoning went like this: as I *can* stay in the ashram and do my writing from there, there is no justification for not staying. If god is on earth and he allows me to be near him, I simply have no other choice. I *have* to stay, never mind whether I like it or not.

On one hand, life had become easier because of this great trust in a loving and almighty god next door and on the other hand, it was harder because life in the ashram was full of challenges. Leaving Sai Baba was not an option though earlier 'leaving' had been my favourite way out of any difficult situation. It would have meant running away from what I felt was my best chance of finding spiritual fulfilment. So I trusted that everything was 'his' will or happened because of my karma. It was an ideal situation to learn "Thy will be done".

The accommodation office and roommates were a major cause for irritation. I was dreading that knock at the door: a foreign woman with her luggage would be standing outside, show me a chit from the accommodation office and say, "I have been allotted to this room". In the beginning, I made the mistake to show up in the accommodation office asking if my new roommate could move into the vacant room next door. "No!" was the curt reply.

Sometimes, when a festival was coming up and we were already four in a room, we found a chit at the door. "Come to the accommodation office". It meant we had to shift to one of the big halls. There were 30 of them, separate for women, men and couples; and again separate for Indians and foreigners, as Sai Baba did not encourage close contact between them. They resembled refugee camps with over hundred inmates. During daytime, they turned into an oven due to the tin roof and at night, they became the hunting ground for mosquitoes and rats, with mosquitoes outnumbering the rats. Only once it happened that a rat sprang on my pillow and landed in my hair.

Yet the atmosphere during festivals was special. Indians have a wonderful way to celebrate: Everywhere decorations; people in their festive clothes; children running and playing; a lot of chatting, a lot of laughter; far less serious and far less self-righteous than we foreigners, and far more accommodating. Food counters were put up and long queues were leading to them. We sat in small groups in the sand under tents, eating with our hands from plates made from leaves. Ten thousands, hundred thousands, even over a million was said to have come. It was difficult to estimate. The ashram was definitely packed to capacity, but the area was probably less than a square kilometre in size. It was encouraging: So many people were his devotees. So many good people among them who followed his teaching "Do good, be good, see good". I felt that I lived in a wonderful place, where everyone converged, and though difficult at times, there was no better alternative.

After the festival was over, the ashram quickly emptied to around 2000 people staying on an average day. There were some weird people among them, too, who fancied to have been famous personalities in a previous life. For example, being the rebirth of Swami Yogananda, Mother Mary and Nefertiti, were all claimed by German women whom I knew. Their claim to fame in their present life was that they had been 'chosen' by the avatar to help in his mission. They were strange but harmless.

Yet there were also some who looked dangerous. Never before had I felt that I should avoid eye-contact with another person. But in the ashram with certain people I consciously avoided it because I felt it could harm me. It was just a feeling that I could not explain nor substantiate, as I did not get to know those persons.

Once, however, I landed in a room with one such foreigner. One night I felt that a dangerous, diffuse, huge 'energy ball' for want of a better word tried to roll on me while I was lying on my mattress. I was in a state in between dreaming and waking. With all my strength, I fought against it, trying hard to roll it off. "Om namah Shivay" repeated itself nonstop within me. I knew that the continuous repetition of the mantra would save me. Finally, the energy ball left me.

After sharing a room with her once, I flatly refused sharing again a room next time—in front of some foreigners, as I had no other option. She probably hated me for that.

A few years later, in the early 1990s, I had a vision of this woman who always looked very holy, spoke very sweetly, had her hair neatly combed and was dressed in starched white saris. It was in early summer. Sai Baba had left for Whitefield, his ashram near Bengaluru, and only 7 or 8 foreigners were still in the ashram in Puttaparthi. One of them was this woman. In the evening around eight o'clock, I was meditating in my room with eyes closed. Suddenly I 'saw' her in her white sari at my door in a karate posture, with bent knees, threateningly stretching out her fist towards me. I usually don't have visions and opened my eyes a bit confused, yet alert. It was dark outside; the door was open, only the mosquito screen was closed. There was, however, nobody, so I forgot about it.

Next morning, the baker was the first who exclaimed, "Thank God, you are alive! I thought they had killed you." Several others also came up telling me they had feared that it was me who had been murdered the previous evening around eight o'clock. The reason was that a Hungarian woman who was based in Switzerland and whose description fitted mine had been killed in the ashram. Two youngsters from the village had brought back a cassette player that she had given for repair. It was speculated that seeing her purse full of money had prompted them to attack her with a glass bottle.

In the evening, I was sitting behind the temple when that woman in the starched white sari came up to me. "Maria, I have cried the whole night. I thought it had hit you", she said and did not sound sincere. I got up and walked towards the shops. She walked by my side and proposed, "Let us forget the past and be friends."

Soon after, I got to know a foreigner who had been taken in by this woman's pious appearance and had been friends with her. Meanwhile, however, she had distanced herself completely. She told me that her former friend had learnt black magic from a Tibetan monk in Sikkim and was according to her responsible for the death of an officer in the accommodation office. This officer was one of the few nice persons who did not intentionally make life difficult for ashram residents. He might have been in his fifties and died completely unexpected within a few days.

This former friend told me that the officer had once greatly annoyed the woman in the white sari by not giving her the room she wanted. She was mad with anger, checked into a hotel in the village and locked herself into her room for three days. During those days, the officer became weaker and weaker until he died. Then she came back to the ashram and attended darshan, sitting next to her former friend, who narrated this to me. Sai Baba came out on the veranda and appeared very upset. He looked around as if searching for somebody and spotting her gave her a furious look.

Where there is a lot of light, there is a lot of shadow", Sai Baba explained the fact that not only virtuous people lived in the ashram.

The great majority of visitors in the ashram, however, were friendly and good-natured. They came from all over the world—from Chile to Japan and from Greenland to Fiji—and for all of them the one centre of attraction was Satya Sai Baba.

CHAPTER 24

Murder in the temple

I lived in Satya Sai Baba's ashram from November 1986 until November 1993—full seven years. For a part of that time I, like thousands of other visitors, roughed it out in one of the big sheds, or shared a bare room with three other women and their luggage. However, in 1991, life became easier for me, as I was allotted a room of my 'own'. It was a great privilege. By far not everyone who wanted to pay the donation got onto the waiting list. Every room in the ashram had an 'owner' who had the right to stay in his room whenever he was in the ashram. When he was out, however, it was used for visitors. Now, for the first time in my life in India, I enjoyed the luxury of a gas stove and a refrigerator.

I did not feel bad in the ashram but also not happy. Life seemed tedious. On my wish list, which I presented Sai Baba at regular intervals, I often pleaded that life may not last too long anymore. My encounter with Anandamayi Ma, as well as the loss of Abdullah had changed my attitude towards death quite early during my stay in India. Dying was no more the final end, but rather a break to recuperate.

Yet my life was not all heavy. There were many plus points: I lived in a warm climate in relative comfort in a clean environment and barely needed any money. In addition, I met nice people from all over the world. After some time I hardly noticed that the people I closely interacted with were all women. Only occasionally, I chatted with a man. Earlier I could not have imagined living only among women, but meanwhile I did not consider it that tragic. "If you want me to sit here for the rest of my life, it is also okay", I offered internally. Apart from sporadic doubts, I was sure that Sai Baba knew what I told him.

Not much happened in our lives, yet a tight schedule made us feel that we were quite busy.

It started early morning at 5 o'clock in the temple with the chanting of "Om" 21 times, which I usually skipped. Around 6 o'clock, everybody hurried towards an outer courtyard of the darshan place, where 20 to 30 rows of people sitting on the ground slowly built up. Then, the first person of each row took from a bag a chit with a number and those numbers determined the sequence in which we were to march to the darshan place and whether one would sit in front or at the back during darshan. Once sitting there, it usually took up to an hour, till Sai Baba appeared on the veranda, made his round and called some people for an interview into the temple. Now the orderly lines disintegrated and the crowd streamed towards the canteens for breakfast.

At 9 o'clock, the schedule continued with bhajans. Students were leading the singing and Baba appeared on the veranda or sat inside the temple. At 10 o'clock, there was a lecture for foreigners, and at 11 o'clock, the canteens opened for lunch.

After a siesta and a quick shower, we wrapped again saris around us and the same procedure repeated itself: forming of rows in the outer courtyard, the first person of the row blindly choosing a number, marching to the darshan place, waiting for Baba, his appearance on the veranda, making his round.

Then we went for a cup of tea to the canteen and back again for bhajans at 6 o'clock in the evening. Thereafter the shops were open. The pleasant, cool evening atmosphere was ideal to sit outdoors with friends and enjoy some ice cream.

Yet one day this peaceful routine was ruptured. On a Sunday, the 6th of June 1993, at night around 10 p.m., a siren howled in the ashram. I slept already and did not hear it. When I left my room the next morning at 6 o'clock, my neighbour from Malaysia greeted me on our common veranda with the words, "Tonight six people were killed in the temple." I could not believe it. On my way to the darshan place, groups of people were huddling together and whispering. I joined one of those groups and came to know what had happened:

Late in the previous evening, four men carrying knives had intruded into the temple under the pretext of delivering a telegram. They stabbed Sai Baba's driver and one student to death and injured the cook who came running. Then they stormed up the staircase towards Sai Baba's apartment on the first floor. Sai Baba had meanwhile started the siren, gone out to the veranda and bolted the veranda door from outside. The attackers were trapped. The siren had instantaneously alerted the police, as well as the ashram residents and villagers, who blocked their escape. The four men were shot dead by the police.

One fact was especially shocking: all four attackers had been either former students of Sai Baba's college or else trusted people from his inner circle. Strange was also the time when the shots which killed them were fired—namely in the middle of the night, several hours after they were caught.

Ashram officials declared the whole affair as an internal matter. Jealousy had been the motive, Baba supposedly said. He did not specify who had been jealous of whom.

It did not take long and the press stopped reporting on the murder attempt on Sai Baba. A journalist in Bangalore told me that higher ups had placed a lid on the case and nobody would dare to further investigate. Regarding the killing of the assailants by the police, ashram residents speculated that Sai Baba himself must have given the order for the attackers to be shot. Nobody believed the official version that they were shot because they tried to escape.

"Sai Baba knows what he is doing", was nevertheless the prevalent attitude amongst his devotees. We were convinced that Sai Baba did not do anything out of personal interest and whatever he did was for the best. After all, murder and killings happen everywhere in the world with god's permission. So why shouldn't they occur in the immediate proximity of the avatar?

A few weeks later, the Indian President paid again a visit to Satya Sai Baba. It was a sign that nothing had changed. Yet metal detectors graced now the entrance to the darshan place and two security officers followed Sai Baba on his rounds. The volunteers who even earlier had not deserved a prize for friendliness seemed to enjoy their new task of treating everyone as a potential murderer.

"Sai Baba says, 'Help ever, hurt never'" one of the nicer volunteer women once said while we were waiting for the bag with the numbers. "Here we follow", and to stress it she pointed her index finger towards the ground, "Help never, hurt ever." Those who heard it laughed.

Life in the ashram continued as usual, but the number of visitors had shrunk. Mainly Indians stayed away—not foreigners, because most of them did not know anything about the murder attempt. Yet for the first time, people from the village came in big numbers for darshan. They shouted slogans that Baba may live long. Probably they realised that the prosperity of Puttaparthi was intimately connected with Sai Baba. Would he not be there, all the shops, as well as the restaurants and hotels could pack up.

Four weeks later, Sai Baba gave a talk. The auditorium was jam-packed. Some friends and I were sitting outside in the sand, listening to his talk via loudspeaker. Sai Baba mentioned several aspersions, which I had never even heard of, and which genuinely surprised me: "People claim that millions and millions of Rupees disappear in wrong channels", he said for example, and, "This is a lie. Every paisa is used for sacred purposes."

He also commented on the fact that he had not saved his 41-year-old driver, who had served him day and night for years and who, so was rumoured, wanted to marry a devotee from Italy in near future.

"I had told him at 7 o'clock to come upstairs, but he did not want to. He said he did not want to sleep yet. See, everything that Swami ('Swami' referred to him) says is for your best."

In the end, he listed all the items that he would gift away at the occasion of his 70th birthday in November 1995: 70 tractors, 70 sewing machines, 70 houses, and so on.

His talk was printed and sold like hot cakes. Already while listening I felt a certain uneasiness and more so, when I saw his lecture before me in black on white. An avatar, who defends himself against aspersions? Who tries to project himself in a positive light by announcing gifts, which would be given only two years later? Yet the uneasiness slowly disappeared. Most of us considered it as a test for our faith. Sai Baba himself had said that he would soon separate the chaff from the wheat and many would leave him. Who would not prefer to be wheat rather than chaff?

Moreover, Sai Baba still seemed to have the power to do miracles. A French friend one day whispered to me that Baba was doing a miracle for her. She had an extremely low count of platelets and every small injury was life threatening. Though she had tried all kinds of remedies, nothing had helped. So I told her about Sai Baba and she came with the hope of getting healed. She was a pretty woman with blond, long hair in her late 30s. In the beginning, Sai Baba ignored her and did not take her letter about her illness. She was greatly disappointed, had hoped so much that he would heal her. Yet slowly he took notice of her and accepted her letter. She then had psychic experiences and an inner communication with him. When she made the next blood test, the number of platelets had dramatically increased. She was convinced it was thanks to Sai Baba and had now absolute faith in him.

Yet my strong faith had got a crack after the murder attempt and his talk. A few months later another, final crack was added.

CHAPTER 25

Intimate with the Avatar

Karin, a doctor from Munich came to my room one evening, "Maria, I have to talk to you", she said looking very upset. The reason: Karin had heard it for the first time—that Sai Baba rubs oil on the penis of young men. I knew it already since long. It was an open secret that Sai Baba frequently called a young man, Indian or foreigner, to a separate room and asked him to down his trousers. Sai Baba would then rub oil on his penis and ask him not to talk about it—an injunction that not all followed. "I now also belong to Sai Baba's darlings" a young German told the German group once at its regular Sunday meetings—clearly flattered that Sai Baba had found him worthy of this special treatment and that he was on such intimate terms with the avatar.

Even Sai officials like the central coordinator for Europe, Bernhard Gruber, did not deny the fact as such. He gave me an explanation, "Sai Baba activates the Kundalini in this way." Kundalini is the tremendous energy that lies dormant coiled up at the base of the spine, the muladhara chakra.

I could imagine that this was possible. Since ancient times there existed spiritual practices that used the powerful sexual energy for self-realisation. Karin was not prepared to accept the Kundalini explanation. She wanted to find out more.

Next evening she came again and told me about her enquiries. "It is worse than what you can imagine," she started. "He does it even with small boys of the primary section and they are ashamed to talk about it. But they feel sick and some even vomit, the parents of schoolboys told me. The boys depend on him, that means, what he does is criminal."

Now I also got doubts, because the ancient Tantra texts state that the awakening of the Kundalini with the help of sexual energy is to be practised only by spiritually highly advanced disciples and certainly not by schoolboys. Karin then said something, which I could not accept, "I owe Sai Baba a lot and he will remain my friend. But in this matter, I believe, he needs help."

An avatar who needs help? Then he is not an avatar and not a guru for me.

Karin's thorough enquiries regarding the 'boys' stories' spread in our friends' circle like wild fire. The topic surfaced now in all conversations. Susanne, a down to earth, confident German woman of about sixty, whom I had invited for breakfast, said, "I told my husband already on our first visit here: 'He (Sai Baba) is not only white." And she added liberally, "but why not let him also have some fun."

The rubbing of oil was one thing, but now other, more indicting stories surfaced—all second hand and not verifiable, told by the boyfriends of some Western women.

I talked about it with Tamara, a Russian. She had been into Theosophy and was clairvoyant. One evening in Russia, she had had a vision of Sai Baba. He asked her to come to him to India. She came—without money and without knowing why he had called her. He told her in an interview that he would give her a good husband but so far, no husband was in sight. (Many years later on an Aeroflot flight, I happened to meet a common friend who told me that she had married a Sai Baba devotee from Canada). We sat for hours in my room and talked. I liked Tamara. She was one of my few close friends. However, I did not have the strong faith anymore that she still demonstrated. She defended Sai Baba, and no doubt was right in one point: we cannot judge whether someone is enlightened or not. Further, we simply don't know why an enlightened being does what he does.

There are stories about ancient Rishis who did not conform to the usual standard of morality, for example Rishi Parashara, the grandson of Rishi Vasishtha. He passionately loved Satyavati, the daughter of a fisher-king, in a kind of one-night stand and then departed, leaving her pregnant. She gave birth to a son. This son became a Rishi—the great Veda Vyasa, whose grandsons were the Pandavas and Kauravas, and who compiled the Vedas and wrote the Mahabharata. His birthday is even today celebrated every full moon in July as Guru Purnima.

I wrote to Sai Baba that I could not justify what I heard about him and needed to know whether he was genuine. My row picked the chit with the number one. Sai Baba graciously took the letter and smiled at me. During the next darshan, I sat again in the first row, which was unusually lucky. Tamara is probably right, I thought. He is genuine.

On the following day, the 3rd November 1993, Sai Baba gave a lecture. He talked about the lack of morality and discipline in today's society because of too much attachment to the body. I was cynical; thought, that Sai Baba's lectures are uninspiring and do not have any effect, because he himself does not do what he preaches. Not interested in listening, I casually took a book from the woman sitting next to me. It was in German—a book with sayings by Satya Sai Baba. I opened it at random and my glance fell on a line: "The reason why disciples do not make any progress is because the gurus nowadays don't do what they preach."

I was stunned. The same sentence I had just a moment earlier thought about Sai Baba though he surely had not referred to himself. I looked at myself, asked, whether I had made any progress and did not see any. I looked around; saw the long faces of the ashram residents, none of whom looked happy, always waiting for something in the future. It became clear to me that it was the beginning of the end of my stay in Prasanthi Nilayam—my strong faith in Sai Baba had suddenly slipped away—now, when for the first time in my life, I called a fridge and a gas stove my own.

I made an inventory:

If I was honest, I had often not felt anything special during darshan. Once I even completely missed seeing him while sitting in the much-desired first row. I had become engrossed in writing and when I looked up he had passed me already.

When, however, he had come close, looked at me or taken a letter, I had felt that subtle vibration that I had earlier felt with Anandamayi Ma or Devaraha Baba. And when he had ignored me long enough, I had felt tremendous pain in my heart.

I never really knew whether he was what he claimed to be. And I always was somehow aware that I was not happy in the ashram. Yet slowly an absolute trust had taken root in me. I simply had not seen any reason why I should not believe him. I trusted that god would not let me down and hook me on to a false guru.

I wrote into my diary: "Earlier I sat here and saw all kinds of things in Baba. Now I sit here and see something altogether different. It is now a matter of not thinking, not wanting to understand, letting things be—and taking responsibility for myself."

I had unconsciously slid into thought patterns, which I had not wanted to slide into and which reminded me of my youth when I had believed in the dogmas of the Church. When I was stuck in those thought patterns, they appeared logical and normal. I had believed so much that I could not know and that was not necessary to believe.

For example, Sai Baba's claim that he will establish dharma, the right way of life, on earth and correct the evil doers. Nothing could impede his mission, he said. We would certainly see that he was successful. In 1993, it was rumoured that on his 70th birthday two years later two hundred heads of states would come to Prasanthi Nilayam to honour him. Sai Baba himself had supposedly said so. "Soon" the whole world would come to realise that the avatar is on earth. On the other hand, he said in an interview to John Hislop, an American, in 1968 that the Kali Yuga, the darkest of all ages, would still last for 5320 years. Then again, he predicted that after his physical departure around 2021, he would be reborn as Prema Sai Baba and an age of love will dawn. As Prema Sai, he would marry, he foretold, and many women in the ashram prayed to be the lucky one in their next birth.

He kept us focussed on the future. We always waited for something to happen. This was no doubt against the basic rule of spiritual life: Be as much as possible present in the now.

I had also justified the manner in which Sai Baba courted VIPs and even corrupt politicians and had believed the official explanation given in the lectures for foreigners: "In the world he follows the laws of the world."

Another point were his promises which he did not keep. Often they were harmless, like the assurance to call someone for an interview "tomorrow" or "before the departure". 'Baba is not bound by our time concepts', some devotees tried to overcome the disappointment. Yet he also raised greater hopes, when for example he promised a friend of mine that her little son who suffered from diabetes would be all right when he starts attending school. "Did he mean high school or maybe college?" Most devotees were good-natured and tried to find convincing explanations.

Now I heard even concerning the materialisation of objects, Sai Baba's visiting card as it were, that not all were genuine, and the lockets, which he gave away during interviews, came in cardboard boxes to the ashram. A friend once told me that she saw Sai Baba taking a watch from under the cushion on his chair, before he 'materialised' it.

Now my viewpoint had changed, not the situation as such. People still kept streaming into the ashram—full of faith in Sai Baba. Many Russians were among them and recently many Japanese who stood out as they all wore the same yellow shawl over their shoulders. VIPs also came in great numbers for blessings. A conference about human values in education was organised and the vice chancellors of some 20 Indian universities took part. Different projects continued to be initiated, for example improving the water supply in the district, which turned out to be a great boon for the area. The new super speciality hospital got an additional department for nephrology.

No doubt, Sai Baba was doing a lot of good. He inspired his followers to serve the poor and many were convinced that he would finally lead them to enlightenment.

Tamara was now worried about me. She felt it was serious and I was on my way out. "I will ask Baba to give you back your faith", she said. "Please don't do that. I am glad I got rid of it", I had to answer her.

Indeed, I felt relieved and knew at the same time that nobody who still believed in Sai Baba could understand me. Tamara probably felt sorry for me. A German told me that Sai Baba had told her that until 1995 many will leave as he is separating the chaff from the wheat and only those with a pure heart will stay. I felt annoyed that he so self-righteously declared me as chaff and my heart as impure.

It, however, became clear to me that I do not have to judge who Sai Baba is, what powers he has and whether he is genuine. I only have to judge for myself whether his presence and my strong focus on him is still helpful. And as I sincerely felt relieved, when I lost faith in him, it was obviously time to leave. A recurring dream supported it: I was in a room and noticed that it was dark. Then I realised that all the curtains were drawn, and I pulled them back. One night, even after pulling back all the curtains there was still not enough light and I thought of shifting to a room on top of the building.

Strangely, there was no feeling of having been betrayed, neither was there emotional pain. It was plain relief—at least in the beginning while still at Prasanthi Nilayam. I told my French friend, who felt that Baba had miraculously increased her platelet count, that I was leaving. She was shocked. "How can you do this?" she asked in disbelief, convinced that Sai Baba was the avatar of our age and that I made a big mistake.

Some seven years later, however, many more foreigners started to leave Sai Baba. In Scandinavia, a few Sai centres closed down completely, when young men came out with their experiences in private encounters with Sai Baba. Internet facilitated disseminating the information. Some ex-devotees from abroad demanded a probe into the activities of Sai Baba. In the cyber world, a war of words was going on between ex-devotees who turned critics and representatives of the Sai Organisation. Sai Baba still was in favour with the Indian government. The President of India, Mrs. Pratibha Patil, visited Sai

Baba in 2009 and a photo showed her bowing to touch his feet.

In November 2010, Prime Minister Manmohan Singh came to attend the convention of the Sai Institute of Higher Learning. I watched it on TV. Sai Baba sat in a wheelchair and looked glum, frequently wiping his mouth with a handkerchief. He was 85 at that time and seemed like a prisoner of the coterie around him. I felt sorry for him that he might have to live like this till the age of 96, as he said he would. I did not guess then that he had only five months left and would die ten years earlier than foretold.

In early April 2011, Satya Sai Baba was admitted to the intensive care of his own hospital in an extremely serious condition. For three weeks, the news bulletins focussed hardly on the state of his health but on the 40,000 crore Rupee (about 6 billion US dollars at current rates)) empire of the Sai Trust of which Sai Baba was the president. Who would be the successor and what would happen to the wealth was the main question.

Devotees suspected that Baba had died already. They became restless and demanded to see him. Police was deployed in strong force, and on April 24th, Easter Sunday, it was announced that Sai Baba had died. It was a shock for the devotees. Apart from the emotional trauma that he had left his body ten years earlier than predicted, they had to deal with the fact that around 100 kg gold, even more silver, and currency valued over two million dollars were found in his private chambers. His body was interred in the same hall where he used to give darshan and the traders and businessmen of Puttaparthi fervently hoped that his samadhi would turn into a pilgrimage centre.

Yet this was still far off in the future when I lost my faith in him in 1993. Now I felt much better in the ashram. I felt free and did not regularly go to darshan any longer. And when I went for darshan from a sense of obligation, I came late und stood outside behind a low wall just for the short time when he made his round—and noticed then only that many Indian women, who permanently lived in the ashram, did the same. I postponed leaving from one day to the other, as I did not know where to go. However, as the situation did not feel right I had to leave.

Ten days had passed since I read the sentence in the book during his talk, when I finally took the early morning bus to Bangalore. I sneaked out of the ashram with a small bag over my shoulder, so that I did not attract the attention of the office, as I could not possibly move my luggage as yet. Volunteers were busy decorating the darshan area with banana trees and flower garlands, as I walked past. Diwali, the great festival of lights would be celebrated today—in memory of the day when Ram returned as king to Ayodhya after 14 years in exile.

CHAPTER 26

Karunamayi's motherly advice

In Bangalore, I checked into a small hotel, a colonial style villa situated right in the heart of the town. It used to be the transit point for Baba devotees from overseas and has meanwhile been demolished. At the reception, there was a notice regarding Vijayeshwari Devi or Karunamayi as she is usually called. She has an ashram in Andhra Pradesh and also tours the West. The notice read that at present, she was staying in Bengaluru and on Diwali evening, there would be a celebration at the given address.

As I had nothing else to do, did not feel particularly great and did not want to sit in my room on that great festive night, I started off in an auto rickshaw in the late afternoon. It took one hour to get through the city. The traffic near the city market was chaotic, and I admired the people there who calmly and quite cheerfully carried on with their chores in small stores and workshops on the roadside—in the midst of deafening noise and extreme pollution from exhaust fumes.

Karunamayi had a hall at her disposal on the first floor of a building in a quiet residential area. It slowly filled with visitors, while preparations were still underway. People sat in small groups on the floor and threaded flower garlands. Others pulled petals from flowers, which were lying all over in big heaps. The whole room was filled with fragrance and with soothing, devotional music. At the entrance, there was a table with books and cassettes for sale. The atmosphere was welcoming. There were about hundred people, in contrast to the thousands at Sai Baba's ashram. Some nodded encouragingly and smiled at me. I was the only foreigner. As I did not feel like pulling flower petals, I sat down on the floor and waited.

To mark the occasion the thousand names of Lalita, the divine mother, were recited and with each name a handful of flower petals were offered, which slowly grew into a big heap. Karunamayi sat down on the floor in front, facing us. She looked motherly with her 35 years at that time. There was no special fanfare, when she entered. After she sat down, she gave me a long, compassionate glance and tears fell on my yellow silk kurta, and made big, dark stains.

My life suddenly seemed so wasted. I was now in my early forties and had neither achieved success in the worldly nor in the spiritual sense. I neither enjoyed the love and security of a family, nor had I found love and security in god. All of a sudden, I felt very alone. Everyone around me seemed to belong somewhere. Without doubt, nobody had come to the celebration alone—except me.

The glance of Karunamayi (Karunamayi means "permeated by compassion") made me cry. I had always asked god whom I mainly called Shiva or Bhagawan, not to lead me on a wrong path. Had he taken me for a ride? Have the seven years with Sai Baba been in vain, thrown away? Had I become more tense and inhibited due to the many rules in the ashram instead of becoming freer and wider? I did not know and felt no ground under my feet.

At the end of the function, Karunamayi put kumkum, the powder made from red turmeric, on everyone's forehead. This dot (called tilak or bindi) on the third, intuitive eye is meant to protect and stimulate it. When it was my turn, Karunamayi said, "Come again". I was glad, because it gave me at least something to do. I bought a booklet about her life at the entrance. Her cousin, who looked after the sales, suggested I should talk to Karunamayi tomorrow morning in private.

On my way out, while looking for my sandals in the pile of footwear in front of the door, a man accosted me:

"You are with Satya Sai Baba, aren't you? I have seen you in Puttaparthi."

"Yes, I have been there, but I am not anymore with him", I played down my seven long years in the ashram.

The next morning, when I went again to Karunamayi, the city market presented itself in a different light. The traffic flowed smoothly, no jam yet; the noise was bearable. The stores and workshops looked fresher in the morning sun. Some still had the shutters down. The people, too, seemed slower and got ready for an eventful and towards evening hectic day filled with exhaust fumes and deafening noise. They were right in the middle of action and I did not know who was better off—they or their colleagues in the West, where noise and other pollutants are under control and the working conditions are generally better and more hygienic. Yet where no cups with sweet milk tea are supplied by young boys, where the place is not teeming with, by and large, friendly people and where smiling faces and laughter are less frequent.

At Karunamayi's place, it was quiet. Her cousin at the book table ignored me. Maybe he felt embarrassed that he had given me hope for a private talk today. As I soon came to know, Karunamayi would remain in prayer and meditation for the whole day and not meet anybody. Instead, I met her mother. She looked straight and calmly at me for quite a while, as it happens often in India, before she asked in Telugu, the language of Andhra Pradesh, where I came from. I did not know who this old, small woman was, till someone introduced her.

I had already read about Annapurnamba, her mother. She got married as a child of eight. At 17, when she was already the mother of two daughters, she paid a visit to Ramana Maharshi in Tiruvannamalai.

"Do you like to live in an ashram?" he asked her.

"Your grace, Bhagavan", she answered reverentially.

"Not now and not in this ashram. You will live in the ashram of your daughter, and you need not go anywhere else. Everyone will come to you. You will give birth to the divine mother", Ramana Maharshi told her.

Annapurnamba was too shy to ask the great Ramana for clarification on what he had said.

In 1958 on Vijaya Dasara, the big festival that precedes Diwali for about two weeks and which celebrates among other events the victory of Ram over the demon king Ravana and the liberation of Sita, whom he had kidnapped, Annapurnamba gave birth to her fourth child. It was a girl and she was called Vijayeshwari.

About the young Vijayeshwari, too, miraculous stories were told, not quite as spectacular, as those about the young Satya Sai Baba, but spectacular enough to make people take notice of her. Once, for example a family friend was visiting. Her son had left his home ten years ago and since then had never given any sign of life. Naturally, his mother suffered from this loss, and when she was visiting that day—it was the 14th June 1968—she started crying. Vijayeshwari, who was sitting over her homework in a corner, came over to her, caressed her cheek and comforted her, "Your son will come back to you day after tomorrow." "If this is true, I will worship you as a goddess", the woman reacted and, in all likelihood, did not believe that Vijayeshwari could be saying the truth.

On 16th June, in the morning around 6 o'clock, when the mother was just saying her prayers, her son came walking through the door. She promptly took him to the house of her friends and fell at the feet of the 10-year-old girl, whose mother protested against her doing so.

Vijayeshwari's father had her horoscope made. It said that Vijayeshwari was a divine person, would spread wisdom and give refuge to the poor and deprived. She would not marry, but settle in the forest.

Her father was horrified to imagine his daughter living alone in the forest with all its inherent dangers. Vijayeshwari just came back from school, when he was brooding over the horoscope, and addressed him, "Father, why are you so depressed about a small thing?" "Which small thing?" the father wanted to know. "Because of my life. That I will live in the forest for some time." The father was more than amazed. His little daughter could not know anything about the horoscope.

Her father died when she was eight and did not live to see, that for 12 years—from 1980 to 1992—she meditated deep in the forest often for days without food, and that indeed she became the refuge for the poor and deprived by founding orphanages and schools.

Some days later, I had a private talk with Karunamayi.

She stood in a room, which was empty except for a small shrine in a corner, and waited for me with a fountain pen in her hand. "You are a daughter of Saraswati", she said and gave me the pen. Saraswati is the goddess of wisdom and learning. I was happy about the unexpected gift and we both sat down on the stone floor. I told her that I had spent several years with Satya Sai Baba, and now did not know what to think of him. I probably talked too fast and was not sure whether she could follow me.

"What about the faith in a guru? Is it necessary?" I finally asked.

"Try to have the same faith as before", she answered.

"It is not possible anymore", I said.

She seemed satisfied with my remark.

"The reason is, because you want the highest", she said. "You are in truth Atman, infinite. You are the one self. I want all human beings to realise their self. Meditation is necessary for it. Your self is like thousand suns. Everything is in you. Atman is *in*-visible, that means", she explained, "He is *in* you *visible* during meditation."

She only briefly mentioned the ashram of Sai Baba and did not make any comment about him. "In Satya Sai Baba's ashram meditation is not given a proper place. That is the reason why there is so much competition. You must meditate and go inside", she urged me and promised, "I will help you. It is my responsibility."

At the end, she asked me to walk around her three times and do pranam. After I had finished and stood in front of her, she handed me a 5 cm high statue of Saraswati Devi. The metal was vibrating hot, yet not in a manner, that one would get burnt. Later, I sometimes tried rubbing the statue between my hands or keeping it on my body, but did not succeed in generating that type of heat.

Was Karunamayi hinting that the miracles of Sai Baba are not so special, that materialisations or transportations are possible for her, as well, and not worthwhile talking about? During materialisations and transportations, heat is supposedly generated. I had a hunch that the statue had not reached her hands in a normal way. Karunamayi smiled and I did not ask her about it, because at that moment it felt not worthwhile talking about. Only later, certain curiosity cropped up.

While I was taking leave, she said again, "You are a daughter of Saraswati. Write about the divine." When I was almost at the door, she added, "Consider my ashram as your home. You are always welcome."

It felt good to hear this, because I did not have a home. My gas stove and refrigerator were still in Prasanthi Nilayam and I had no idea, to which place I would transport my belongings. Not to an ashram, so much was clear. But I was grateful that she made me feel welcome. In the night after the meeting, I had a dream: I lit candles and knew that it was New Year.

I took Karunamayi's advice to meditate to heart. I noticed then only how much I had neglected meditation during the years in the ashram. Sai Baba once said that meditation was useless, since we would only sit and think about all kinds of things. Instead, we should rather serve our fellow human beings. I felt he had a point. Yet maybe mediation is not useless, even if thoughts dominate.

Now I sat down regularly for one hour in the morning and evening and sometimes also in the silent night, if I happened to wake up. The meditation kept me going at that time, when I rather wanted to be dead than alive. I had lost my home, my friends and whatever structures my daily life had had and sometimes felt as if I was floating in mid-air—without any support.

Karunamayi had recommended a simple, but in the Indian tradition basic breathing exercise, called Anulom-Vilom, which I practised before meditation: Closing the right nostril with the thumb of the right hand and breathing in through the left nostril. Then closing the left nostril with the ring finger and breathing out through the right nostril and breathing in again through the right nostril. Now again the thumb was placed on the right nostril, while the ring finger was lifted while breathing out through the left nostril and again breathing in through the left nostril. This cycle was to be repeated five times. Karunamayi placed great importance on this pranayama and had given me a list of all its benefits. The list was long.

Still, my meditation was not conforming to my idea of a 'good' meditation. Again and again, thoughts took me on excursions and only occasionally some peace was felt. However, now there were often beautiful experiences in the morning in between the state of sleeping and being fully awake.

It had happened earlier, too, that in this state all my cells were vibrating with bliss. Once I saw Shiva before me, with a peaceful countenance and long hair, as he is pictured on posters. Brilliant light shot out from his third eye on his forehead and entered my third eye and I heard "Om namah Shivay". I felt ecstatic. Each cell in my body was in jubilation. I was lying on a berth in a train with over 80 people in the second-class compartment and possibly could not have stood more bliss. Such wonderful feelings came now more frequently. They came as a surprise gift and helped me to become gradually certain that there is truly something great and loving alive inside me.

When Karunamayi went back to her ashram in Andhra Pradesh some 200 km north of Chennai, I did not join her. It took me fourteen years until, in January 2008, I visited her ashram at the foot of the steep Garudadri hills and close to the temple of Sri Narasimha Swami. The place is literally at the end of the road.

After reaching, I sat quietly in the spacious temple dedicated to Lalita, when a woman called me. I thought she wanted to see my passport and followed her—and ended up in a small room where Karunamayi was sitting on a couch. It felt as if no time had passed since last seeing her. Her eyes narrowed to sparkling, black slits—so big was her smile.

"Those hills are special. The seven Rishis have meditated here, and the place is as holy as Arunachala Mountain in Tamil Nadu", she said in a soft voice, smiling. She knows those hills in and out. It was in those hills where she had meditated for 12 years.

Karunamayi at her ashram at the foot of the Garudadri Hills.

In her ashram, a weeklong meditation retreat had just ended and only a few Russians and Americans were left over from it. The spacious ashram looked empty, but the priests performed their daily routine of worshipping the main deity of the temple. They chanted the Vedas for several hours, performed homa, and recited Lalita Sahasranama every day.

A few days after my arrival, however, the ashram was teeming with people and wore a festive look. It was a Saraswati festival and Karunamayi gave initiation into the Saraswati Mantra to students. Thousands had come. Right from the ashram gate up to the temple visitors lined up, proceeding slowly. They filed past her from 7 in the morning till 7 in the evening. Karunamayi dipped a small tulsi twig in honey and wrote a mantra on the tongue of the student, while the parents stood by.

On my last day in the ashram, a big group of village folk filled the temple in the evening. It was obvious that they had never seen a foreigner and some of the children, after discovering me, pointed excitedly or shyly towards me. Karunamayi sat among the villagers who were crowding around her. "Sri Lalita is in the form of consciousness", was one of the few sentences I understood during her talk in Telugu. It struck me that only in India such highly philosophical statement can be made even to villagers. In the West, in contrast, even educated people might have a blank stare on being told that god is in the form of consciousness. There, hardly anyone wonders what the basis for this world is and here, in the deep interior of India, simple villagers are taught the highest wisdom. Karunamayi then initiated us into the Sri Chakra mantra. She kept chanting it and we all repeated it, till the last person got the pronunciation right.

Suddenly she talked in English. I was the only foreigner and she addressed me directly. "Layers of karma will be burnt up by meditation", she said and "The mantra has to be given by a guru to be effective in the right way." She exhorted me "Go inside with the right insight. You are Atmaswarup." And in the end a comforting assurance: "Wherever you go, wherever you are, I am with you."

I was leaving the next morning. She did not come with me, or did she? "The physical body which you see is not real", she had earlier explained. "I am not this limited body. I am the auspicious, divine Light and not the bodily, material form. On the ordinary level of consciousness, you see Amma and yourself as different. Yet if you go above that, you will see yourself and Amma as one. There is no difference between the Atmas."

It was the same message that all Indian sages give: that, what she essentially is, is definitely always with me. It has to be, as it is my essence, too, and the essence of everyone.

CHAPTER 27

Shantivanam—a Christian ashram

Shantivanam is an ashram right on the banks of the river Kaveri about one hour by car upstream from Tiruchirapalli. The ashram belongs to the Catholic Church though outwardly it looks like a Hindu ashram. The monks and priests wear saffron or white, like Sadhus. Even the chapel looks like a temple, except that the figures on the dome are those of Jesus and Mary. I had met the head of the ashram, Father Bede Griffiths, at the conference on ancient wisdom and modern science in 1982, where he had portrayed Shantivanam as a meeting ground of Christianity and Hinduism. He felt Christianity could learn from India.

It sounded interesting, and Abdullah and I planned to visit. Yet then I came alone, after his death, and spend several months there in the following years. In 1993, after leaving Sai Baba and meeting Karunamayi, I went there again to have some quiet time in beautiful surroundings to sort out what I should do next.

When I reached Shantivanam for the first time in 1983, I was awed by the beauty of the place and by the easy, friendly contact with fellow travellers. It seemed I had found the ideal base in India. The ashram blends into the lush, tropical environment with simple, thatched huts, a cow shed, a big round meditation hall also with a thatched roof, a well-stocked library and an open-air dining hall.

There were some minus points, too—like common bathrooms with only cold water, thin, hard mattresses, scorpions and even snakes which had free access to the huts. Yet these things did not deter young travellers and rather added to its charm.

Path to Shantivanam, the Christian ashram at the banks of Kaveri river.

Shantivanam was originally founded by two French missionaries, Jules Monchanin and Henri Le Saux. That was in 1950. Jules Monchanin died already in 1957 and Shantivanam became a burden for Henri Le Saux who took to Hinduism, had a Hindu guru, took a Hindu name (Abhishekananda) and dreamt to be free like a Hindu Sanyasi. Yet he belonged to the Church, had to read mass every day and owned a bank account. In his letters, his struggle is obvious. When he wrote to friends, he sounded like a Hindu. When he corresponded with clergy, he used Christian terminology and acknowledged Christ as the saviour of all humankind. It seems he did not have the strength to break away from the financial security that the Church guaranteed.

When in 1968 Bede Griffiths, an English Benedictine monk arrived in Shantivanam, Henri Le Saux left for northern India, never to come back. Father Bede, as Griffiths was called, had no problems concerning loyalty. His commitment was to the Catholic Church, which he had joined as a young man to the great distress of his

Anglican mother. He once told me, "For me Christianity—the relationship to God in Jesus—has a fullness and finality that I don't find anywhere else".

Most visitors in Shantivanam were from the West but occasionally, groups of Indian novices or priests came for retreats. While cutting vegetables or during the tea breaks I had many inspiring talks.

Yet very soon, I discovered a jarring note. Whenever Bede Griffiths gave a talk, I felt a certain lack of intellectual integrity. He would appreciate the basic principles of Indian philosophy, and then claim, that those very principles had been there in Christianity all along. Yes, there were also Christians who realised the oneness of all. Meister Eckehart is an example. But the fact that he has been excommunicated and so far not yet rehabilitated, shows how the Church treated mystics who were close to Hindu philosophy.

I realised that "learning from India" meant to take over Hindu philosophy, rituals and mantras ("Om namah Shivay" had become "Om namah Christay") so that Christianity has a better chance of being accepted in India. Bede Griffiths was open about it. He felt that Christianity had not been presented in the right way for Hindus to see its worth, and he wanted to change this.

He took off his brown, heavy monk's robe and wrapped an orange cotton cloth around his hips and threw another one over his shoulder. His shoes were discarded in favour of walking barefoot in the ashram or wearing sandals outside. Instead of having his meals sitting on a table, he sat now on the ground and instead of fork and knife, he used a spoon. Father Bede was tall and slim, with long, white hair and a long, white beard. He looked like an ascetic and could be mistaken for a Hindu swami. He even took a Hindu name "Swami Dayananda" which however did not stick and was rarely used.

Every prayer started with OM. Before mass, the ancient Gayatri Mantra and other Vedic mantras were chanted. Aarti was performed in the end and everyone put a finger into a bowl of kumkum and placed a dot on his or her forehead. Bede Griffiths had even an edition of psalms printed, where those psalms, which sounded too offensive and violent, were missing.

This enculturation, as Father Bede called it, made him popular with new age groups in the West. His books were well received and he was invited for seminars.

In India, however, many traditional Christians eyed him with suspicion. They loved their Western ways and wanted to be distinguished from the heathen Hindus. A young woman was so shocked that she was expected to put a red dot on her forehead—a mark she considered 'Hindu'—that she refused to enter the chapel again. She was married to a Hindu and the marriage was in trouble as she did not approve of the rituals which her mother in law observed. Her local priest had told her that Hindu rituals are from the devil, Hindu gods are devils and she should not even look at a temple (she herself told me this), and now she was supposed to conform to a Hindu custom which she vehemently resisted.

Father Bede adjusted his daily talks depending on who was listening. As most of the visitors were Western travellers who were appreciative of Hinduism and Buddhism, Father Bede was liberal and did not condemn those faiths. Yet once I happened to come to the hall while he was talking to Indian novices before their final vows as nuns. I was shocked how differently he talked and went afterwards straight to his hut. "Father Bede, how can you talk so badly about Hinduism?" I blurted out. "I have to strengthen the faith of these girls. Otherwise they won't know where the border to Hinduism is", he justified himself.

Hinduism has no borders because truth has no borders. It does not mind if a Hindu keeps a picture of Jesus in his prayer room. Many Hindus bow reverentially not only when they pass a temple, but also when they pass a church or Sufi shrine. They are sure that there is only one Supreme Brahman. Such openness is threatening for a religion that claims it has the duty to herd all humanity into its fold to save them from eternal hellfire—without any proof of course.

Father Bede spoke English fast with long winding sentences. I often had difficulties to find out what he meant. Once he was talking to me in his hut and I had again this problem. So I wanted to make sure: "Father Bede, can I summarise that you consider Christianity as superior to other religions?" Nodding his head, he agreed. "Yes, you may say so."

On the next day, Father Bede distributed among the visitors their mail, as usual. "Maria, this letter is from me", he said handing me a note in an envelope. I was curious and started reading: "Regarding our talk yesterday, I would rather not say 'superior'." Then he went on to explain that in his view other religions are becoming *fulfilled* through Christianity, whereas Christianity is becoming *enriched* through other religions.

Well, does it not mean superior?

He is of course entitled to his opinion. Yet it was insincere to create the impression that Christianity is basically not different from Hinduism, except for the additional advantage of having Jesus Christ as the saviour. He initiated an Interfaith Dialogue in Tiruchirapalli in the 1980s and took me a few times along. Everyone was friendly, yet it fizzled out. Christianity and Islam were not prepared to question their dogmas and to open their borders, and the Hindus present there, unfortunately did not challenge them.

Father Bede's birthday was celebrated on 17. December and the ashram was always full at that time. In 1992, I was there during his birthday celebration. He turned 86. An Australian TV crew made a film on him. He was put in a bullock cart for a bumpy ride and driven around the village on uneven tracks. Further, he was interviewed for hours in front of the camera. He cooperated, but it was tiring for him. The film team left shortly before Christmas. On the morning after their departure, everyone waited in the chapel for Father Bede who usually was exceptionally punctual. He did not come. Someone went to his hut. He had suffered a stroke.

He recovered somewhat, yet a second stroke followed. He died on 13. May 1993.

When I reached Shantivanam in December 1993, Father Bede was missing. Missing were also many of the guests. The place was as beautiful as ever. Yet my discomfort regarding the lacking intellectual integrity was still valid. The talks continued, conducted by Brother Martin who had been groomed by Father Bede. "Shantivanam's main objective is now to prevent foreigners from immersing themselves too much in Hinduism or Buddhism," an Indian Christian told me. It may be true, but it did not work in my case.

CHAPTER 28

A coffee planter guru in Kodagu

While reading newspapers in Shantivanam, I kept noticing 'Madikeri' in the weather column. Madikeri had always some 6 degrees Celsius less than Tiruchirapalli. I concluded that it was in the mountains and probably a good place for meditation. So I started off—by train to Bangalore and then by bus for six more hours towards the Western Ghats. The last hour the bus pulled up the mountain on a winding road.

Madikeri is located in the Nilgiri Mountains at a height of 1200 metres and sprawls over a hilly area in midst of lush vegetation. It has around 35,000 inhabitants and is the capital of Kodagu, a wealthy district, where coffee and pepper grows.

I took a room in the Tourist Bungalow. The government hotels usually had the worst service, yet the best location. In Madikeri, too, the location on top of a hill was great, the rooms were spacious, the view over the mountains fantastic but the place looked run down, the geyser did not work, the restaurant was as bare as a canteen on a railway station, and the preparation of breakfast took an hour. Even my request for toast with jam and butter was—untypical for India, where usually everything is possible—turned down.

"Not available," the waiter said.

"Available!" I insisted with my German logic. „Look here 'Toast with butter', and here 'toast with jam'" and pointed with my finger triumphantly on the items on the menu.

"But toast with butter and jam we don't have."

I ordered toast with jam and toast with butter.

A young couple from Munich joined me for breakfast. The girl had a beautiful face, long blond hair and gave me a sweet smile when her partner pushed her in a wheelchair out on the veranda. She was paralysed from the neck down.

"We are in India for the second time", she said. "I love India. People are so natural and warm here. When they see me, their first question is: 'How did this happen?' This feels so good. In contrast, in Germany everyone pretends as if I am completely normal. Everyone tries hard and somehow embarrassed to overlook my condition. Nobody dares to mention it."

Until then I also had not dared but now I asked her. When she was 16, she had attempted suicide by throwing herself in front of a car. In the hospital, she had fought for her life with all her strength.

"I so much wanted to live, even if I am badly handicapped. I realised how precious life is", she said and sounded surprisingly cheerful. Meeting her helped me to see my situation in perspective. My life situation had collapsed and I have lost my home and my friends. So what? Life goes on and I still have a functioning body and mind, not to speak of the spirit.

In the evening I went to 'Raja Seat', a nearby park, high above the valley, where people gathered to admire the sunset behind the undulating nilgiri, blue mountains ("nil" means blue and "giri" mountain). Many, mainly elderly coffee planters strolled up and down and went afterwards to the nearby club for a drink or a game of bridge. At the entrance of the club used to be a signboard until the end of the British colonial rule in 1947: "Only for Whites".

I sat down on a bench and noticed a foreigner. She noticed me too. Her name was Trudy, she was born in America, but her parents were Germans. She was happy to talk in German.

"I was a teacher and retired a few years ago", she narrated. "And now I am only interested in meditation."

"Do you know "I am That" by Nisargadatta Maharaj? I asked her, because I thought she might like this book as she was interested in spirituality. It was my favourite at that time. She seemed surprised and kept quiet for a while. Maybe she pondered whether to tell me.

"We have a meditation group under a guru here in town and we are reading this very book under his guidance. Our guru is in the same lineage (Nath Pant) as Nisargadatta Maharaj. We meet tomorrow. Would you like to come?" she finally asked. I said yes.

This 'yes' was the beginning of five years under a new guru, although I had not intended that. This new guru, however, was in many aspects the exact opposite of Satya Sai Baba:

With Satya Sai Baba, there were thousands of people, with Guruji, as he was called, only around fifty. Sai Baba was wearing day in day out the same long, red robe, Guruji was dressed in tailor-made shirts and trousers, a sleeveless vest and sometimes a stylish tweed cap. Sai Baba was unmarried and lived in the ashram, Guruji had a wife and three children and lived in a luxurious bungalow. Sai Baba had caught the attention of people because of his miracles and had attracted followers fully on his own; Guruji had taken over the leadership of an established meditation group, after his guru had passed away. With Sai Baba I talked in seven years only five times for a few minutes, with Guruji I sat already on the very first day, alone with him, for a whole hour in his room.

Maybe this contrast was the reason for me to stay once more with a guru. The familiar surroundings and the easy contact with him came much closer to my idea of a guru-disciple-relationship.

Or was it even destined that I had to have another guru?

Tamara, my clairvoyant Russian friend in the ashram of Sai Baba, had once dreamt about me: She and many others were on the beach trying to get their boats ready to venture out into the sea. Her boat had no oars and she was at a loss what to do. When she looked up, she saw me already far out in the ocean. A man was rowing my boat. She saw only his back, described that he "still" had black hair, and wore a "coffee brown" shirt. I wondered at that time why she said 'coffee brown' and not just brown. She had rushed to me immediately after her afternoon nap and looked agitated. "It will come true", she was sure. She felt the man in my boat indicated that

I would marry and leave Sai Baba "after about two years" (it turned out to be exactly to the day two years), yet at that time leaving Sai Baba seemed highly improbable.

My new guru, in spite of being 57, had still mainly black hair and was the owner of a coffee estate.

Trudy took me to the meditation centre. It was a small house on the outskirts of the town. Guruji had built it for his own guru. Around 30 people were there already. Some women were cooking in the kitchen. Trudy and I were the only foreigners. Everyone was very friendly and welcoming. After a fantastic lunch, we all gathered in the biggest room. Guruji's sister read out from Nisargadatta's book 'I am That' and Guruji repeated it in his own words.

After some time, he told his sister to stop and asked his disciples to tell how they had benefited by their sadhana (spiritual practice) under his guidance. Everyone had enormously benefited. I felt ill at ease, and in the group, too, several seemed to feel ill at ease now. They felt pressured to say something positive. Guruji expected praise for himself and this was embarrassing. Even more embarrassing was that I felt he did it to impress me.

Afterwards, Guruji invited me for a talk to his room. I told him that, in my view, by asking his disciples about the benefits of their practice he had encouraged dishonesty, as nobody would want to admit that he had not benefited as much as those who spoke before him or her. Guruji however brushed my concern aside and explained that it is important to evaluate from time to time, where one stands and how far the goal is away. I accepted his view because he appeared likeable and almost charming.

"Maria, you need once more a guru. As long as you have not attained self-realisation, you need guidance from a guru", he destined. "Sai Baba has not taken you to self-realisation. A guru can lead you only as far, as he himself has reached", he continued, and I was surprised that he considered a world famous guru like Satya Sai Baba below his own stature. He gave me several examples of well-known saints, who had several gurus. "Only the last one has led them to enlightenment", he explained. "On an average it takes five years to reach self-realisation. My guru took five years and I took five years. You, too, can reach the goal in maximum five years."

"But I don't want any more a guru, because the guru can do whatever he wants and I have to swallow it", I said and avoided addressing him, as I could not bring myself to call him Guruji. He laughed and sounded trustworthy: "Maria, the guru is your friend."

I asked him for tips on meditation. He explained already during this first meeting the Soham mantra, which he gave to his disciples, yet without the formal initiation, which is supposed to pass on the power of the mantra though the guru. I was grateful, because I had never received so much attention from any guru so far. After leaving his room, I told Trudy that I liked her guru.

Guruji threw a spell on me, yet I wanted to take my time. A friend had recently told me about a guru in Lucknow whom he held in highest esteem. Several books had been written about him and he had become popular in the West. Before committing myself, I wanted to meet H.W.L. Poonja, as this man in Lucknow was called.

CHAPTER 29

"Don't think!"—Poonja's good, difficult advice

On a hot Sunday morning in April 1994, I arrived in Lucknow and took an auto straight to his centre because at that hour, Poonja, also called Papaji, would give darshan. Yet there was no guru anywhere in sight. Instead, the hall had been converted into a bazar. Fancy long dresses, skirts, blouses, trousers, jewellery were for sale, as well as brown bread and other homemade delicacies. Some of Poonja's disciples made some money in this way.

I found a room in a bungalow, which a German had taken on rent. She made a living by renting out rooms to visitors. Earlier, she had been with Osho and after he had died, she came, like many others, to Lucknow. A Brazilian moved into the room next to mine at the same time and we teamed up for the four days that I stayed in Lucknow. I benefitted from having a male companion when we went out in the evenings to eat at some stalls in town and he benefited from the fact that after 15 years in India, I knew my way around and could give him helpful tips. Furthermore, we both were no devotees of Poonja and clearly in the minority.

On the next morning, about 400 foreigners were pushing into the hall, meanwhile cleared from the bazaar, under supervision of strict, neat and clean looking volunteers (also foreigners) who seemed to be high up in the hierarchy that exists around every guru. Apparently, everyone wanted to sit right up in front.

The hall was packed. It had been a long time since I was exclusively among Westerners and I noticed that people looked around in a different way than Indians do. Apart from some who obviously had already found each other and exchanged loving glances, many pairs of eyes looked around as if searching for their soul mate. The Brazilian, too, dark, tall and at 40 in an attractive age, received direct, long glances from women, as he himself told me. He was not happy about it. Once, when we were in town, he surprised me.

"Did you notice that no Indian woman looks at me?"

It was true. They did not look directly into his eyes.

"Yet almost every Western woman looks directly at me and in Brazil it is the same. The women there make themselves cheap and the culture is finished. The way Indian women conduct themselves is admirable. It shows that their culture is still intact."

Poonja came into the hall accompanied by a group of neatly combed Westerners dressed in white. They looked like his bodyguards. He sat down in a low chair, closely surrounded by his devotees, looked around and smiled at some. A bunch of letters was lying next to him and he took one of them and started reading. He asked whose letter it was and the person who had written it got up and sat down right in front of him.

Relationships were a subject, which often figured in the letters. For example, somebody had written that his girlfriend had left him and now he was desperate. He sat there with his head lowered as if waiting for a scolding. The scolding came:

"You claim that you want self-realisation. Yet when the boyfriend or girlfriend leaves you, you fall into a deep hole and you want to die. That is complete nonsense. Have you still not understood that you are the self? That you need nothing and nobody to be happy?" Poonja reacted.

Then he became softer and gave usually the same advice. "Be still, here and now, without any effort and don't think." He asked the person to close his eyes and be still—simply be himself. After a while he asked, "How was it?"

"Great! I felt so much peace", was usually the answer and Poonja said, "See you discovered it. Now stay with it and don't lose it again."

Then he took the next letter and the next disciple came up to sit before him.

I realised why Poonja was so popular among Westerners. He propounded pure advaita, doubtless the highest philosophy: you are the self. You do not have to look for the truth because you are the truth here and now. You *are* that what you look for. The self alone is. Everything is fine as it is.

And the logical conclusion: no meditation, no mantras, no effort and no need to change your lifestyle. It is enough to simply be still and not to think—and enjoy the good food in the garden restaurants, which had sprung up all around the place to cater to the Western taste.

Poonja is right from his point of view. The truth is always present and its realisation cannot be forced, not even by meditation. Yet did Poonja really do us a favour with his advice: "Don't make any effort." To be still and not to think might not be possible for the great majority of his followers. At least one should be ready to drop thoughts off and on, not to be concerned too much with one's own problems and not to take one's own person so seriously. Normally, Westerners take thoughts, their own person, and their own body very seriously.

Poonja himself admitted in the hot hall, "Maybe I do not discern properly. I give to everyone the same truth. But the truth will reject those who are not worthy of it."

Surprisingly, Poonja himself had put in tremendous effort—for about 25 years. As a boy of eight, he had had an enlightenment experience of great bliss, which however left him after some days. He was longing for this state again and his mother advised him to worship Sri Krishna. His mother was the younger sister of Swami Ram Thirta, a well-known saint, as well as a brilliant mathematician. Poonja, however, had not met his famous uncle, because he had drowned in the Ganga in 1906 at the age of only 33 years– four years before Poonja was born.

Poonja took the advice of his mother to heart and devoted himself fully to Krishna. Later, after marriage, he repeated Krishna's name almost non-stop. He even took his food in the pooja room.

Then one night, he had a vision of Ram, Sita and Lakshman. Poonja was disappointed. His whole life he had dedicated to Krishna and now Ram stood before him instead of his beloved Krishna. After the vision had disappeared, Poonja could not continue with his spiritual routine. He was worried and went to Tiruvannamalai, to request the great Ramana Maharshi for advice.

Ramana asked him how he had come to Tiruvannamalai.

"By train", Poonja answered.

„And what did you do when you arrived in Tiruvannamalai?"

"I got down from the train."

Maharshi then explained to him that his spiritual practices have brought him to his goal and he did not need them any longer—similarly as the train had brought him to Tiruvannamalai and he did not need it any longer. Thereafter, he narrated, the glance of Ramana Maharshi purified all his cells and he became aware of his self that, as he realised, had been there all along.

Understandably, Poonja now advised "No effort", because he had realised that the ego makes the effort and the ego consists only of thoughts. Therefore, the activities of the ego lead away from the self, because it is thoughts that veil the self. Only when the ego is still, the self emerges from the depths of one's being. Maybe it is like with those pictures in which a figure is hidden: either one sees it or one does not see it. Activity, pondering, analysing or waiting for the future will not help to see it.

On the other hand, Poonja seemed to have forgotten that his intensive search over 25 years might have been a vehicle, which carried him to the point where he only had to open his eyes. The long preparation was probably necessary to be able to realise that what he searched for was always right here. It may not be logical, but logic is valid only in the realm of thinking and not wherefrom thinking arises.

On the next morning, I handed over a letter, to get an opportunity to sit in front of Poonja. I asked in the letter how I could get rid of thoughts, which obstinately crowd my mind especially, when they are useless. For example, when I try to take a nap, my mind would suddenly start writing an article and search for appropriate expressions. And often I just cannot stop the flow of thoughts.

Poonja did not pick my letter. Also not on the next day. Yet on the last day of my stay, he started reading it. I crossed over the tight rows of people and sat down in front. Poonja smiled and said, "I will give you now some homework. Tomorrow you report to me how it went."

"Tomorrow I won't be here, because I leave tonight", I said.

"If you are here for only such a short time, I can't help you", he responded slightly annoyed and sent me straight back to my seat. I climbed again over the rows—embarrassed and awkwardly—and missed the enlightenment which seems to have been granted to several persons there in front.

Poonja's declaration "You got it", after they had sat still for a while before him, was for several Westerners the start of their career as a guru. Many Western gurus who go on tours even to India had been sitting once in front of Poonja who confirmed their enlightenment.

Yet it also happened that Poonja withdrew his confirmation of enlightenment. Andrew Cohen, one of his most famous disciples, split up with him after years of deep devotion to his guru. Andrew blamed Poonja that he was jealous of his success and popularity. Poonja had said that he could create a thousand Andrew Cohens, but Cohen could not create a single Poonja. Earlier, however, Poonja had declared Andrew as his beloved, enlightened son. I read in Andrew Cohen's book about the goings-on between them and got the impression that power can corrupt even spiritually highly aware personalities.

I was not inspired to become Poonja's disciple, neither was the Brazilian. One reason might have been that only Westerners clustered around him. There was only one Indian in that big hall and he turned out to be from Canada. I felt that Indians might have a better sense about who was genuine and who was not. Around Guruji, there were only Indians, except for Trudy and me. Further, there was no pushing to sit close to the guru, as the guru was anyway easily accessible.

CHAPTER 30

Life in Kodagu

It was foggy, cold and wet when I reached Madikeri. The weather had changed dramatically on the way up the hill shortly before our destination. It was a big surprise. In March, the climate was sunny and the temperature ideal. Now, it was June, and the monsoon had set in. I did not know that with around four metres of rainfall per year, the place figured among the wettest places on earth. However, I enjoyed wearing a raincoat and boots, braving storm and rain in heavy fog, as we were literally living in the clouds.

With the help of Guruji's disciples, I found a bungalow near the meditation centre. The living room was 11 meter long. There were two verandas and six doors, which led outside, and the house was everything else but burglar-proof. It was far too big and unfurnished except for a few beds, but the rent was reasonable with less than 50 Euros at that time in 1994. Finally, I had a place for my belongings, which I soon fetched from Puttaparthi.

Now, I was the only foreigner. Trudy had fled from the rains back to the USA, and I was fully included into the social life. There were invitations for lunch or dinner. The women exchanged recipes, while their husbands talked about the price of coffee and pepper and discussed whether it was advisable to sell now, or whether frost could hit Brazil, which would damage the coffee crop there and push the price up.

My spacious, rented bungalow in Madikeri.

Kodagu is a wealthy district, and as Guruji himself was a rich coffee planter, many of his disciples belonged to the same class. I was amazed at the plush bungalows in wonderfully located coffee estates, where not only coffee berries grow on bushes, but also pepper winds climb up tall trees that provide shade for the coffee berries. I had not imagined that the region 'where the pepper grows' would be so exceptionally beautiful. In Germany the phrase 'go where the pepper grows' means more like 'go to hell'.

Wealth and luxury, however, were limited to the family of the estate owner. The workers lived in simple housing lines. Yet they were not badly off, compared to unskilled workers in towns. Living in the midst of nature had its advantages—and also disadvantages. Tigers and leopards were on the prowl and elephants crossed through the plantations. The villagers were aware of the dangers. Guruji narrated an incident that happened when the first movie was shown in Madikeri. A tent had been put up. Tribals from the surrounding hills flocked to the town and sat on the grass in front of the screen. In the movie, an elephant appeared. The villagers shouted, "Run", and all ran outside, with some throwing slippers at the screen.

Weddings were another important event on the social agenda. Two thousand guests were not unusual in the class of the coffee planters and the expenses, which were covered by the parents of the bride, accordingly high.

Further, there were condolence visits when someone had died. In my whole life, I had not seen as many dead bodies as I did in those five years in Kodagu. Was the deceased young, there was a lot of weeping.

Visiting sick people was another requirement in the social schedule. There was always some acquaintance in hospital, and he, too, was not left alone, whether he liked it or not.

There was a friendly, pleasant atmosphere among the members of the meditation group. We met twice a week in the centre and listened to Guruji talk. On Sundays, we often drove in a long caravan of cars on bumpy roads to one of the coffee estates, whose owner served us lunch with at least ten varieties of vegetarian dishes in an immaculately groomed garden. It did not seem to fluster the host that we were some 50 persons. I had to get used to having so many contacts, because I was more of an introvert—a character trait, which Guruji slowly cured me of.

"Maria, you are too much of a recluse. You have to get out of your shell and engage yourself more in society", he advised and probably was right. He took me to functions in a school, which his father had founded and made me distribute prizes. Once he asked me to describe my life in India before coming to Madikeri in front of the whole group. I felt panicky, but in retrospective, I am grateful for this, at that time unwelcome, nudge.

A few weeks after my arrival in Madikeri, Guruji said at the end of his birthday celebration all of a sudden, "Come, Maria, let's get serious." He called me to his room, closed the door, took the telephone receiver off the hook, sat down on the carpet opposite me and gave me initiation into the Soham Mantra that he had explained already during our very first talk. He then demanded that I meditate for one hour in the morning and evening. Now, I was fully part of the group and he was officially my guru.

It took some time until I had the same trust in Guruji that I used to have in Sai Baba. Yet slowly, I slipped again into the same thought patterns as it had happened with Sai Baba. Again, the faith developed that Guruji was enlightened. One aspect that probably helped was that, initially, I had a very good position with Guruji. He praised me at the slightest occasion and told the others to follow my example, which, though embarrassing, ultimately flattered me.

When Trudy came back, Guruji treated her very harshly, far more harshly than he treated any Indian in the group. He often ridiculed her in front of everyone, used insulting language and even threatened to throw her out of the group. When she was alone with him in his room, she often stormed out crying. Guruji smilingly explained that she was a tough nut to crack and needed this type of treatment. Trudy herself was—when the pain of it was not acute—proud about this special handling by Guruji. "He knows that I am strong enough to take it. That's why he does it with me. He can't do it with others", she told me.

'Guruji treats her in this way to hurt her ego', I used to think and wondered whether I could bear such treatment. It was a theoretical question. For more than three years, Guruji never uttered a harsh word to me. This was painful for Trudy and she occasionally showed me her frustration. By now, she regretted that she had introduced me to Guruji, but prophesied, rightly, that Guruji would drop me also one day.

Guruji and I on Arunachala Mountain, when our meditation group visited Tiruvannamalai

Guruji often talked about the role of the guru. He maintained that the guru does not do anything out of personal interest and acts only for the benefit of his disciples. "The guru does not make any mistake" and "the guru can see till eternity, and the disciple only till the tip of his nose", he even claimed.

"I had unshakable trust in my guru", Guruji said. "If he had asked me to jump into the temple pond, I would have done it." Nobody asked him whether he could swim.

Oddly, gurus and also leaders of other religions are rarely questioned about their claims. The reason may be that the 'ordinary' person does not consider himself competent in the realm of transcendental reality. Who knows what it means to be enlightened? Who knows whether 'God' really has spoken to some gifted men, called prophets or even had a son? I have swallowed many unverifiable claims in my life based on what I took to be an 'authority' in the field, starting as a child when I was taught that only Catholics were right. I had been convinced that Sai Baba was an avatar and now again I believed that Guruji was enlightened—without any proof.

Of course, the most important thing in life—my own existence—also cannot be proven. But the difference is that it is self-evident. If, however, alarm bells are ringing ever so softly regarding blindly believing anything, it is better to heed them. When I told a Swiss friend about Guruji's claim that a guru makes no mistake, her reaction was, "I don't want another Pope."

The alarm bells that I had heard ringing at the very first meeting when Guruji questioned his disciples about their 'progress' under his guidance had been too soft for me to heed. They seemed negligible compared to the positive aspects of this new phase in my life.

Life looked bright in Madikeri in spite of the dark rain clouds from June till September, and I attributed my happiness to Guruji. I was grateful that finally, I had found the 'right one' and projected my love and reverence on him as the visible form of the invisible Divine, and he undoubtedly did give helpful inputs.

For example, Guruji stressed the importance of knowing the qualities of Atman. "In spiritual books one often reads that Atman cannot be described, as it is beyond thoughts and words. This is true, however only to a certain extent", he said and explained, "Can you describe the taste of vanilla ice-cream? No. There are no words for it. Yet one can approximately describe it—sweet and not sour, salty or spicy. Cool and not hot, melting on the tongue and not liquid. Similarly, Atman cannot be described in words, nevertheless one can say something about it, for example, it is conscious and vast, expanded till infinity. It is without beginning and end, unchanging, eternal, formless, indestructible, fully independent, extremely subtle and eternally blissful." And his advice: "Be aware of those qualities and meditate continuously on Atman which is your Self."

Guruji knew how to motivate me. "The desire for self-realisation has to be on top of your priority list", he insisted. "By now you know everything about vanilla ice-cream. It is high time that you taste it."

I told him that my life has already become much more worthwhile simply by *knowing* about the oneness of all. Many fears have disappeared. Further, the trust has grown that everything is just right as it is. Yet Guruji was adamant, "This is not enough. You have to really experience the truth; you have to know that you *are* this Oneness. Self-realisation is not reserved for people with complicated Indian names. It is attainable also for Maria."

I meditated regularly for long and had for the first time out-of-body experiences. Earlier, I used to be very sceptical towards such experiences; maybe, because the first person, who told me about astral travel allegedly from own experience, was a rather unpleasant foreigner.

I had assumed that out of body experience and astral travel are accessible only for highly accomplished spiritual masters like Babaji. Yet now I experienced it myself and came to know that self-realisation is not a prerequisite. I had, however, no influence on it. It just happened and the first time I was on the outset even a little afraid. Yet the fear soon evaporated when a wonderful feeling spread throughout my being. I was full of bliss and felt fully awake. Yet it obviously was not the normal waking state. As soon as I slipped back into the normal waking state, the blissful feeling slowly vanished and only a vague memory was left.

For some time, I had many such experiences and was already looking forward, when I noticed the first signs that I would slip out of my body, because the feeling which went along with it, was beautiful. Not to be compared with anything in this world. The normal reality seemed so grey and drab in comparison. In fact, I dreaded to come back to it. However, intense observation seemed to shorten the experience. Once, for example, I wanted to know how I go through the ceiling. I watched myself floating towards it, then it felt as if my shoulder touched it and then I suddenly found myself back in my body lying in bed, regretting that I had obviously used my mind too much.

Guruji advised me not to take these experiences too seriously. They were simply proof that I was going along the right track. For me they were also confirmation that I was with the right guru. So I was willing to try, what Guruji demanded now more insistently during the satsangs, as the group meetings were called, and also in private talks: to completely surrender to the guru, to be totally devoted to him, to give him, as it were, the power of attorney for one's life. This 'Guru Yoga' was the highest form of yoga, Guruji claimed.

In ancient times, when there were no books and when scientists did not yet question the reality of sense perception, the guru was the only bridge to the truth. Truth cannot be known in the usual, dual sense, as in 'I (the subject) know That (the object). Truth is outside duality. It is a thoughtless or I-less way of being, where I and That merge into one. Therefore, the means to discover the truth are unorthodox. Sometimes the disciple needs a shock. Sometimes the guru ridicules the disciple in front of others.

Guruji told me how his guru, a retired army colonel, had treated a respected, elderly coffee planter who still was in our meditation group. One evening, several disciples were sitting around the guru. That elderly man got up asking, "May I go?" "Sit down!" the guru commanded, and he sat down. After a while, the guru said, "Now you may go." The man got up, yet before he could take the first step, the guru ordered, "Sit down!" This was repeated several times until the guru finally let him go. Doubtlessly a tough teaching!

And if the guru was not genuine and just enjoyed ordering people around?

In all likelihood, most people consider this elderly gentleman a weakling who too obediently did the bidding of some assumed authority. Yet could one look at it from a different angle? 'A yogi is even-minded in heat or cold, in praise or blame, in joy or pain', Sri Krishna tells Arjuna in the Bhagavad-Gita. Even if the guru was fake, that man took him to be genuine and passed through that humbling experience without an angry reaction. He had the chance to watch himself in this embarrassing situation and he might have learned something. Being the same in blame and praise, in pain and joy does not come naturally. It comes through introspection, understanding—and by being tested.

Meanwhile, I had great trust in Guruji, yet he did nothing to hurt my ego. My life was all sunshine for three years. As a foreigner I had a privileged position in the group and Guruji often praised me and gave me a lot of time. As he had asked me to type his talks from a cassette, there were many chances to connect. Guruji was truly like a friend.

The outer circumstances of my life were also to my liking. My bungalow was spacious and surrounded by lush vegetation. A stray dog had adopted me, and a wild cat came for food. But the greatest joy gave me cows, who during the monsoon took shelter on my veranda. I loved seeing them, closely huddled together. However, on their first visit it lessened my joy somewhat when all of them, as on cue, dropped cowpats before moving out. While I was wondering how to remove the wet dung without making too much of a mess, some women from a nearby settlement passed by. They noticed the cowpats and asked whether they could collect it. With pleasure! I handed them plastic bags and they scooped the precious droppings with their bare hands. They used them to disinfect the mud walls in houses and after drying, they serve as fuel. Maybe the cows left those dung-cakes which they consistently dropped only when they were about to move out as a thank you gift.

The cows came often, till my landlord had a fence put up around the compound. Yet I stayed in touch with one young white cow. Whenever we met on the road, she came with an energetic pace and—so was my impression –joyfully towards me and gazed at me with her calm, good-natured eyes. In the West, I occasionally hear a sentence like "Indians should eat their holy cows". In the Indian context, this sounds coarse. Moreover, it is not a sign of good understanding of the economic situation, either.

CHAPTER 31

Surrender and testing times

One day my landlord came with the news that his brother wanted to move from Chennai to Madikeri as soon as he would recover from an accident. It was a notice to leave, albeit without a fixed date.

Guruji came to my help. He not only offered but urged me to move into the almost ready basement of his new house, which he was building right next to the meditation centre. I did so before the rains started. A few months later new tenants settled in my bungalow. The brother of my landlord had died.

Simultaneously with moving, a difficult time started which dragged on for two painful years. It was not that tragic that the new flat would have fitted into my former living room. It was also okay that there was no electricity yet, and I had to manage with a gas lamp for one full year.

Worse was that above my ceiling, carpenters were making the window and door frames for the house and kept working till late hours in the night. I consoled myself that the carpenters, too, had to bear the hammering and banging—not only temporarily, but for the rest of their lives, whereas in my case it hopefully would end someday.

Another thing was as bad as the hammering: two young Doberman dogs of the neighbour, tied up at a distance of about 5 meters from my bedroom, were barking uninterruptedly through the night. Even earplugs did not help. It was luck, when I slept for an hour at a stretch.

My outer circumstances had badly deteriorated from one day to the other, and almost every night I made up my mind to move out, but by daylight, I could not justify capitulating before dogs and carpenters. Besides, Guruji himself had provided me with the flat in his own house, which was no doubt a privilege.

Yet not only were my living conditions now difficult. My relationship with Guruji also underwent a radical change. Already at the very first meeting after my move, he appeared almost hostile. "You only have book knowledge. You have no idea what it is really about", he threw at me. He certainly had a point, yet the tone and the way he pushed me aside, were completely new. He became increasingly more unfriendly and the change in his behaviour could not be missed by the others.

"You belong now to the inner circle", his sister tried to soften the blow. "Earlier he has treated you like a guest—friendly and hospitable. Now he attacks your ego, and this is only for your good." I was inclined to believe the thing about the ego. "The association with an enlightened master consists in getting blows for the ego", Anandamayi Ma had said. For three years, Guruji had cleverly created a strong bonding—so strong that I would not run away at the first assault on my ego. And now, he finally played the role of a guru and I did not run away.

Yet I suffered. Guruji had several devotees from Bangalore, all of them women who had one thing in common: their husbands objected to them falling at the feet of Guruji. Yet these had no scruple telling white lies and Guruji approved of such excuses for his sake.

Some of these women enlightened me now that Guruji *had* to treat me badly, because no one else did it. In their own case, their husbands would hurt their egos and take on as it were the role of a guru. I realised that I indeed lived a rather free life, was not answerable to anyone and not obliged to listen to any reproaches from anyone.

Except from the guru. Because the guru, so is assumed, has only the well-being of his disciple in mind and knows what is best for him. Therefore, one is required to absolutely obey the guru, provided one is interested in one's own good.

I learnt humility, learnt to accept reproach without defending myself and over time without being angry or terribly sad. I lost my embarrassment about the fact that Guruji had a lot to criticise about me and gradually did not mind anymore to play the role of the black sheep in front of others. Yet I kept conscientiously typing from a cassette everything that Guruji had said during the meetings. It was a lot of work and did not bring any appreciation. If there was a mistake in the text, I got a big scolding far out of proportion. My ego was doubtlessly under heavy fire, yet it was still alive. It hurt.

One day I mustered courage, went to his room and asked, "Guruji, what can I do, so that you don't have to lash out at me so hard?"

"What! You doubt the actions of the guru? That is the greatest crime of all!" he erupted like a volcano. "You are not fit for this path. It is the highest path of all. For you, there is no hope. You can only analyse and rationalise. I will throw you out of the group…"

I did not comprehend what happened and had no other option than to quietly let his outburst pass. It ended with, "From now on you are not allowed to talk to me, unless spoken to. Go now!"

I walked out from his room dazed. At the door, a young woman was beaming with joy, waiting to go in. She had been selected by a national airline as an airhostess and wanted to tell Guruji about her luck.

I had felt that it could not get worse, when I had asked Guruji my question. Now it got worse. Guruji not only did not say a single word to me, he did not even look at me during the meetings. I realised that I had only two options: accepting the situation or leaving.

I felt it was wrong to leave hurt and in a huff. I had to accept it.

It helped to follow the news on radio at that time. During the winter of 1998/99, Pakistanis had stealthily occupied several Himalayan mountain peaks on the Indian side. In the same winter, the Indian Prime Minister Vajpayee had inaugurated a bus service from Delhi to Lahore as a gesture of friendship, had travelled along with the first bus and had shaken hands with his Pakistani counterpart. End of April 1999, however, the Pakistanis opened fire from their advantageous position on top with the goal to capture the Srinagar–Leh road and isolate Ladakh. The Indian soldiers faced an almost impossible task to dislodge the Pakistanis, as there was a gradual ascent to the mountain peaks from the Pakistani side, yet a steep drop to the Indian side. Moreover, they were inadequately equipped for the cold climate. Nevertheless, they did the impossible. The whole nation stood behind the soldiers and their commanders, many of whom sacrificed their lives. There were daily reports about the incredible heroism of the young men who, in the night at sub-zero temperatures at 5000 metres, climbed up the rocks and came under fire from the top, with many of the soldiers wearing only canvas shoes and carrying heavy equipment on their backs.

This naturally made my suffering pale in comparison. Yet it kept bouncing back and I lived in great tension—mentally and bodily, because the hammering of the carpenters and the barking of the Dobermans continued. Yet I was determined not to run away. Somewhere deep inside I had the trust that it was a chance to give in and to completely surrender to the situation as it was. "Don't think that there is no growth now", I kept hearing.

After almost six weeks, Guruji called me to his room. He started off, "The search for the self is an extremely serious matter. Do you really want the self? Think about it! You are free to leave. If you stay and you are not serious, I will throw you out. I have tested you now for one month. Here it goes according to me, not you!"

Then he became gentler. "I know it is difficult. We (and he meant himself) went through similar things. You must never judge the guru. The guru, too, has a human side and if you are close to the guru, you can see it and you judge. My guru has told me not to see any intentions in his actions and I have done it and benefited."

"Once", he continued, "I found my guru drinking whiskey and was shocked. "Don't judge your guru!" he demanded. I obeyed and benefitted."

"You must never judge the guru's action. You must be ready to do everything, absolutely everything, that the guru demands of you", Guruji stipulated.

I felt immensely relieved that Guruji talked to me again. Now he also drew me into the discussions during satsangs. I enjoyed the normalcy as one enjoys washing dishes after an illness. It had been a hard test, and it was over now. I did not run away, had gone through hell and came out at the other end in one piece. And I had the best intentions to accept in future, whatever my guru would do. I was sure it would be child's play, because the toughest part, I believed, lay behind me.

Things, however, turned out differently. Only three months later I suddenly got doubts whether Guruji had really our well-being in mind or his own. I got doubts, whether he is really competent to help his disciples to realise the truth.

My faith in Guruji got the first crack, when he suddenly felt weak and dizzy shortly before lunch in the meditation centre. He lay down in the guest room and seemed extremely anxious about his health—something I had not expected. He was taken to the hospital and tests were done. It was nothing serious, only overexertion.

In the hospital, at one end of the corridor, workmen were busy. The noise disturbed Guruji and he changed his room. I was surprised and wondered whether he really knew how much noise I had borne in his house for two years. I had once told him about it, but he had replied that I was overly sensitive.

Soon after the hospital episode, I further got the impression that he had personal, human preferences while observing whom he called for private talks outside the usual bi-weekly meetings. "You must never judge the guru. The guru, too, has a human side and if you are close to the guru, you can see it and you judge", Guruji had told me. Judging was one thing and could be controlled, but losing faith and getting doubt was another, which could not be controlled.

Doubts are the end of blind belief, because only proof can drive doubts away. Once more I was not ready any longer to believe something I could not know. This time, however, I was sure that he was the last guru whom I had placed on a pedestal and to whom I had surrendered full of trust. At the same time, I was grateful to him—for drawing me out from my shell and especially for the heavy bombardment of my ego. It was an incredibly intense time and I remembered Kunti, the mother of the Pandavas. In the Mahabharata it says, that she preferred suffering over happiness, because in suffering, she would always think of Sri Krishna and not forget him even for a second.

Guruji looked completely surprised, when I told him that I would not come anymore to the satsangs and would move out from his house. He had not noticed that I had internally already moved away from him and he tried to make me stay. "Maria, the last steps on the spiritual path are tough", as if I was close to the goal and it would be foolish to quit now. Yet I was clear. I had lost my faith in him and had to move on.

CHAPTER 32

Does one need a guru?

I have pondered a lot how this strong faith in a guru develops, which manages to justify everything that the guru does, which no rational argument can shake, and which seems to narrow down rather than broaden one's mind. Was my personal, psychological makeup at fault or is it a general human or maybe more specifically a female trait? Is there a desire to trust in a perfect guide who takes charge of one's life? I don't know.

Undoubtedly, a human being needs teachers. "You need a guru to learn higher mathematics. Just by reading books, you won't understand it. Similarly, you need a guru to show you the way to the truth", Anandamayi Ma had claimed. She is not alone in stressing the necessity of a guru. Adi Shankara from the 8th century, Sant Jnaneshwar from the 12th century, Kabir from the 15th century and Nisargadatta Maharaj of our time, they all praise the guru, and especially their own, in highest terms. They also stress that one need not search for a guru. "The guru comes when the disciple is ready", is the accepted view.

Since ancient times, gurus held a high place in Indian society because they could give knowledge that made life truly worthwhile. Kings would pay their respects. Yet I wonder whether traditionally, the guru has been idolised the way he often is today, especially by Westerners. The ancient Indian scriptures maintain that the same consciousness plays different roles in the different forms on this world stage. It is teaching through the guru and receiving through the disciple. Guru and disciple are, as it were, two sides of the same coin. "See Atman in the guru", is advised. Yet this does not imply that one should degrade oneself. "See Atman in yourself, too," could be added and genuine gurus will stress this point. Certainly, the guru deserves respect and gratefulness from the disciple. However, there is no superiority involved. In the Upanishads, many encounters are recorded where the guru encourages intelligent questioning from the disciples.

Yet there are no hard and fast rules regarding the behaviour of a guru. He may even throw stones at his disciples, as Shirdi Sai Baba has done. Allegedly, those who were hit were healed of some disability they had suffered from.

The Tibetan tradition also has a famous example of incomprehensibly harsh behaviour of a guru, which finally proves to be a blessing for his disciple. The guru was Marpa and the disciple Milarepa. Milarepa had acquired bad karma by doing black magic early in his life. Marpa, through his harsh treatment, so is believed, gave him a chance to get rid of this heavy load of karma. Milarepa was not allowed to listen to his guru's teaching but had to slog like a donkey to build a house for him, only to be told when he had finished, that the guru wants the house now at a different place. So Milarepa started anew. Yet when he finally received the teaching, he was immediately enlightened.

It all depends on the integrity and competence of the guru. To judge his integrity and competence is difficult, for an outsider rather impossible. Test a guru thoroughly before you accept him, is a common advice. But, how is one to test the integrity and competence of a guru?

'The guru is genuine if one feels peace in his presence.' Ramana Maharshi endorsed this criterion. I have met many gurus in my life. However, I can't say that I felt perceptively more at peace in the presence of, for example, the great Anandamayi Ma, than when I was alone with nature or in my room. The reason is to be found in me: when I worry about how to give the flowers, which I brought for her, or whether I should bow down, then peace won't reach me even if she radiates a lot of it.

Paul Brunton described how he felt deep peace during his first meeting with Ramana Maharshi. But probably not everyone in the room felt this peace, even if Ramana radiated it. The psychological state of the visitor and his expectations certainly affect what he sees and feels as much as does the actual presence of the guru.

The expectations towards a guru are often too high and the notion of what all he is capable of is exaggerated. His disciples, who praise him to the skies and credit him with miracles, are largely responsible for this.

There is no doubt that nowadays, there are fake gurus among genuine ones. Today it does not endanger one's life to teach India's ancient wisdom, as it did during the long Muslim rule; on the contrary, it can be lucrative. As there is no definite way to know whether a guru is truly enlightened or only pretends to be, it may encourage some to take up 'guru' as a profession.

"It is easy. I also could do it," a colonel with a booming voice once joked during a long train journey. "I only need to quote from the scriptures, look around knowingly and play the game of divide and rule by praising some and ignoring others. My future would be secure. The devotees will look after me", he laughed. In a country where old age pensions are rare and meagre, the prospect of a financially secure future by teaching scriptures and posing as a guru may indeed be a temptation.

This temptation is also there for foreigners who spent many years in Indian ashrams, and often have no other source of income. They reside in places like Rishikesh and their clientele is usually exclusively from abroad.

Apart from such gurus, there are also gurus who are convinced that they are spiritually superior if not enlightened. I count Guruji among them. Judging from the stories told by older disciples, he had been an earnest seeker, meditated for long hours, and had many spiritual experiences. He was greatly devoted to his guru and even had, against his father's wish, a house built for him from his inherited money.

When his guru shortly before his death appointed him as successor, Guruji felt at first shy about being treated reverentially. Yet over time, he must have realised that he could do no wrong in the eyes of his disciples. He became used to having power over them and seemed to enjoy it. His stress on Guru Yoga as the highest path to enlightenment secured his position as the absolute authority.

"Please don't get involved in a personality cult", my sister had cautioned me long ago, probably, because she also was influenced by the negative press which Indian gurus got. In the late 1960s and 1970s, after the Beatles were inspired by Maharishi Mahesh Yogi and Transcendental Meditation (TM) became popular in the West, the Church frightened people that Indian gurus brainwash the youth and were a danger for our societies.

Meanwhile, however, the Church changed its tactic regarding gurus. It happened several times in recent years that I came across books about gurus in ashram libraries and realised only slowly that they were Christian propaganda material. Deceptively, these books or leaflets describe the lives and teaching of well-known Hindu gurus and only in the end come to the point: Jesus Christ is the only true guru. He is the perfect one. Only he can save. One better follows him. All others are imperfect.

There is of course nothing wrong in following Jesus. Yet others may prefer to follow Krishna or Ramana Maharshi or any other guru. The problem is that the West, Christianity and also Islam, lack the knowledge that all is One Consciousness. They lack the knowledge that it is the one consciousness that shines through all and is behind the greatness of all world teachers. It has shone through Krishna and through Jesus. It shines through Guruji and through you and me. How much light comes through in each bodily form is however different depending on the degree of egolessness. In some persons, the light is dim, in others bright. Yet nobody and nothing is without this all powerful and all-knowing consciousness. It is one's Self (Atman). It is the ever-present inner guru.

Ramana Maharshi once said, "There is a guru for everyone. I admit a guru also for myself." His devotees were surprised, as he did not have a guru in a human form (though he had earlier hinted that he might have had one in his previous life). "Who is your guru?" somebody asked. "Atman" he replied.

Guruji had once claimed, "The guru never leaves his disciple, even if the disciple leaves him." At that time, I had thought that Guruji would always keep the thread intact, even if a disciple would distance himself. I was wrong. After leaving him, we chanced to meet once at his sister's place. He was friendly, as one would normally be. When I was leaving, he made an odd remark. "You may wonder why I am so friendly now", he said. "The reason is that I am free of you now. I am not responsible for you anymore" and he slipped one palm over the other as if washing his hands off me.

I realised that an outer guru is there only for a while. He comes into one's life when the time is right. Yet the inner guru is always there. He never forsakes one and guides one through life in the best possible way and even better if one listens to the subtle promptings and stays present in the now as far as possible.

CHAPTER 33

Mata Amritananda or Amma

Only after leaving Guruji, I realised that several people whom I knew in Madikeri had been critical of him all along. They shared their views only after I had lost faith in him. I was surprised that they never had felt the need to voice their opinion earlier. They had allowed me to see the enlightened master in Guruji, while they themselves considered him rather ordinary.

Even in the meditation group, two women confided to me now that they had lost trust in Guruji many years ago, but could not be open about it due to social pressure. One of them gave me the biography of Mata Amritanandamayi or Amma, as she is called. Her life story touched me, more so perhaps, as it referred to a time, when I was already on this earth. When she was born, I was already here, three years old.

She proved psychologists wrong who tend to believe that lack of parental love will make a person distrustful and neurotic for the rest of her life. Sudhamani, as she was named, was the fourth of nine children of a poor family of the fishing community, who lived on a small stretch of land between the Arabian Sea and the backwaters in Parayakadavu village in Kerala. Her mother resented her right from birth on 27. September 1953. The reason: the new-born was unusually dark, besides being a girl.

After the 4th standard Sudhamani had to quit school to take over the household chores, as her mother had developed arthritis. Her brothers and sisters continued their education, while she, as the darkest of them, was treated as the family servant. Her day started at 3 a.m. and lasted till 11 p.m. and her mother was an unkind supervisor. She would beat her up even if one leaf was left in the courtyard after sweeping. Sudhamani also received many blows for giving away provisions from the family storeroom to villagers who were hungry. Yet Amma did not blame her mother for those numerous beatings. "She could not help it and did not know better", she later said.

Sudhamani learnt early that the world had not much to offer. Yet she did not break, because she had tremendous support from within. It was her great devotion for Sri Krishna, to whom she poured out her heart at night in soulful songs.

It is inexplicable why this little girl had so much devotion for Krishna. Her family did not encourage it. Amma later said, "I would repeat Krishna's name incessantly with every breath, and a constant flow of divine thoughts was kept up in my mind irrespective of the place where I was or the work I was attending to."

Yet Sudhamani not only repeated Krishna's name, she cried out to him, when she felt he was hiding from her and danced in ecstasy when she felt his presence. Her devotion was so intense that her family and villagers considered her strange, if not crazy.

In September 1975, at the age of 22, Sudhamani was on her way home from cutting grass for the cows. While passing a neighbouring courtyard, she heard the Srimad Bhagavata in praise of Sri Krishna being recited. Amma stood transfixed. The bundle of grass on her head fell to the ground and she rushed into the congregation. She felt that she was Krishna and this identification with Krishna expressed itself in her features and behaviour.

The villagers were convinced that Krishna had come to them in the form of this dark girl. The news spread like wildfire and sceptics came as well. Those sceptics demanded a miracle. When they promised they would not ask for any further miracle, Sudhamani relented, 'Come next month when Srimad Bhagavata is recited again. I will show you a miracle.' They came in droves; everywhere, in the courtyard, on trees, on the roof people had gathered, many expecting to expose the girl as a fraud.

Sudhamani asked for a pitcher of water and sprinkled the water on those present. Then she asked one of the sceptics to put his fingers into the water and lo, it had turned into milk. Another sceptic was called to put his fingers into the milk. Now the milk had turned into panchamritam, a type of sweet, with raisins and banana bits.

It sounds incredible. Yet times are changing or rather, science is changing. Some 40 years ago, when 'scientific' was the last word in the West, nobody dared to believe that miracles could really happen. There was the general view that miracles simply are not possible. It was the politically correct view. Today, quantum physics itself suggests that miracles are indeed possible and that strong thoughts have the power to manifest. People who witnessed this miracle are still alive and Amma herself would certainly not tolerate falsehood in her biography.

From then on, Amma showed herself as Krishna several times a week and people flocked to her from afar. Yet her tribulations even increased. During her identification with Krishna (Krishna Bhava), Amma danced in ecstasy and embraced everyone, women and men, young and old, high and low. This was too much for her elder brother, who was an avowed atheist and who regarded the family honour at stake.

Together with the sons of the landowner of the village, he founded a "Committee to Remove Blind Beliefs". They recruited about 1000 'rationalists' from the surrounding villages for their committee, which probably was not difficult in Kerala, which had been ruled by the Communist Party for long. Those 'rationalists' did everything to make life hell for Amma. "Here comes Krishna!" they taunted her when she passed by and even threw stones. They filed cases against her, got negative articles published in the media, offered her poisonous milk to drink (which she smilingly accepted and then vomited in front of them), took the help of a black magician and even hired a killer. Yet all their attempts to take her life and drive away her devotees failed.

Her own brother, with the help of some cousins, even tried to murder her. They lured her to an uncle's house and locked themselves into a room. Sudhamani stayed calm, said they could kill her but only after she sat quietly in meditation—a last wish, she insisted, they had to grant her. This infuriated her would-be killers. A cousin advanced towards her and was about to stab a knife into her chest, when he himself collapsed on the floor with acute pain in his own chest. He died some days later, with Amma by his side consoling him. She did not have vengeful feelings. "He had to reap the fruit of his action", she later said.

Amma meanwhile was even more intense in her devotion. Now, after having realised her oneness with Krishna, her longing was for Devi, the Divine Mother. She lived outdoors, as her brother had thrown her out of the house. She had only animals for company, neglected her body and behaved like a child desperately crying for her mother. One day, Devi appeared before her and, becoming dazzling effulgence, merged into her.

"From that day onwards, I could see nothing as different from my own formless Self," Amma later said.

Slowly her opponents exhausted themselves and many even became devotees. Her elder brother contracted elephantiasis and committed suicide in 1978. Her father was greatly distressed about the death of his son. Amma consoled him. "Your son will be reborn in three years' time as the son of Kasturi (his eldest daughter)." And she gave him already his future name, Shiva.

In February 2008, I happened to be in Amma's ashram when she conducted a wedding. Members of the wedding party told me that it was Shiva's wedding!

In the same year, 1978, when her brother had committed suicide, several young, educated men came to Amma, determined to live a spiritual life under her guidance, in most cases against the wishes of their well to do families. Amma's father, however, did not allow them to stay near Amma, fearing for the reputation of his still unmarried daughters. In 1981, when more people came, among them some foreigners, he relented and Amma agreed to form an ashram though she was not in favour of it earlier.

The Mata Amritanandamayi Math and Mission Trust was registered in May 1981 and started with a hut under palm trees on her father's land. Her ashram has grown enormously over the last four decades. Some 2000 people reside there now, including around 500 foreigners, and as the land is limited, the pink buildings rise up 18 stories high. Colleges, schools, a hospital, even a swimming pool—for the students to learn swimming in this area full of water bodies—have come up and a bridge for pedestrians was constructed across the backwaters after the tsunami in 2004.

Amma as a young woman.

Amma is getting a lot of attention abroad. She represented India at the World Conference of Religions in Chicago, received a number of awards and was invited to speak at the United Nations. For the Cannes film festival in 2005 a film about her life was selected—made not by an Indian but by a Finn.

She has initiated a vast number of humanitarian and environmental projects and she is also in a unique position to improve the standing of women in society. She stresses the great potential, which is in them—she herself being the best example.

Reading her biography was amazing, yet it was the story of Dattan, the leper, which touched me most and which inspired me to travel to her in Kerala:

Dattan from the village Perumpally in Kerala became a victim of leprosy in his youth. His family turned him out of the house and he had to beg. The disease advanced and his whole body was covered with infected wounds oozing pus. He covered his body with a cloth which would stick to the wounds. Flies would constantly buzz around him. Other beggars would not let him eat or sleep in their company and villagers would hold their breath when they passed him. He could hardly see anymore, because his eyes had become narrow slits. For years on end, he did not hear a kind word. "I led a dreadfully miserable and despairing life. All my hopes had ebbed away", he said.

Then he heard of Amma. He came during Devi Bhava to the temple, but the people around her urged him to go away. His wounds had a foul smell.

Amma however noticed him and called him near her. She pressed him to herself and comforted him. Then she licked the infected wounds and sucked the pus and blood from them. Some of her devotees, who witnessed it, vomited, others fainted and again others cried because of so much love and compassion.

From then on Dattan came to each Devi Bhava. Prior to it, Amma gave him a bath and rubbed holy ash over his body. His wounds healed, only the scars of his terrible sickness remained.

Amma said about Dattan, "Amma does not see his outer body. She sees only his heart. He is my son and I am his mother. Can a mother forsake her son?"

CHAPTER 34

In Amma's Ashram

In December 2000 I crossed over the backwaters by boat to the narrow strip of land full of palm trees right on the shore of the Arabian Sea. It was my first visit to Amritapuri. The sun still stood low on the horizon as I had reached the nearest railway station by night train.

The first person I came across was a woman whom I had met in the ashram of Satya Sai Baba. She looked similar to what I had looked in Puttaparthi: thin and unhappy. But she was kind and helpful. "Come and put your bag into my room. The office opens only at 10 o'clock. You can take a shower and then we go for breakfast." She camped with two other women in a room—for the last two years.

I knew from own experience that one can get used to such circumstances. Moreover, the lingering, constant unhappiness may finally turn out as a blessing. It is a passing phase. Yet I was glad that I had left this phase behind me. As much as I was impressed with Amma's life, I was sure that I would stay in the ashram only for a few days. Now, I drew my support not from an outer guru but from my self—the one Self that permeates everything. Yet this self was doubtlessly more translucent in Amma's form than in mine, so I appreciated the fact that I had a chance to be in her presence.

On the forenoon, Amma came to the temple, gave a short talk and started guiding a meditation. She appeared soft and motherly and her face was beaming. There were many foreigners present, because Christmas was near. Amma talked in Malayalam, her mother tongue, which a saffron robed sanyasi translated into English. "Breathe in love and breathe out light", she advised. "While you breathe out, the light spreads far and wide."

In the end, some people formed a queue in front of Amma and she took the first one into her embrace.

"Did you arrive only today?" a foreigner asked me.

"Yes, this morning."

"Then you can join the queue."

I hesitated. Somehow, I did not feel prepared for an embrace. There were only about five people left in the line, when she urged me again. "Go to her. It is your chance."

Amma pressed me to her shoulder and whispered something into my ear that I did not understand. I looked up to her. Then she pressed again my head to her shoulder. When I was sitting down afterwards, I felt extremely blissful. I did not want to get up when everyone got up and left. I knew it was time for lunch and I might miss my meal, but I did not mind—rather untypical for my usual self. I was alone in the big room and enjoyed the feeling of bliss. Finally, someone came and swept the floor. I had to get up. Lunch was already over.

On the next day, there was darshan day, which meant that Amma would embrace everyone who came. The ashram was full of visitors, about two to three thousand, and Amma sat for 5 hours in the same position and took one after the other into her arms. I wanted to save her at least one embrace and did not join the queue. Yet unexpectedly, someone called me to help out: I was asked to sit directly next to Amma and hand her small envelopes with sweets which she gave to each person after the embrace.

On the following Sunday, I joined the queue for an embrace. It was a special day. Amma identified herself with the divine Mother, called Devi bhava.

All day long, people streamed into the ashram. There was a festive atmosphere. In the late afternoon Amma gave a talk and then sang bhajans with great devotion.

View of the temple from a high-rise apartment block in Ammas Ashram.

At around 7 o'clock she disappeared for a short while. She changed from her white cotton sari into a red silk sari and returned with a small crown on her head. The outer appearance gave a finish to her identification with Devi, the divine Mother.

Meanwhile, in the big, open hall two long queues were building up—one for men and one for women. Amma sat down on a cushion on a small pedestal on the stage and one person after the other kneeled down in front of her and she took him into her embrace. First in the queue were handicapped children. It was touching to see them in Amma's arms. On a big screen, everyone could observe Amma's facial expression. She looked very soft, very loving.

Each person had taken a number and the turn of my number would be only at around 2 o'clock at night. At 10 o'clock, I went to my room, which I shared with three women, and slept for a few hours. When I reappeared, Amma had been sitting already for six hours on her cushion in the same position and pressed men, women and children to her chest. Her face was still as soft, loving and radiating as six hours ago and she gave every single person full attention.

I felt a little bad that I had slept. The queue moved slowly towards the stage. When it was my turn, Amma pressed me close to her and whispered "my daughter" into my ear. "Sit down behind me on the stage", she indicated, before I got up. An assistant showed me a place at an angle directly behind Amma.

The feeling after the embrace was not as intense as the first time. The circumstances were probably responsible: the first time, the queue was short and Amma took her time. During the Devi Bhava there were about 10.000 people in the ashram who all wanted to be embraced. Understandably, her assistants urged everyone to get up as quickly as possible after the embrace to make room for the next person.

During the following hours, I sat only about 2 metres away from Amma and could closely observe her. What she did was humanly impossible. She welcomed everybody with the same, loving smile, pressed him resolutely to her chest, whispered something into his ear and gave him prasad. Some took more time, asked questions or confided to Amma a problem, but most people were content with the short embrace. Only once, she briefly interrupted her routine and took a sip from a cup which an assistant offered her. At around 5 o'clock in the morning a woman started massaging her back, yet Amma did not take notice of it. She kept sitting in the same position, until the queue finished. That was at 8.30 in the next morning.

Amma however still kept sitting, and now around hundred people came again to her, who had asked Amma for a mantra. Each one had written on a chit his Ishta Deva, the form of the Supreme he or she loved most. Indians have many gods and goddesses, and everybody is free to choose the one to whom he feels most attracted. These gods are connecting links to the formless Brahman from a higher plane, for it is not easy to love the formless. There are many stories about the gods, they are like good friends, ever ready to listen and it is easy to love them. Moreover, it helps to have a loving, intimate partner, as long as we do not yet realise that we are one with everything and ourselves divine. Amma gave corresponding mantras, depending on what was written on the chit.

At 9 o'clock Amma finally got up. I hardly could believe that her legs carried her. She stood on the stage, beaming, without any trace of tiredness and looked at us who were still left over from the night. Most people had gone back to their villages and towns and were probably already at work.

This night was no exception for Amma. She hardly needs any sleep. Once someone asked her how she manages to endure those long sittings. She answered, "Where there is love there is no difficulty."

"God is not a limited individual, who sits on a golden throne in the clouds. God is pure consciousness that is in everything. Understand this truth and learn to accept and love everyone in the same way", Amma advises.

She does what she preaches. To a question of a journalist, how she manages to embrace even sick people and criminals in the same loving manner, she replied: "If a honey bee buzzes around the flowers in a garden, it does not see the different flowers, but the honey that is in them. Similarly, Amma sees the highest Self in everybody."

Amma is in all likelihood the most accessible person that has ever graced this earth—a mother to all humanity. Whoever wants can walk right up to her, feel free and embrace her and many million people from around the world have done so till now. He or she might have to wait for some hours for his turn to come, but he will not be refused.

On this first visit in December 2000, I was sure that she could not go on like this. Her body would not stand it much longer—bending forward and taking into her arms a man, a woman or a child thousands of times for ten or twenty hours in a stretch. Today, in 2018, Amma is still giving her unconditional love to everyone with a strong motherly hug. She is not concerned about her body but goes about her task:

"Devi told me to ask the people
To fulfil their human birth.
Therefore I proclaim to the whole world
The sublime Truth that She uttered
"Oh man, merge into your Self"."

CHAPTER 35

Happy through breathing: with Sri Sri Ravi Shankar

Sri Sri Ravi Shankar is another great brand ambassador of India. Typically enough, both he and Amma are spiritual personalities. India still is the spiritual teacher of the world.

Sri Sri, as Sri Sri Ravi Shankar is called, was born on 13th May 1956 in a village in Tamil Nadu. His was an easier childhood than Amma's. He, too, showed a fondness for meditation early and started reciting verses from the Bhagavad-Gita, when he was only four years old. His parents however supported him. They allowed him to study the Vedas as well as physics.

Several gurus influenced him, most of all Maharishi Mahesh Yogi. Sri Sri lived in his ashram in Rishikesh on the Ganges for some time. Once, when he retreated in meditation for several days, he had an idea. This idea is spreading today around the world and goes by the name of Sudarshan Kriya. It is a breathing technique that is supposed to purify internally. Sri Sri has imparted it to millions of people so far—and the numbers are steadily increasing.

Already in the 1980s, a man sitting next to me in a long-distance bus gave me the address of Ravi Shankar's ashram some 20 km south of Bangalore. He told me that the Sudarshan Kriya had helped him a lot. "Sudarshan Kriya" did not mean anything to me, so I ignored the entry in my address book for years.

In the 1990s, however, I came across an article in a German magazine about Sri Sri and his centre in Bad Antogast in the Black Forest. His youthful, relaxed face beamed over a whole page—his long, black hair falling over his shoulders, a beard, a calm expression in his eyes and a likeable countenance. I remembered my address book. However, I felt that Guruji might consider it as disloyal, if I went to see another guru. Now, after I had left Guruji, I went to Bangalore.

In my early years in India, while practising yoga, I had noticed, how often I unnecessarily held my breath, how shallow I was breathing and that I never fully breathed out. Even while doing simple chores my breath would stop. I had the best intention to observe my breathing, but most of the time I forgot about it.

Now finally I wanted to do intense breathing under professional supervision. Intense breathing was the core of Sudarshan Kriya. That much the person next to me in the bus had revealed.

In the large ashram, which spreads over hilly terrain, I saw a number of young men who all looked like Sri Sri: their black hair fell over their shoulders and their beard over their chest. They were slim and wrapped in white cloth. They were friendly and likeable, except for one person, who fell somewhat out of line with the usual appearance—the portly, short-haired and very determined cashier in the office. He decreed that I had to pay the fee for foreigners, which was much higher than that for Indians. The fact that I lived already for 20 years in India and did not draw a monthly pay check from Germany did not cut ice with him. Yet, I fully understood the directive that foreigners were to pay more. We anyway benefit immensely from the low cost of living in India.

During the registration, I was asked whether I had any illness, especially if I had any heart problem, and had to sign a form that I will not hold the Art of Living Foundation (that is the foundation which Ravi Shankar had set up after his inspiration of Sudarshan Kriya) responsible, if something went wrong.

I was a little nervous. My health had never been robust, and I was not sure what the Sudarshan Kriya would entail. At the medical check-up before admission into primary school, the doctor had diagnosed a 'hole in the heart'. I was not to cycle or climb mountains. This injunction remained in my memory, even though, of course, I rode a bicycle and walked, slowly though, even at the height of 5600 metres, the highest motorable pass in Ladakh.

I did not mention the hole in the heart. It was too vague. Probably I did not even have it. And if my heart was meant to fail, then let it fail, I thought. I signed the form, which included an injunction not to divulge the content of the course.

We were 44 participants, all Indians except for me and an Indonesian, and men and women equally represented. Our teacher was a young doctor by the name of Jayshree from Bangalore. In earlier times, Sri Sri himself conducted the courses, yet those times were over. He established a wide network of teachers whom he selects and trains. They work on a voluntary basis.

Sri Sri Ravi Shankar.

"You can feel in every situation as much at ease as if you were sitting on a couch in your living room", says Sri Sri and he surely speaks from experience. Once during bhajans with around 500 people present, I felt that he had slipped into a nap. Occasionally his head fell to the side; he put it up again, until it fell again. He was supposed to give a talk and his assistants exchanged partly amused and partly helpless looks with each other, as his talk was already overdue. Finally, when the music all of a sudden stopped due to some resolute decision and when unusual silence prevailed, Sri Sri slowly opened his eyes, briefly orientated himself, smiled and started his talk. No embarrassment, no wanting to hide anything. He felt like being in his own living room in midst of his family.

Jayshree sat in front on a cushion—calm, confident and beautiful with her huge, dark eyes and draped in a green sari. She, too, seemed to feel like sitting in her living room and belonging to us. Sri Sri greatly values this feeling of belonging. It makes sense, if we all are basically one. The first thing Jayshree asked us to do was to get up and introduce ourselves to each other. Everyone should talk to everyone else—and end with the phrase, "I belong to you."

Afterwards we talked about how uneasy we had felt with this last sentence. Some had mumbled it quickly. Some had not said it at all. Some had said it loud and clear. I had taken the easy route out: I reacted to the person opposite me in the same way, as she introduced herself to me. The others walked quite naturally up to me and I did not have to take the initiative. If somebody mumbled it quickly, I also mumbled quickly. When somebody dropped the sentence altogether, I also was immediately ready for it. And if somebody said loud and clear, and Jayshree was one of them, "I belong to you", I managed to say it loud and clear, as well.

We started with preparatory pranayama, the ancient Indian breathing techniques. "How do you feel", Jayshree asked after the first exercise. "Dizzy", I answered. My capacity for air and prana, the life energy contained in the breath, was obviously not much. The dizziness left after some time.

Jayshree created a familiar atmosphere with a combination of yoga, pranayama and psychological methods and soon we felt that we indeed belonged to each other. On the first evening, when we had arrived at the reception with our bags, we sceptically scrutinized each other. While saying good-bye, we all were grateful for the time spent together.

The core of the course is the Sudarshan Kriya. It is an intense breathing technique, about which a number of medical and psychological research papers have been published. During a conference on Indian psychology, medical doctors gave presentations about how the Kriya helps curing not only depression and psychosomatic illnesses but also reduces diabetes and high blood pressure.

For me, the Sudarshan Kriya had a big impact. Maybe, because earlier I never had done such long and conscious breathing and my system was flooded with so much oxygen for the first time. Occasionally I even felt that I reached my limits. But I followed strictly the instruction: "Keep breathing! Come what may!" Sometimes drowsy thoughts overwhelmed me, and I forgot to breathe. We were however under supervision. Immediately some assistant was by my side and loudly breathed into my ear. This woke me up and I continued breathing.

While relaxing flat on the floor afterwards, I had a similar feeling, as I had had after the embrace with Amma. Absolutely blissful. All my cells felt alive and throbbing with ecstasy. I was grateful to Sri Sri that he had gifted us the Kriya.

Sri Sri himself was present in the ashram during the time of our course and came for bhajan every evening to an open round hall situated on top of a hillock. He sang with his clear, high pitched voice and afterwards answered questions. The singing, accompanied by clapping and sometimes dancing, is very common in spiritual India and makes for a joyful atmosphere.

I followed the request of Jayshree to practise a short form of the Kriya, which takes half an hour, for at least 45 days at home. I even practised it for full eight months because the Kriya gave me more energy, increased a feeling of general well-being and reduced my inhibition to get in contact with others. Earlier, during my psychology studies, I used to label myself on questionnaires regularly as "introvert". Yet today I would rate my behaviour fairly extrovert. No doubt, India has helped to effect this change, because one is embedded in a huge human family wherever one is. Guruji, too, had helped to get me out of my shell. And now, the Sudarshan Kriya strengthened this feeling even more: yes, I belong to you and to everyone.

I realised that another claim of Sri Sri is also true: nothing and nobody can make you unhappy, if you have decided to be happy. There are only two conditions for happiness: on one hand, a stress free and relaxed body and mind are required and the Sudarshan Kriya takes care of that. On the other hand, your decision "Yes, I want to be happy". That is all, claims Sri Sri.

It is amazing what far-reaching consequences the idea of one single man has had. I read on a pamphlet, who all had benefited from the course: scientists at NASA, WHO officials, computer engineers at Microsoft, students and professors of reputed universities, the football team of Manchester United, Oil barons in the gulf, actors in Hollywood and Bollywood, politicians in Costa Rica, hoteliers in Singapore, musicians in Australia, and so on.

The list continues: Rickshaw drivers, porters on railway stations, terrorists in Bihar, inmates of Tihar, the biggest prison in Delhi, residents of Dharavi, the most densely populated slum in Mumbai, refugees in Kosovo, tree cutters in Siberia, belly dancers in Brazil, street children in South Africa, and so on.

The list is impressive. Furthermore, Sri Sri, as well as Amma, has initiated countless projects to uplift the underprivileged. Members of his organisation work in tens of thousands of villages and also are involved in the rejuvenation of several rivers.

Amazing that many in the West get it so wrong and believe what the Church conveys: Hindus care only for themselves, because they believe that everyone deserves his fate due to his karma.

Sri Sri also involved himself in political issues, for example in the Columbian peace process and in finding a compromise for building the Ram Mandir in Ayodhya. A mistake, however, which Hindus, including their leaders, generally make, is on one hand to assume that everyone has the same mindset as they have—to be well-meaning towards everyone -, and on the other hand not wanting to court controversy by touching sensitive, yet central issues.

So, when I once had the opportunity to meet Sri Sri, I asked him to please not overlook the fundamental differences between the religions in Interfaith Dialogues, as the Abrahamic religions need to be confronted with their unacceptable dogmas. I suggested, that he could ask the Christian and Muslim clergy in his inimitable way, "Will I (Sri Sri) go to hell if I don't convert according to your doctrine?" However, Sri Sri felt it is better if I, an insider in Christianity, take up these points. Yet aren't Hindus at the receiving end of those faiths, and don't they have every right to demand answers regarding the proof or otherwise for their alleged eternal condemnation?

In Mach 2016 the Art of Living foundation organised a spectacular World Culture Festival to celebrate its 35th anniversary. Almost four million visitors from 155 countries came to Delhi and 37,000 artists from around the world presented the amazing and beautiful diversity of cultures on the world's largest floating stage of seven acres. It was a mega event in every respect.

Yet, strangely, some people worked overtime to prevent it, even petitioning the court to ban it just a few days prior to the event though all permissions had been given. The National Green Tribunal (NGT) which seems to have a penchant to object to anything Hindus are doing (in 2017 it even forbade chanting mantras in front of the Amaranath cave, a pilgrimage place high up in the Himalaya, which later the Supreme Court struck down), objected to the festival being held on the banks of the Yamuna. It imposed a huge fine, which was highly unfair, because thousands of Sri Sri's volunteers had cleaned the floodplains of the Yamuna before and after the event and in all likelihood left them in much better shape than before.

CHAPTER 36

In Gangotri

In 2001, I moved from Madikeri to Dehradun, the place I had always felt most familiar with since I had come there with Anandamayi Ma in May 1980. Rajpur Road, where Ma stayed, was quiet then—a bus every 20 minutes, some scooters, off and on an Ambassador or Fiat car and a truck carrying lime from the quarries in the mountains. Meanwhile, Rajpur Road is not recognisable any longer. It looks like a highway with occasional traffic jams even. Not only the traffic and the car brands have multiplied, the population has also doubled from the 1980s till now.

Settling now on the outskirts of Dehradun was not easy for me. My life felt empty in spite of a few friends from my early years and a kind landlord family. I was lacking a structure in my life. For the first time I was not linked to a spiritual group. To top it all, the German magazine, which was financially my mainstay, became insolvent soon after I reached there. I sat in my flat and asked myself, what I was meant to do.

I went to the source of the Ganges to escape this feeling of emptiness. While travelling, every day brings new people and new experiences. Only when someone asked me "What are you doing in India?" it hit me that I actually had no ground under my feet.

The journey to the source of the Ganges leads through an impressive landscape. After a 6 hours bus ride I stopped for the night in Uttarkashi and stayed in one of the small hotels near the bus stand at the foot of a hill. Two years later, those same hotels were destroyed during a massive, yet slow landslide.

From Uttarkashi I took a share jeep, packed with 10 people, for the last 100 kilometres up to Gangotri. My bag was on top of the jeep and obviously not properly secured, because, when the driver made a crash halt a few hours later, it landed directly in front of us on the road and thankfully not deep down in the gorge of the Ganges.

Gangotri is situated at a height of 3140 metres near the border to Tibet and is a popular destination in India. Many pilgrims want to take a purifying bath in the young, bubbly Ganga Ma, as Indians call the Ganges, high up in the stillness of the mountains, surrounded by snow-capped peaks. Even young, modern Indians have great reverence for and trust in Ganga Ma, which may be difficult to understand for Westerners. She symbolises for them the female, caring aspect of the universal power, which governs all our lives. That is why she is pictured as a young, beautiful woman with long, flowing hair.

Temple dedicated to Ganga Ma in Gangotri. Gomukh, the glacier from where Ganga springs, is 18 km away.

"Just see, how this lady overcomes obstacles—calmly, coolly and graciously. She has no fixed behaviour pattern, reacts according to the situation. She has inspired me since long and I have learnt a lot from her." An engineering student from Hyderabad in South India explained his admiration for her to me, when we stood at the bank of the Ganga. By "lady" he meant Ganga Ma, and I was surprised, how naturally he, 21 years young and not a poet, invested the river with aliveness, which we in the West usually reserve for human beings and animals.

It was a rishi, a wise seer, by the name of Bhagirathi, who according to the ancient texts brought the Ganga from the heavens down to the earth thousands of years ago. As the mighty impact of the fall would have been disastrous, Shiva caught "her" first in his hair. Whoever stands near the mouth of the glacier 18 km to the east of Gangotri and witnesses the immense power, with which the newly born river surges out of the icy cave, will not be surprised that it needed a god to soften its fall.

The bus stand in Gangotri presented a colourful picture: thin, poor, old and young people from the plains slowly moved in their family clans from shop to shop towards the temple, comparing the prices for the offerings, which they would make in the temple. They were without pullovers and often barefoot, carrying their few belongings on their head and holding their children by the hand.

Members of the middle class in contrast looked big and stout, well equipped with windcheaters, caps and sneakers, yet the elderly among them seemed to have hardly any stamina. Especially corpulent women gasped for the thin air and took a break after every ten steps.

Then there were lanky sadhus with matted hair and ash smeared in their faces. They, too, were barefoot and wrapped only in thin cotton cloth.

Last, there were tourists from abroad, on one hand young backpackers, who searched and found cheap places to stay, and on the other hand older, wealthy foreigners, who arrived by taxi and lodged in the most expensive hotel of the place.

I found a wooden hut in Yoga Niketan on the other, quieter side of the Ganges. Yoga Niketan is an ashram with its headquarters in Rishikesh and is known for its yoga courses. It was July and warm. The thermometer climbed up to 23 degrees Celsius in the shade. Flowerbeds and apple trees beautified the surroundings of the huts. I even discovered rhubarb plants, and felt like having landed in a German summer. However, the sun was merciless. My skin turned bright red in no time.

Some tourists from Israel, Korea and Japan also stayed in Yoga Niketan. The atmosphere was good and life simple.

A young sadhu taught us yoga. His name was Yogananda. He was calm, likeable and a good teacher. Once, over lunch, he told us his story:

He had studied psychology in Varanasi and had finished his studies seven years ago. His parents were happy, when he went home to present them with his academic degree. They did not suspect that they would lose their son the next morning. The father was determined to arrange his marriage as soon as possible, now, after he had obtained his degree. He had already selected the bride. She was the only daughter of a wealthy friend. The father himself, too, owned land and three houses.

Yoga Niketan, where I stayed in a hut for 3 months in summer 2001.

Yet Yogananda did not want to marry. He wanted to become a sanyasi. As a youth, he had already declared his wish. The father knew it, but he had put his foot down. And Yogananda had no other choice. Early in the next morning, he sneaked out of the house and never came back.

He looked for a guru and took sanyas. Then he called his home. His sister in law picked up the phone. He told her that he had renounced the world and would now start wandering around as a sanyasi. She started to cry, and he put the receiver down. Since then he had never again contacted his family.

"They will miss you. Why don't you at least call them", I suggested.

"Why should they miss me? My family consists of 19 members. Each day we need 20 litres of milk, for us and for the numerous teacups that are served to visitors. Furthermore, Indian parents secretly are pleased at having a son who has dedicated his life to a spiritual life, though they do not admit it and even put roadblocks in his way. He brings blessings for the whole family and they know it", he argued.

Nevertheless, I felt that he could at least call them. He himself also had thought of it already. "Maybe I do it, when I am in Rishikesh next time", he said.

On Yogananda's example, I could observe during the next few months that even an ascetic continues to live in the world and has to deal with its problems.

Yogananda was good natured and helpful. A Japanese man, for example, wanted to write a book on yoga and requested Yogananda to demonstrate the different yoga asanas one after the other. He took photos of each yogic asana viewed from the front, as well as from the side. Yogananda patiently held the position until the Japanese was satisfied with his shots. I occasionally watched the demonstrations, as the project went on over a long period.

Several times it happened that other swamis, mainly heads of different ashrams, wanted to use Yogananda for their own purposes. Yogananda declined. Once, a woman from Delhi came to his cave in the forest with a suitcase full of money. Yogananda knew her from his studies. He, as the son of a wealthy landowner, had occasionally supported her financially. Meanwhile she had acquired the status of a guru and had travelled to Gangotri with a great number of devotees in tow. She was determined to have Yogananda as a yoga teacher in her ashram in Delhi. No doubt, he would have been an attraction in her ashram, yet she had to leave disappointed.

Another swami was more successful. He wanted Yogananda to manage his ashram in Gangotri, while he went to America and England to collect donations.

Yogananda said no. I also would not have liked to become involved with the affairs of that particular swami. The swami took revenge and sent a forest official to Yogananda's cave. Sadhus are permitted to build a cave under the ledge of a rock, provided the wall of the cave does not protrude from the rock. The forest official declared that the cave protrudes a little. Yogananda denied it, because it was not true, but he had no money to convince the forester, who was obviously bribed by the swami to give him trouble. Yogananda asked me to take photos of his cave from all angles. He then went to Dehradun, the state capital, to sort matters out. After that incident, I saw Yogananda often in the ashram of the swami, looking after the guests.

Yogananda in front of his cave in the forest near Gangotri.

Yogananda told me that he had ruined his health during the last, hard winter. He had stayed in Gangotri without any heating. Moreover, he had meditated very intensely for 17 days and had taken no food, only tea, during this time. That had proved too much for him. Even his eyes had suffered.

When I mentioned this to some other sadhu, he immediately retorted, "And you believe the story with 17 days only tea?" "Why would he tell a lie?" I replied and added, "It is obvious that he is not healthy."

The sadhu nodded derisively and continued to criticise, "He stayed up here in the winter only, so that later he can tell in Rishikesh that he has spent the winter in Gangotri."

It seems sadhus, too, are confronted with negative emotions like envy and not everybody realises the danger.

The stories, which Yogananda narrated to me, showed that "the world" had caught up with him. No doubt, he was one of those sadhus who had ideals. Nevertheless, he had to pay for the provisions he needed. He did not beg, but occasionally invited foreigners to his cave for lunch, because he cooked well and knew that we were lacking in good food. In all likelihood, the hope that his guests would show their gratitude by leaving behind some money played a role. Not all guests did. Others, however, were generous. His cave was narrow, but cosy—located about 20 minutes on foot from Yoga Niketan. It resembled a room in a students' hostel because of the numerous books.

It surely was not easy for Yogananda, from one day to the other, to live as a sadhu in a cave in the forest, fetch every single drop of water from afar and develop the necessary trust that whatever he needs will somehow be provided, especially as he had not experienced any lack in his earlier life. I wished him from my heart that no negativity would arise in him in spite of difficult circumstances and difficult sadhu-brothers.

One day, with a small backpack, I started on my trek to Gomukh, the mouth of the glacier. The sky was clear and blue, and my nose smeared with sunscreen. At first, I had to climb many big steps behind the temple, which steeply led up to a path. After 15 minutes, I was already out of breath. Yet from then on, the trek was easy—a climb of only about 800 metres over a distance of 18 kilometres. It was wonderful to walk in this grandiose landscape. The snow-covered peaks were near and overpowering.

People sitting on mules kept overtaking me with ease. The local horsemen were walking fast. The sadhus however moved slowly. Once, a sadhu came from the opposite direction. He had only one leg and supported himself with a stick. I was amazed, and he noticed it. "Ganga Maya ki jay!" (Victory for Ganga Ma!) he shouted the customary salutation with a big smile on his face, and swiftly moved on with the help of the stick.

Since some time, a boy was following me. He wore only a shirt and trousers, had no bag and probably not a single paisa. During the lunch break, I questioned him. He was from Nepal, 11 years old and had come alone. He did not have any money.

How do you want to manage without money?" I asked. The boy turned his palms upwards, shrank his shoulders and smiled. I offered him food and then asked him to move on.

In the ashram of Lal Baba in Bojwasa, about 4 kilometres' distance from the source of the Ganges, I saw him again. He held a hot tea cup, like everyone else. Whoever entered the ashram was straight away given hot tea, which was gratefully received especially by the thinly clad sadhus. Lal Baba, an old sadhu who exuded authority now questioned the boy and then sent him to the kitchen to help.

On the next morning, after a sleepless night in a tiny, windowless cubby-hole, next to the much-frequented toilet, I trekked the last 4 kilometres over rocky terrain to the mouth of the glacier, which is called Gomukh (= cow-mouth).

Then I stood at the source of the river. What immense power, with which Ganga Ma starts her journey. I sat down on a rock and for a long time let myself be enveloped by the thunderous roar of Ganga in midst of silence.

Close to Gomukh, the origin of Ganga Ma, almost 4000 m high in the Himalaya (July 2001).

Suddenly the Nepali boy sprang up to where I was sitting. He had come with a group of sadhus and had spotted me. He looked happy, wearing an oversized pullover and holding two blocks of ice in his hands. “Photo, photo!” he demanded urgently.

On my way back, a German caught up with me. He was in his early thirties and except for the whiter skin indistinguishable from his Indian sadhu colleagues. His hair was matted, he wore several malas around his neck, was barefoot in flip-flops and fluent in Hindi. But when he switched to German, his dialect gave him away as a native from Nuremberg, my home district. He has been a sadhu for ten years, he told me. At first, he took drugs. Then a sadhu advised him not to waste his life. He underwent a rehab and became the disciple of a guru, who earlier was an officer with the secret service “and even today does not trust anybody”. We trekked together to Gangotri, where he stayed in a small room by the Ganges.

I went back to my hut in Yoga Niketan. It looked now comfortable and life in Gangotri seemed almost city-like.

CHAPTER 37

Insights from a VIP sadhu

On the compound next to Yoga Niketan, right above the gorge of the Ganga, three sadhus were living in simple huts. One of those sadhus sat the whole day on his tiny veranda and devotedly scribbled into a big book placed on a wooden stand before him. Two more big books were spread out near him. He translated the Yoga Vasishtha into English using both the Hindi and Sanskrit versions for reference. The Yoga Vasishtha is an ancient teaching, which the guru Vasishtha imparted to Ram, the prince of Ayodhya, when he came back from a pilgrimage and had lost all interest in worldly life.

Prior to my trek to Gomukh, James, an American, who also lived in Yoga Niketan and daily visited the sadhu, had taken me along and introduced me to him. James asked questions and recorded his answers on a cassette. He wanted to make a book out of it. "Answers of a sadhu, who has lived high up in the Himalayas near the source of the Ganges for 20 years and who even spends the harsh winters there—that certainly will have a great appeal in the West", James told me.

Meanwhile James had left; and I went alone to Brahma Chaitanya or BC, as the sadhu was called. He was an impressive, powerful character in his late fifties, tall and strong, his matted hair so long, that he could use it as a cushion, his laughter louder than even the roar of the Ganga and his eyes sparkling with humour and charm. He was quite naturally a VIP among the sadhus and the president of the sadhu community in Gangotri. As he came from a wealthy family and had been an engineer, confident behaviour and commanding authority came easily to him and this self-assured conduct stayed with him as a sadhu.

Early in life, he became interested in spirituality, read a lot and practised pranayama, but he was young and did not want to be celibate. So, he married and had two children.

When he was in his late thirties, he however had enough of family life and, one fine day, left his wife and teenaged sons. He had thought about it for a long time and had tested himself, he explained. Then he was sure. He wanted to become a sadhu.

However, his wife traced him in Uttarkashi and was adamant that he came back home with her to sort out some heritage issue. He yielded. Yet soon after, he left his family for good. His wife discovered him in Gangotri, too, but now she respected his wish.

He told me, what happened, when he begged for the first time:

It was in Haridwar. He still had a few hundred Rupees in his pocket, but now wanted to start his new life—without the safety net of a bank account and with full trust in providence. He stretched out his hand towards an elderly gentleman. As a reaction, he did not get any alms but a furious rebuke. "You should be ashamed, young man! Go to one of the ashrams which offer free food for sadhus!"

The newly baked sadhu was greatly annoyed, went straight into a restaurant and ordered a meal. Then he checked into a hotel. In the night, his conscience troubled him. "So quickly am I offended? Only because of a passing remark?"

Next morning, he gifted his travel case to a boy in the hotel and threw the rest of his money into the Ganges. "I now fully belong to you. You have to look after me now", he told his Ganga Ma. From then on, he did not face any problems. He went to the centres, which served food to sadhus. He specifically mentioned that he joined the queue like everyone else.

The talks with him were highly interesting and he had, unexpectedly, an exquisite library in his hut—books by ancient and

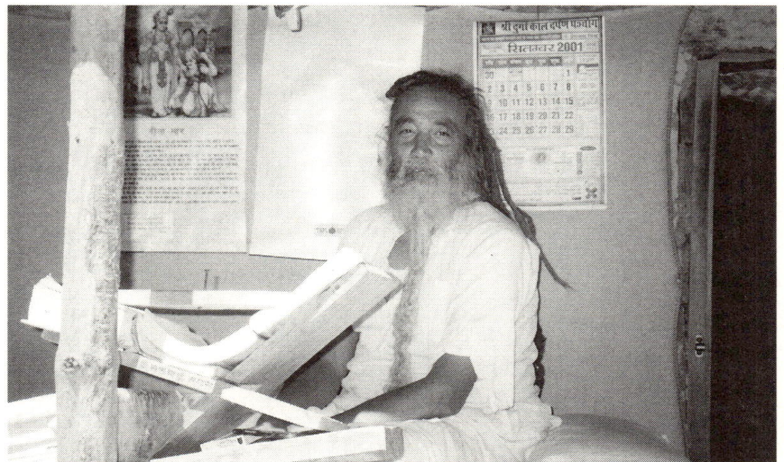

Brahma Chaitanya, translating the Yoga Vashishta in front of his hut.

modern Indian and even Chinese masters, and by Zen- and Tibetan Buddhists.

Our conversations in the afternoon became routine and I looked forward to them. Afterwards he often dived into his hut and came back with a book in his hand. The first book that he gave me to read was "Jnana Yoga" by Swami Vivekananda. It was that very first book that I had bought in Kanyakumari at the Vivekananda Memorial. Strangely, now it did not touch me so much anymore. Books like the "Shiva Sutras" or the "Spanda Karika" about the philosophy of Kashmir Shaivism, which flourished in Kashmir in the 11th century, I found now more appealing and enjoyed studying those texts in the beautiful surroundings at the height of over 3000 meter with snow-capped mountains standing guard.

BC made fun of the important looking, but unnecessary activities in the world and advised me, "Turn inward. You will enjoy it." He handed me a poem of Chuang Tzu, a Chinese master, who had quite accurately described the 'Active Life' already over 2000 years ago:

"What would become of business without a market of fools? What would become of labour, if there were no superfluous objects to be made?" he asked for example already at that time. And his ironic advice: "Produce! Get results! Make money! Make friends! Make changes! Or you will die of despair!"

On BC's advice, I bought a mala, a kind of rosary, made from 108 beads from the sacred Rudraksha tree in one of the shops near the temple and sat for hours on my bed repeating mantras. I was generally feeling well and when I woke up at night, I heard the mantra repeating itself. Yet sometimes I also felt heavy and down. How would my life go on?

One day BC suggested, "Now I will cure you from feeling small and unwell." Then he asked, while pointing around himself with a sweeping gesture of his hand, "Whose world is this? Yours or mine?" And he answered himself, "Mine! You appear in it. In the same way is everything what you perceive your world. Everything in your world is there to help you. My world is different. You are alone. Nobody influences you."

On one hand, he was right, but only on one hand, as everything that is put in words touches only one aspect of the truth. Certainly, no sentence can hold the truth.

Later, when he talked about virtual reality and informatics, he suddenly declared: "We all are only mechanic robots." He mentioned scientific research, which claims that emotions depend on genes, hormones and so on. For example, the attraction between man and woman is based on testosterone and oestrogen. "It just happens. You don't have a part in it. You simply watch. Don't get involved in what happens", he advised.

I remembered that I had brought a bar of chocolate for him. "Do you eat chocolate?" I hesitantly asked. Because sometimes he looked very holy, for example said, that he does not like conversing on worldly topics, and I considered it possible that he had renounced such worldly pleasures of the palate. "Yes, of course I eat chocolate", he immediately replied.

He told me that once an American accused him of wasting his talent. "You should give lectures in the West", he had said. BC answered him, "I have here everything I need. I get daily two meals."

"Meals okay. But if you want chocolate, you have to do something for it", the American had replied.

"Look! I even get chocolate!" he exclaimed and once again burst into roaring laughter.

BC was nice to me. He did not like to talk to other sadhus, because they were not really interested in spirituality, he said. "Most of them are sexually frustrated and some even keep women. They give an excuse by saying that the ancient rishis also had women." He suddenly became loud and thundered, "If someone has not finished with his sex drive, he has no place here."

"Do you shout at me?" I asked.

"No, never", he suddenly became very quiet, friendly, explaining. I felt that he might have shouted at himself. It probably was not always easy for him to stick to his vow of sexual abstinence.

"What happens if a sadhu breaks his vow of celibacy?" I asked and thought of the punishment, which in Buddhism was ordained for a monk—the expulsion from the monastery.

"Nothing happens. He falls, gets up and falls again." He had made a slip of the tongue and hurriedly corrected himself, "and tries again."

"Only few are really interested and do their work properly", he said. "A doctor from Amma's ashram, who runs up to Gangotri whenever Amma travels overseas, is one of them. He is genuine. A young woman is also genuine. She flew to Paris when she was 17 to learn fashion design. But this fancy world did not suit her. She informed her parents that she wanted to take sanyas. They were not at all pleased. They had money and wanted a comfortable life for their daughter. Yet she was determined and got her way. She lives now under very simple conditions here in Gangotri", he said. "You will meet her."

"You also belong to those who are genuine", he flattered me and suggested to come earlier so that we had more time for our conversations, as he daily left at 4.30 in the afternoon for his food in an ashram.

I liked BC. He had exactly those traits that I was lacking: strength, confidence and a loud voice. I had always been on the quiet, shy side and my voice does not become loud, even if I try.

"All spiritual seekers are unhappy", BC declared out of the blue one day. "You, too", he said and hit a tender spot. Was I happy? Not particularly, I had to admit. "They have the knowledge, but something holds them back", he continued. "Be like a lion! Break free! What can the world give you? All faces are like in a movie. Don't get entangled in the plot! When you die, the movie ends anyway. Throw the film roll away—now already! Throw out your thoughts! You are greater than the film, which consists of thoughts. Do your work well and sincerely. Let the others think what they want. Follow your conviction. Help is always available", he encouraged me.

I sat either in front of my hut and studied ancient scriptures or inside and meditated. During the first few weeks in Gangotri, I made hardly any contact with others. It was an intense time, and it slowly became clearer to me what 'pure awareness' signifies.

"Look at those snow-capped peaks over there, but nevertheless stay with your awareness inside", BC advised me. "Try to be aware of the unity behind the apparent duality—be aware of the white paper and also perceive the black print on it. Be attentive! Give your attention not mainly to the objects, but to attention itself", he demanded. I tried it and got an idea what he meant.

Once he gave me the 'Golden Letters' by Garab Dorje, an ancient Tibetan master, after he had again dived into his hut. They were a treasure, like the Shiva Sutras, and I copied them by hand into my diary, because there was no copy machine in Gangotri.

The content of those letters is simple, yet very subtle. The main thing is to recognise that this fresh, immediate awareness of the present moment is the truth that is sought after. It is ever present—this ordinary, thought free awareness—now in this moment. Realise this ordinary awareness as your true nature and stay with it, because everything else, which means all appearances in this world, are only modifications of this basic awareness and therefore secondary.

BC shared my excitement regarding the Golden Letters. He suggested that during my next meditation I completely relax and then suddenly and loudly shout "Phat". This would cause the pure awareness to rise up. In the evening, I tried it and it had a tremendous effect. It felt so beautiful that I didn't want to move. Joy mixed with gratefulness. As if something had opened—an insight into my Self.

In the next morning a hint of bliss was still felt. Later it disappeared, yet now it was easier to discover it again. My own immediate, ever-present awareness had now become more familiar. I was sure that with time it would become dearer and dearer. I was grateful for this gift and better understood Ramana Maharshi's saying: "You are always enlightened." The true, inconceivable basis on which the mind builds its dreamlike castles is indeed always lovingly present.

BC suffered since long from back pain. One morning the pain became unbearable and he could not get out of bed. The doctor from Amma's ashram advised him to go to the hospital in Rishikesh for a check-up and accompanied him.

When BC came back after a fortnight, he felt better and decided to stay in Gangotri for the winter as usual, even though everybody advised against it. It was only end of September and already ice-cold.

"Last year a Frenchman paid for my winter provisions", he told me, and I knew why. I felt obliged.

"I will pay for it this year", I offered. "How much is needed?"

"5000 Rupees are enough."

I had not expected that much but had forgotten the cigarettes which he smoked one after the other.

Later I came to know that every November before the temple closes, a businessman from Punjab sends a truck with provisions up to Gangotri, which supplies the seven or eight sadhus who usually stay through the winter with their basic needs. BC had not given out this information. Yet I did not mind. He simply needed more than others. I was grateful, and money could not possibly compensate for what he had given me. Pure awareness as my own inner being had become more recognizable through the contact with him and his books.

Four years later, in August 2005, I went once again to Gangotri and looked forward to seeing BC.

"Brahma Chaitanya is no more", the manager of Yoga Niketan

informed me, even before he unlocked a hut for me. "He died completely unexpected last month in Delhi."

I really felt sorry. He had been so full of strength and life. I did not understand how he could have gone to Delhi in the hottest season. He himself had told me that he would not leave Gangotri again. Only his ash would be carried down into the plains by his Ganga Ma.

I heard two versions why he went to Delhi in the peak of summer:

A well-known, 'big' Swami from Delhi wanted to meet him and sent two of his followers to Gangotri to request him to come. BC declined. However, they came again and urged him. That time he yielded, maybe because the Swami had offered to arrange an Ayurvedic treatment for him. Yet nobody knew why the Swami wanted to meet him.

The other version said that BC wanted to go to Delhi on his own wish for Ayurvedic treatment and the Swami arranged it for him.

It would surprise me, if BC had wanted to do a treatment in Delhi in the hottest time of the year. I had been in Delhi in that same June for a short while. The temperature was 46 degrees Celsius and took a huge toll from every body, even more from a body that, since a couple of decades, was used to the cold climate at the height of above 3000 meters.

"Death called him to Delhi", a sadhu neighbour of BC said and thus put any speculation that there might have been some foul play into a different perspective. "His time had come."

BC's sons came to Gangotri and took the translation of the Yoga Vasishtha out of his hut. Their father had given his life to this work. The ash of BC was immersed in his beloved Ganga Ma—in Haridwar, where he had started his sadhu life. The circle had come full round—an inspiring life had ended.

CHAPTER 38

With Eckhart Tolle in Rishikesh

For three months, I had blended in with the life in Gangotri. The shopkeepers knew me, the postman, the doctor and some priests of the temple. I came to know about the relationships or rather enmities between the rich swamis, realised, that the ego survives even in an orange robe and listened to the latest gossip. No doubt, the world was up there, as well, and yet, it was easier to dive into oneself and be aware of the priorities in life. The 'active life' that Chuang Tzu had so well described over 2000 years ago was less active at the height of over 3000 metres with snow mountains watching.

Back in my small flat on the outskirts of Dehradun, I got a surprise visit by a friend from Vancouver. Arthur had a book with him: 'Practising the Power of Now' by Eckhart Tolle. I read the first pages and became fully engrossed. Eckhart expressed Indian wisdom clearly and simply by focussing on the ever-present NOW— the same 'present awareness' that BC had helped to make me discover.

Arthur knew Eckhart Tolle from Vancouver and was sure that he was enlightened. "Next February he gives a week-long retreat in Rishikesh. He comes to India for the first time ever", he said. I hesitated, because the fee was high, but for Indians, it was much less. I signed up, but the retreat was already fully booked.

End of December, however, I slipped into the list of participants. There had been many cancellations due to the terror attack on the

Indian parliament on 13th December 2001 and the build-up of troops along the border to Pakistan. The situation was tense, and war seemed imminent.

I had offered to help with the registration, to feel better about paying 'only' the fee for Indians. Around 130 persons from mainly English-speaking countries from Hong Kong to Hawaii gathered in the spacious Paramarth Ashram on the banks of the Ganges. There were only about twenty from India.

Eckhart reached the ashram with a group of people, some of whom I happened to know—for example Kim Eng from Vancouver. I had met her in Mumbai at a satsang of Ramesh Balsekar, and again in Tiruvannamalai and Puducherry. Kim, a beautiful woman of Chinese origin, was now Eckhart's girlfriend.

An Englishman tried to trace his room key which he had handed over to a watchman who was nowhere in sight and I helped him out with my Hindi. His name was Philip and he had lived with Eckhart in the same house in Glastonbury, when the latter was writing his famous book "The Power of Now". Our paths kept crossing several times that first evening, and once we stood talking. My difficult life situation suddenly hit me: I had left my guru in South India and in the process, had lost my friends and the structure in my life. I had moved to a new place all alone and the magazine I wrote for and which had paid reasonably well had become insolvent. I felt without ground under my feet and confided it to Philip.

"Great!" he said. "You couldn't have a better starting point for the retreat with Eckhart."

I knew he was right.

When the ego cannot hold on to the old, anyhow false identities any longer there is a chance that it becomes weak and finally disappears. And when the illusory ego is not projected anymore, the real Self shines forth. Nothing else is needed, because the self is always there. It is hidden beneath the ego, as the ocean is hidden beneath the waves, or the rope beneath the imagined snake or the desert sand beneath the mirage.

Eckhart defined the ego or phantom self, as he called it, as the unobserved mind. The stress is on 'unobserved'. It determines one's life completely, as long as one is not present as the observing consciousness. Then one is not 'there' and reacts unconsciously according to the strategies of the ego. There is no choice and one *has to* be angry or sad or resist the moment in some other way, because "the ego feels better if it is against something", Eckhart—chuckling—revealed one of its characteristics.

Eckhart Tolle takes part in a yagna (fire ceremony) at the banks of the Ganges in Rishikesh.

The ego, however, is in a weak position, when I *know* that I am sad or angry. Then it cannot order me around. I am awake and have the choice whether I want to allow dark thoughts and feelings to take hold of my mind. And who would voluntarily choose to be unhappy?

We need to know the crucial difference between 'being aware in the present' and 'being lost in thoughts'. It is a fundamentally different way of life to consciously accept the now. It is the state of an enlightened being. "An enlightened being doesn't put up any resistance towards the present moment", Eckhart possibly described his own state and gave the analogy of swimming:

As long as the ego dominates, the person can be compared to someone, who is learning to swim. He wildly splashes around in the water, exhausts himself, and fights to keep his head above the water. The water is his enemy. He doesn't trust it. In a similar way, the ego sees the whole universe as an enemy and keeps fighting it.

If someone, however, consciously accepts the now as it is and flows with it, he is like an experienced swimmer, who trusts the water and allows it to carry him. The water supports him, is friendly. Similarly, the whole universe is friendly and creates helpful situations, if one doesn't resist the present moment. "Try it out", he said. "You can know for yourself that it is true."

However, *noticing* that one is unconscious is the crux of the matter and not really within one's power. Eckhart often attached the rider 'if you can', when he asked us to be present. You cannot 'do' it, but you can allow it, he said. Allowing things to be as they are may seem trivial, but it opens up a completely different quality of life.

Eckhart claimed that a depressive mood was easier to catch with awareness than anger. It arises slowly with heavy thoughts how dreadful the world is. Anger, in contrast, leaps up like fire, and before one realises it, one shouts already at somebody.

Eckhart himself had been depressed and even suicidal before his transformation. One night—he was 29—he woke up and felt terribly dismayed with the world, and most of all, with himself. "I can't live with myself any longer", kept repeating itself in his mind. Suddenly it startled him: 'I with myself? Am I one or two? Probably I am only one.' He was stunned by this strange realisation. He felt drawn into what seemed a vortex of energy and then into a void. He let himself fall into that void without any resistance.

When he woke up the next morning, his world had changed. He felt connected with something immeasurable. There was deep peace and bliss. The connection with the depressive Eckhart was cut off. He was truly only one.

Most people live with a mind-created self, with whom—would it be another person—they wouldn't live for a single day, Eckhart laughed. They even address it as "you". "What fool you have been!" for example. Some try to improve this self and paste stickers: "I am okay" or "I love myself" and read them many times a day. It will help only to a certain extent. In the world of duality, the other pole will show up at some point and then you won't feel okay or you will hate yourself, explained Eckhart. Yet there is a solution: allow the present moment to be as it is; accept it in whatever form—inside and outside—it presents itself. Never mind if it is not ideal. He asked us to practise this the whole day.

'The now, the present moment, holds the key to liberation. The now is the most precious thing there is, because in the now the whole life unfolds. Life is now', Eckhart explained and zoomed in on a very important aspect of the truth.

It is not easy to recognise the now for what it is. Most people consider past and future more important than this small, fleeting moment, which can't be grasped. Yet the now doesn't refer to a point in time. The now is not in time. It is a completely different category from past and future. To help us understand, Eckhart suggested: "Imagine you ask a bird what time it is. He will answer, 'it is now of course. It is always now!'"

The now is eternal. Everything always happens in the now. Nothing happens in the past and future and nothing *can* happen in the past and future. Past and future are only thoughts in the mind and these thoughts are there now. Past and future borrow their reality from the now, as the moon borrows its light from the sun. Learn from the past and plan for the future, but honour the now, live in the now, and don't resist it. The now is your faithful companion. It is always with you and never forsakes you. It is always the same, infinite and sacred. And Eckhart even went a step further. "You are the now", he perplexed us.

I imagined the reaction of some of my friends in Germany if I told them: 'Do you know that you are the now?'

The ego doesn't like the now, because it needs past and future for its story and requests the now: 'Please, dear now, don't stop me. I am on my way to the future'. Eckhart laughed. It would be funny, if it wasn't so tragic: almost the whole of humankind waits perpetually for fulfilment in the future. Almost everyone steadfastly ignores the now, the present moment, in which life happens. Almost everyone wants to get away from the now, wants to be somewhere else, wants to be with somebody else, wants to do something else and wants the future to come quickly and on the other hand is afraid of it. Yet the future comes always only as now.

Only now can you feel what you truly are, and only when you are fully one with that, you will be happy, Eckhart claimed. Outer circumstances won't make you happy in the long run.

And what are we in truth?

Eckhart quoted from the Vedas: "(Brahman is) not that what the eyes see, but that whereby the eyes can see. Not that, what the ears hear, but that whereby the ears can hear. Not that, what the mind thinks but that whereby the mind can think."

Words and thoughts turn back from it, the Rishis add. It is not about knowing something but about *being* truly oneself. Being cannot be understood by the mind. Yet it can be felt. Enlightenment is, said Eckhart, to regain Awareness of Being and to abide in it.

Eckhart didn't say anything new. Yet his talks had great impact, because for this truth to deeply touch the listener, it needs to be conveyed by someone who is present in the now.

There are warning signals when you are not present in the now—for example when you are irritated, or impatient or unhappy or if you complain about something, even about the weather. "If you are fully present in the now, it is not possible to be unhappy", he stated.

"90 per cent of your thinking is unnecessary", Eckhart claimed. Create a pause in the thought stream, for example by consciously taking a deep breath, or by intensely listening to the chirping of birds or by simply looking without labelling what you see. Feel the inner energy field of the body and become one with it, especially before sleeping and after waking up, he advised.

Eckhart told us that once he was asked what he had achieved in life. At that time he had not yet written his book and had no job.

"Well, I don't have to think anymore", he had replied, and chuckled, "This is not highly regarded in the West".

In India, this type of achievement is more likely to be valued. Eckhart said that after his transformation he felt not like a Westerner anymore but like an Indian. There was a sense of deep connectedness with Ramana Maharshi. "India represents the inner dimension. It is the cradle of the transformation of consciousness."

I wanted to write about the retreat and asked Kim whether I could have a brief one to one meeting with Eckhart, as it would be helpful. She said she would come back to me. However, I did not get a chance to meet him. Like in Poonja's case, there was a protective ring around Eckhart by close disciples.

Yet I was glad I had attended Eckhart's retreat. He seemed rooted in his self when he was in Rishikesh, except maybe for the final talk in the presence of Swami Chidananda, the head of Parmarth ashram. This talk was open to the public. I had the impression that Eckhart wanted to pack a lot of information into this talk and seemed somewhat out of his depth.

Eckhart was catapulted into the limelight after his book was an extraordinary success with many million copies sold. Great adoration came his way and the danger that it may go to his head and activate a 'spiritual ego' is real. "As soon as a spiritual teacher considers himself as someone special—and his followers usually project that he is indeed very special—he is not transparent for being anymore", Eckhart himself told us in Rishikesh. Being is not partial. It doesn't prefer Eckhart over others, but reveals itself wherever it does not get blocked by an ego.

I have not met him since 2002 and don't know whether he is still as transparent and inspiring as he was in Rishikesh.

Meanwhile, 'Eckhart Teachings Inc' has morphed into a business empire and Eckhart is not only one of the most influential spiritual teachers worldwide, but is also on the rich man's list. People in his circle claimed that it was Kim who became very business savvy. The charges for his talks and retreats are exorbitantly high. Talks are on internet, but if one wants to meet him in person, it needs deep pockets. Why would he make his physical presence so costly? In the Indian tradition darshan (seeing, or being in the presence of an enlightened being) is highly valued and granted freely. Amma even gives a hug for free and though there is a comparatively small charge for Art of Living courses, darshan of Sri Sri during talks or bhajan is free.

Anandamayi Ma said that meeting an enlightened being means meeting yourself. Ramana Maharshi gave darshan till his last day.

When towards the end, his assistant told him once that he had asked his devotees not to come for darshan as it would be too much strain for him, Ramana had tears in his eyes, saying "But I want to have *their* darshan."

Eckhart had mentioned in Rishikesh that he feels intimately connected with Ramana Maharshi and had added "If not one". Some slight difference seems still to be there.

CHAPTER 39

Intimations from Beyond

During the retreat in Rishikesh I had a short, but vivid dream. I called up a person and told him that I will move into his flat. I had met this gentleman briefly in real life. A few months earlier, I had informed some people that I look for a place to rent which was better connected to town and did not have an electric transformer humming in front of my window. The person in my dream had recently shown me a flat in his house. It was a grey, cold January afternoon and the flat right next to the forest felt too cold and dark, in spite of big windows. I declined his offer.

Yet when I woke up after this dream, I was surprised how matter-of-factly I had said that I will move and decided to have another look at his flat. After coming back I went to my future landlord and was simply amazed that I had not seen the beauty of his place earlier. A few days later I moved, and felt very fortunate with my new environment—a 'deluxe cave', as a friend dubbed it, and again a kind landlord family.

The financial pressure eased soon after as well. My mother gave me some money to put me on par with what my sister had got over the years. Further, I started writing on a book in German language, most of which is included in this English, greatly expanded version. I was also back to writing articles. My article on Eckhart was published in Germany, India and even Hong Kong. For the first time, I had dared to write in English.

After Eckhart's retreat my focus was, as in Gangotri, often directed to my inner being, to 'discover the white paper under the black print', as BC had put it. I realised that the bliss that I had felt during occasional out of body experiences is always there, even when I don't feel it. It is, as it were, inbuilt in the 'stuff' out of which everything is made. This stuff, which has no material substance, is overlooked because of thoughts, in a similar way, as the white paper is overlooked because of the black print on it.

Thoughts are indeed capable of totally veiling the truth. The Rishis give an analogy: at dusk, when I mistake a rope for a snake, I do not see a rope, only a snake. I am afraid and run away—from a rope! Similarly, I am afraid and run away from the world, though everything in this world in truth is 'I myself'.

Nisargadatta Maharaj, the author of "I am That", had defined meditation as "radical refusal to harbour thoughts". It requires some sacrifice because it is much easier to think than to be still. The mind has great strength and keeps pushing thoughts. It will not give any value to being still. It will argue that being still is boring and does not make use of one's intellectual capacity. "Have a cup of coffee and read the paper. You can sit still later", it will propose. Yet, in all likelihood, the intellectual capacity will even increase, if the mind is still, at least sometimes.

'Not needing to think', as Eckhart put it, is rare and of immense benefit. Great sages from Buddha to Ramana Maharshi were not driven by thoughts. Ramana once was asked whether he thinks.

"Usually I don't think", he answered.

"But I see you reading newspapers."

"When I read newspapers I think of course. But usually I don't think."

"And I see you talking to people."

"When I talk to people I think of course. But usually I don't think...."

If indeed 90 per cent of our thoughts are useless, then there won't be any harm if we refuse to harbour some of them...

There were interesting experiences while trying out Eckhart's advice of not thinking and instead feeling the inner energy field of the body.

For example, once I travelled by train from Delhi to Chennai. It was a 36-hour long journey. An English woman, older to me, was in the same compartment. Right from the start, she proved to be extremely unpleasant and provoked me into getting annoyed with her. I could feel resentment rising. Did I want to resent her for 36 long hours? Certainly not! So I lay down on my berth and tried to feel the inner energy field of my body. It was easy, because there was already a lot of turbulence going on inside. I watched it for several minutes, and slowly, the turbulence gave way to a very pleasant, expansive feeling.

Amazingly, there was now no resentment anymore. I only felt amused at her continued attempts to create friction. I offered her nuts (she refused) and could tell her calmly to take down her feet which, at one point, she placed right next to my face when I was lying down. When I once sat chatting with a young man across the corridor, she protested that our talk was too loud. We smilingly obliged her and whispered thereafter—amused, not annoyed.

I had noticed already in my early years in India that whenever I felt close to my inner being and generally was living according to spiritual tenets, like wishing well for everyone, amazing and pleasant things would happen—on a small and also bigger scale. There were several incidents with their probability as rare as winning the jackpot in a lottery. I mention some of them to show that one can trust that great power. It surely can work miracles.

Probably the most amazing coincidence—meeting Georg by chance in Varanasi, I have narrated already. Yet there were others.

When I flew back to India after my first visit to Germany in January 1982, a German sat next to me. I told him that I had earned the money to come to India by selling Crepes Suzettes, a French type of pancake, during my studies. "It was a great idea and I got it when I bought a Crepes near the railway station on the island of Sylt with the queue of his customers never ending", I narrated. "This stall near the railway station in Sylt—I was running it with a partner!" he exclaimed and we both were surprised at the coincidence.

Another time, I was standing at the reception of a hotel in Bodh Gaya and filled out a form. Next to me, a man put his Indonesian passport on the counter. The receptionist left for some errant, and the Indonesian and I started talking. "You remind me of a friend from my studies in Hamburg", I told him after a while. "But she is only half Indonesian."

"What's her name?" he asked.

"Kunang Helmi", I replied.

"She is my sister."

When Kunang and I were studying in Hamburg, she once showed me photos of her family and told me that her brother has lived in a cave in the Himalayas for a whole year. "Wow, I would like to meet this brother", I had thought at that time.

In 1986, I read "Daughter of Tibet" by Rinchen Dolma Taring. When the Chinese started shelling Lhasa in March 1959, she had two options: either to flee to India or be imprisoned by the Chinese as she belonged to the aristocracy and had been politically active. She fled with a heavy heart, leaving back her old mother-in-law and four grandchildren whom her daughter had left in her care, when she and her husband went to India on some work. Those children were small in 1959—between 5 and 11 years—and their fate touched me deeply.

This story was fresh in my mind, when I travelled by bus from Dehradun to Delhi. A Tibetan sat next to me. I mentioned that I had just read the book "Daughter of Tibet". "Oh, my grandmother has written this book", he said. He was one of those four children who had been left behind at that time and had managed to come to India in 1980.

Sometimes, several pieces of a mosaic gradually form a beautiful picture, like in the following case:

I had heard of "Tripura Rahasya", an ancient philosophical text since long. Ramana Maharshi had encouraged its English translation.

Finally, I got it in a bookstore in Rishikesh and wanted to study it in a quiet place. In Barkot, on the way to Yamunotri, I asked the District Forest Officer for permission to stay in the Forest Rest House. The officer was helpful. "Barkot is a big place and forest officials may come. They have preference over tourists, and then you will have to leave. I suggest you go to the rest house in Gangnani, a small village on the Yamuna. It is about 10 km north of Barkot and there you can stay for a longer time. Nobody will disturb you there." I gladly accepted his suggestion.

The rest house was in wonderful surroundings. A watchman lived there with his family and cooked meals for me. I had the whole day to concentrate on Tripura Rahasya. In the text, Parasuram, an avatar prior to Ram, the prince of Ayodhya, asks questions and his guru Dattatreya answers with parables and logic.

Dattatreya, for example, postulates two criteria for truth. first, truth has to be always—in past, present, future. In one sweep, the whole, constantly changing universe is disqualified as truth. Second, truth must be self-evident. If it needs something else to be perceived, it is not truth. It means only one thing is left—the perceiving awareness as such. Then Dattatreya explains why only pure, thought free awareness is true. It is always present and makes everything else 'shine'. This pure, empty awareness shows up for a fleeting moment between two thoughts or two perceptions. However, it is not recognised because one is not familiar with it, Dattatreya claimed.

I tried to catch this gap, looked at one snow peak and then at another again and again. Sometimes it felt, as if I got a glimpse of this gap, a free-floating feeling. I enjoyed studying this ancient text, scribbled many insights into my diary and moved on only after I was through with it.

A few years later, I stayed in Uttarkashi in the ashram of Tapovan Maharaj, the guru of Swami Chinmayananda, and read his book "Wanderings in the Himalayas". In the book Tapovan Maharaj described his travels in the 1920s, when he was young and strong, and travelled all over the Himalayas. He also came to Gangnani. "In Gangnani on the Yamuna, sage Jamadagni is believed to have had his ashram", I read. "Jamadagni" sounded familiar and I opened the Tripura Rahasya. The introduction starts, "Jamadagni was a Brahmin saint who lived in the forest with his wife Renuka and his sons, of whom Parasuram was the youngest, the most valiant and the best renowned."

I got goose bumps all over my skin. The place, where I had studied the discussion between Parasuram and Dattatreya, was the very place, where Parasuram was supposedly born and grew up! I did not know anything about Gangnani, not even that it existed, and yet of all places, I had landed in this tiny village with the Tripura Rahasya in my bag.

A less spectacular, yet surely rare incident happened only recently, which helped me in making a decision.

A renowned Sanskrit scholar offered an intensive Sanskrit course in Puducherry. I could not make up my mind whether to take part. Only two days were left for signing up, when I had lunch in a South Indian restaurant. I joined a young Indian as all tables were full. Later a young couple from Nepal joined us as well. It turned out that the Nepali was a Sanskrit teacher in Leyden, Holland, his wife was studying Sanskrit at Hamburg University, my own Alma Mater, and the Indian had volunteered at the Sanskrit course of that very scholar in the previous year. That same afternoon I signed up.

Such incidences naturally increased my trust in that great Presence that guides all our destinies. It felt close, personal and responsive. The claim in the Bhagavad Gita—that one need not worry for the morrow if one trusts completely this Presence—sounded realistic. It is definitely present—right here, right now. Yet trusting "completely" is the point and not so easy. Abdullah had amazing trust which I still don't have. For example, once a foreigner in the Aurobindo Ashram needed to reach the airport in the middle of the night and worried how he would wake up as he didn't have an alarm clock. Abdullah offered to wake him up, and the young man gladly accepted. Yet Abdullah also didn't have an alarm clock and I asked him how he was so sure to wake up in time. "Before falling asleep I ask to be woken up and I definitely will wake up", he said.

I also tried it and it works. However, when I have to take a flight, I put an alarm…

I lived now a life independent of any guru or spiritual community. Exceptional however in the sense that I had no close or distant relative anywhere near—in a country where family plays such dominant role. Sometimes, I felt this as a lack. Most of the time, however, I was grateful to be free.

CHAPTER 40

Macaulay's Children

In my early years in India, I used to think that every Indian knows about his great heritage—Sanskrit, the Vedas, the mantras, the ancient epics, Indian philosophy, spirituality, yoga, Ayurveda. Over the years I realised I had been wrong. I realised that many Indians have never read any ancient text, nor its translation. I met Brahmins who didn't even know the Gayatri Mantra.

Yet, living now away from ashrams and gurus, I was in for a big surprise. Several people, whom I met in Dehradun, were not only ignorant, but they demeaned their tradition. They were not Muslims or Christians, where one could explain their disdain because they were brainwashed into it, but they had Hindu names and were without exception the educated lot. How was this possible? It took me long to understand why especially educated Indians and the media, too, pictured everything traditionally Indian in poor light.

Here are the conclusions to which I came:

The reason lies in the history of India—more precisely, in the short span of the last thousand years, for India traces its origin back to remote antiquity. For long, Western scholars, handicapped by their Christian faith, did not date anything further back than around 5000 years because, according to the Bible, the world was created only around 6000 years ago. Slowly however, science has pushed the frontiers back into the distant past and estimates now the earth to be a few billion years old. Even human civilization is now estimated by historians to be 10,000 years old—still falling very much short of Indian standards. Their yugas (time cycles) last millions of years. According to the Rishis, even the universes come and go.

Indian Sanskrit texts are the oldest and most voluminous literature of humanity, and contain deep philosophy and scientific insights in a language that is considered the most perfect language available. Whoever studies these texts in an unbiased way, will be stunned into admiration. Even if someone starts off being biased, he may change his mind, as for example Max Mueller (1823—1900) did.

He was Professor in Oxford who translated the Vedas and brought out 49 volumes of "Sacred Books of the East". At the age of 26, he began his long translation work to prove that these texts are only the babble of primitive people. He was in the service of the East India Company and out to prove that Europe was culturally and intellectually far superior to India.

Yet later in his life, his view changed. In 1884 at the age of 61, he gave his famous talk at the Cambridge University: "If I were asked under what sky the human mind has most fully developed some of its choicest gifts, has most deeply pondered on the greatest problems of life.... I should point to India. And if I were to ask myself from what literature we, here in Europe... may draw that corrective which is most wanted in order to make our inner life more perfect, more comprehensive, more universal, in fact more truly human...—again I should point to India."

However, theses utterances could not make up for the immense damage Max Mueller had already done. His "Aryan Invasion Theory" provided an important tool for the British to divide and justify their rule though it was only based on flimsy linguistic similarities and never backed up by any archaeological or genetic findings. India suffers even today from this fabricated, unreal division between 'Aryan invaders and the Dravidian indigenous population', because political parties rake it up for their benefit. Some even talk of creating 'Dravidistan", separating the southern states from India.

Max Mueller never was in India. The India he knew was the India of the scriptures. From this literature it is evident that ancient India was highly developed—culturally, scientifically, technologically and spiritually. What happened to that India? How did India become so poor and corrupt when it was so accomplished and wealthy in ancient times?

The reason is that the area that comprises today India, Pakistan and Bangladesh, was invaded and badly mauled. The Muslims came first, and they rampaged across the land with brutal force. Islamic historians recorded with pride how infidels were slaughtered or forced to convert, how Hindu women and children were sold in slave markets and how centres of learning and temples were destroyed, and their huge wealth looted. From around 800 to 1700 AD, Muslims invaded and ruled large parts of the Indian subcontinent. It was an extremely bloody conquest.

"All the infidel Hindu men were slain, their women and children and their property and goods became the spoil of the victors", Timur for example wrote in his memoirs, known as Tuzk-i-Timuri, after he had raised Delhi to the ground in December 1398.

When he left for Samarkand, where he would a few months later start building the famous mosque, 90 elephants carried the loot of precious stones alone. Immense quantities of spoils and thousands of Hindu slaves, including skilled artisans and builders, were taken. Many died while crossing over the mountain range called Hindukush (= Hindu killer).

Yet, when I saw some years ago a documentary about the Samarkand mosque on Arte TV, not one word was said about the India connection. How could they miss out on it except intentionally? Did they not want to mention that India was very wealthy and had expertise in building domes?

In the early 16th century, Babar, a grandson of Timur, established the Mogul dynasty that sat on the famous peacock throne (which was taken away to Persia in the 18th century) until the British came to power. The Mogul Empire, Indian children learn, was a glorious time. It was indeed a great and wealthy empire. Yet the Hindu population suffered badly. Guru Nanak, a contemporary of Babar and the founder of Sikhism, cried out to the Supreme and his cry is enshrined in the Granth Sahib, the holy book of the Sikhs:

"Having lifted Islam to the head, You have engulfed Hindustan (India) in dread... Such cruelties they have inflicted and yet Your mercy remains unmoved.... Oh Lord, these dogs have destroyed the diamond-like Hindustan."

Around 1750, the British, who had come as traders of the East Indian Company, seized more and more power and in 1858, after the Indians resisted and fought the British one year earlier, the British Raj took over. Under the British, too, Indians suffered badly. Their economic policies uplifted Britain, yet made India destitute. In the 19th century, four great famines killed over 25 million people, each one of them dying a slow, painful death. Even as late as 1943, over three million Indians starved to death in Bengal, while India had to shoulder the major part of the British World War II expenses, and while over a million Indian soldiers fought on the British side. Without those Indian soldiers known for their bravery (over 75 000 sacrificed their lives) the outcome of the war might well have been different.

Apart from their ruthless economic policies, the British designed a sinister plot to subdue their colonial subjects by brainwashing them. "We must do our best to form a class who may be interpreters between us and the millions whom we govern, a class of persons, Indian in blood and colour, but English in taste, in opinions, words and intellect", demanded Thomas Macaulay in 1835 in the Parliament in London. "I propose that we replace her old and ancient (Sanskrit) education system, her culture, for if the Indians think that all that is foreign and English is good and greater than their own, they will lose their self- esteem, their native self- culture and they will become what we want them, a truly dominated nation."

It is worthwhile to note that Macaulay devised this policy *after* the Vedic knowledge had reached Europe and had greatly impressed the intellectual elite there. Voltaire praised it as the greatest gift to mankind. "We are eternally indebted to India", he said. German thinkers, too, hoped this knowledge would spread in the West. Yet from now on, Indian students learnt that their tradition deserves contempt.

Macaulay could not have hoped for better success of his strategy. It worked so well, that even 70 years after independence, a small but hugely influential section of educated Indians, several of them in Western universities, still despise their ancient tradition and adore the West. They are called "Macaulay's children". Their grandparents and parents were brainwashed that they were a fatalistic people due to the flawed "Hinduism", a term the British coined. Whatever culture they had, had been brought from outside.

It was a lie, yet children could not detect it, as Sanskrit and Indian heritage was not part of the syllabus. They 'learnt' that Britain is the epitome of modernity and science and British rule would raise India from the morass of castes and religious superstition. The students aspired to be like their colonial masters and looked with disdain down on the uneducated masses. They proudly spoke in English, quoted Shakespeare, and had no idea about the amazing contribution to human civilization of their forefathers.

It is inexplicable that even today neither the Bhagavad-Gita is taught in Indian schools, nor the Upanishads or the amazing epics Mahabharata and Ramayana. Indian historians still propagate the Aryan invasion theory, whereas historians elsewhere refute it. Brainwashing is difficult to overcome, but the views of Macaulay's children do not go unchallenged any longer thanks to social media, and a government that at least is not inimical to Hindus since 2014, even though it has not yet removed unjust discrimination in several fields like education, which put the Hindu majority at a disadvantage.

Now, here I was in Dehradun and had acquaintances who spoke only English, and considered Christianity and Islam the better religions, in spite of their Hindu names. Some were taken aback about my Hindu friendly views and my former Bengali neighbour, a self-declared communist, introduced me as 'the local RSS pracharak' to his friends—half in jest, but more than half it was meant to be demeaning. RSS is a social volunteer organization which is in the forefront in helping during natural calamities and close to the BJP (Indian People's Party), but media portrays it as

'Hindu nationalist'. Once an elderly woman reacted, "Oh, in that case I am not pleased to meet you."

'Whoever goes through our education system will look down on the Indian tradition', Macaulay had predicted. How right he was! Now I understood why the media, the education syllabus and politics were biased against Hindus. The people who run institutions, who are in education, media and politics, are precisely this 'educated' class—who learnt what the British wanted them to learn. I could not blame my neighbour. In West Bengal, school children learnt even in the 1990s: "Islam and Christianity are the only religions that treat the human being with dignity and equality." And a circular instructed the teachers not to mention the destruction of temples and forceful conversions during Muslim rule. No religion should appear to be worse than Hinduism.

Macaulay might be laughing in his grave. And those, who treasure India's heritage, might wonder when the Vedic dictum and India's motto "Satyameva jayate" (Truth will triumph) will come true.

CHAPTER 41

English education—a big blunder

In Dehradun, I helped the son of our watchman with his homework and got a glimpse of what I considered a truly terrible education system. His books seemed to be taken straight from a primary class in England. It was about Jill and Jim, about rabbits and foxes and the "London Bridge is falling down". But apart from the inadequate content, the medium of instruction—English—was the even bigger problem. The boy was exceptionally bright and eager to learn, but of course he couldn't have a clue what those stories meant. It seems the educationists forgot that English is not the mother tongue of Indians.

I asked his mother why on earth would she send her son to a school where a foreign language is spoken, which the parents themselves did not speak. Her reply made me realize that I had missed out on a trend:

Under the UPA government between 2004 and 2014, there was a veritable exodus from vernacular Government schools to private English medium schools which sprang up everywhere. Between 2008 and 2013 the enrollment into English medium schools almost doubled. Many of those schools were terrible. Parents who did not know any English were made to believe that only 'English schools' would provide their children with the same opportunity as children of 'big people' who speak English at home.

The parents believed it. They wanted the best for their children. They were ready to pay for the education even if it took a big junk of their income. They even clamoured for 'English schools' without realizing what it entails. Friends, who had established primary schools with dedicated teachers in over 20 villages in the Himalayan foothills, closed them down after parents insisted that they convert the schools to English medium. In my neighbourhood, too, most children go now to English medium school and in the afternoon for tuition. And I truly feel sorry for them.

Where in the world would children be sent to a school where the teachers speak in a foreign language? And why are parents not better advised? Just imagine the plight of the kids. They learn to spell and can read after a while, but they don't know the meaning of the words. I wondered what would have happened, if my parents had sent me to a (luckily non-existing) English medium school. It would surely have been a disaster, even though English is closer to German than to Indian languages. Even today, after decades of plenty of reading and speaking English, I get the meaning of some words wrong. Recently only I discovered that 'callous' is not the same as 'casual', as I used to think.

A lot is made of 'freedom of speech'. Nobody seems to realise that the greatest curb on freedom of speech happens due to English medium in schools and in jobs. The students cannot say what they want to say, because they don't have the words.

Meanwhile, India has a big number of students, who are neither good in their mother tongue nor in English, who had an extremely tough childhood, with long tuition hours, and whose brightness has been blunted by low self-esteem and with no time left to explore genuine interests. Kids just stare at their textbooks when their parents tell them 'to study', and the parents don't realise that no learning can happen. A foreign language cannot be downloaded like an app. Each word needs to be learnt.

Only a tiny minority benefits from this system. These are the children of those who speak English at home and who have English as a poor substitute for a mother tongue. But why would India want to perpetuate colonial policies which were introduced to weaken India?

The argument given is that a link language is needed for the different states with their different languages. True, a link language is needed. But why not make students learn English, if India really wants English as the link and not Sanskrit. Teach the language as a subject from maybe 10 years of age onwards. Make them learn vocabulary, grammar. Motivate them to learn. Don't assume they know the language somehow miraculously. As it is, even with English medium schools around, only about 10 percent of Indians know sufficient English, and not even one percent speak it fluently.

From my outsider perspective, it is incomprehensible that India does not choose Sanskrit as link language and as language for higher education instead of English. Sanskrit would be the better option, because it is, though most ancient, also most perfect. Foreigners meanwhile learn Sanskrit in droves. Indians would have a big advantage as their own languages are related to Sanskrit and it is much easier for them to learn. And anyway, English is slowly losing its 'world language' tag, with Asia becoming economically more powerful.

Sanskrit would not, as English medium does, dim the naturally high intelligence of Indians but increase it. Students also could again decode the vast knowledge that is contained in their Sanskrit heritage. India could stop copying Western education, which definitely has not covered itself in glory, and instead devise an education system more in tune with the deep insights of Indian wisdom. Indian texts can be the basis for this important overhaul in education.

As it is, much what students learn in school is useless. From my own experience I know that most of what I learnt in school did not stay with me much longer than until the exams. Yet the desire to know is deep-rooted in a human being. It was so in me, too.

After high school, I was dismayed that I knew so little, in spite of good grades. I became a voracious reader, wanted to know everything. At that time I did 3 years training with Lufthansa and the world was open to me. I wanted to know the political and economic situation in every country or at least in those which I visited, and I visited some 40 of them. I made files for South

America, Africa, Asia, etc. and whenever I found an article in one of the major German weeklies regarding those countries, I read it and filed it. After some time I only filed it, resolving to read it later which, of course, never happened. Slowly it dawned on me that I can't know everything.

One morning I was sitting in a railway restaurant for breakfast, when suddenly a picture came to my mind: I 'saw' all knowledge being lined up on the circumference of a huge circle with me in the centre. It would never be possible to learn all this out there. And then I wrote a sentence into my diary that surprised me: "I believe there is a point inside me, and when I reach that, I know everything."

This certainly was a strange sentence for a young German. And what a surprise when I came to India several years later! Here I read in the Chandogya Upanishad that the goal is 'to know THAT by which everything is known.' Well, it felt like home.

If it is possible to know That by which everything is known, then of course it must have priority in education. The focus should definitely be on this one thing. Yet there is a difficulty now, because it becomes very subtle and is not anymore only in the realm of reason. There has to be openness for spirituality. 'That' is namely our core; it is the intelligence, power and life in everyone. It is not an object to be known. It is the invisible essence, pure consciousness without content. And if That can occasionally get an opening through the maze of constant thinking, then inspiration and worthwhile knowledge happen.

The Rishis claimed that this intelligence can be approached by being still, by being fully present, by devotion. Putting attention on 'That' has been the tradition in India since ages and is called dhyan, or meditation. And it may not be far-fetched to assume that this was the main source for the amazing knowledge the ancient Indians had.

In March 2018 the Indian education ministry announced that the syllabus for CBSE (an English medium board) will be cut down by half. Such de-cluttering of the textbooks is a very welcome step and a big relief for the students. The space that is freed in this way could be used for dhyan (meditation), yoga and other means which help to be fully present and not to be constantly lost in thoughts. It could be used to give India's heritage its due. India is in the best position to take the lead in education. Does India again want to wait till the West appropriates her knowledge and makes it into an "international phenomenon", like yoga?

The philosopher Hermann Graf von Keyserling, a German, who traveled through India already in 1911, wrote: "I can say from own experience that this seemingly useless and often ridiculed 'being still' (meditation) is of great importance… all great personalities are masters of their mind and not slaves of their automatism… a few minutes every morning of being still have more effect in increasing concentration than the strictest schooling."

The great mathematician Srinivasa Ramanujan felt that Namagiri Devi, the goddess he worshipped, helped him solving mathematical riddles. Even on his deathbed he dreamt of a mathematical formula that did not make much sense at that time but was validated in 2012, some hundred years later.

Einstein also had his path breaking insights in quiet moments. It all points to the fact that great intelligence is within us, which means, it is very close. This intelligence can be tapped into. How this tapping is best done, has to be enquired into and experimented on. This should be the major concern of education. In all likelihood it is not done by more thinking, but by occasionally stopping to think. And the motivation also needs to be right. It may not work if the motive is to outshine others. Maybe also certain qualities like humility and genuine gratefulness to that inner intelligence are required. It would be worthwhile to find out, wouldn't it?

CHAPTER 42

Mischievous accusations: 'Hindu terror' and 'rape culture'

In Dehradun, I got now also, for the first time in my life, a TV and a daily newspaper. This again was a revelation. I could not believe the speed in which the frames changed on screen especially on news channels. To be able to read the bar, I had to wait for several pop ups, as they too quickly disappeared. There might be subliminal messages embedded, as well. Once on NewsX I discovered in the right lower corner for a fraction of a second a hand holding a pistol, shooting a bullet across the screen. I focused on the spot and after some 20 seconds it briefly popped up again. I tweeted about it and somebody else had also noticed it.

Compared to Indian news channels, the international ones are less speedy. Yet on one of those channels I detected once also a subliminal message. In the right lower corner of the screen "Quran" popped up and something underneath. Yet it kept disappearing so quickly that I could never make out what it was.

The crowded, flickering, speedy, innumerous Indian TV screens are surely not good for the brain. I wished a neurological study would be conducted and the effects of this constant bombardment of one's brain cells brought to light.

Apart from the form in which the news was presented, its content was also disturbing. In the months before the attack on the

Taj Hotel in Mumbai on 26th November 2008, there were insinuations that Hindus had committed acts of terror. The terms "Hindu terror" and "Saffron terror" were used with ease by politicians, who would not use the term Muslim or Islamic terror. Suddenly "Hindu terror" showed up in headlines and in debates on TV frequently. Hindus were implicated in bomb attacks in which Muslims had died, even though originally the trail had led to Muslims. Hemant Karkare, chief of the Anti Terror Squad (ATS) in Mumbai, was quoted in the Times of India that most of his time and energy went into investigating Hindu terror.

And then the unbelievable happened. I had come home from a bhajan session, when I switched on the TV and saw the attack on the Taj Hotel and other landmarks in Mumbai happening live. It stretched over three days and on the internet soon the first hints came that the attackers were Hindus. "They wear red wrist-bands" was said. "They speak Hindi, not Urdu", "They don't have a beard". And then the news broke that Hemant Karkare and two other top police officers had been killed by the terrorists. "Hindus eliminated Karkare because he was after them", was the reaction on the net.

I felt pained and suspected a conspiracy. Hindus would not attack a hotel or railway station or café and kill at random. I was sure about it. Yes, Hindus also killed, for example Udham Singh killed the Lt. Governor O'Dwyer, who had approved of General Dyer's action, to shoot at many thousand unarmed Hindus who were trapped in Jallianwalla Bagh during Baisakhi festival in 1919 in Amritsar. Udham Singh was one of those trapped who escaped wounded, but alive. Around one thousand people were not so lucky. They died.

Hindu Dharma allows killing cruel despots. But Hindu Dharma does not allow shooting at random at innocent people. It is plain and simple against Dharma, which means righteous behavior. And Dharma is the backbone of Hinduism. Yet now certain people wanted the world to believe that Hindus also, like Muslims, commit terror in the name of their faith. In fact, Rahul Gandhi, who was projected as the future Prime Minister, wanted the USA to believe that "*Hindu* extremists pose a greater threat to his country than

Muslim militants". These were his words to Timothy J. Roemer, the U.S. Ambassador to India in 2010, which came out in the open thanks to Wikileaks. Yet neither Rahul Gandhi nor media explained what purpose Hindu terror was supposed to serve. After all, Hinduism is not known for demanding a Hindu type of Khalifat.

Then something went wrong for those who tried to pass off the 26/11 Mumbai attack as Hindu terror. At a roadblock, the police constable Tukaram Ombole managed to fiercely hold on to the gun of one of the attackers—long enough for his colleagues to overpower him. While holding on, Ombole took several bullets into his body and died. Yet through his sacrifice, he did an immeasurable service to his motherland. Nobody had expected that a terrorist on a suicide mission could be captured alive. But now there was one alive. And he was a Pakistani Muslim, Ajmal Kasab.

So the terrorists were not Hindus, yet the talk about Hindu terror continued. In December 2010, incredibly, a book was released by Digvijaya Singh, a prominent Congress leader, titled '26/11—RSS ki Saajish (RSS conspiracy)?' Several Hindus had gone already to jail in 2009, including a woman ascetic, Sadhvi Pragya and an army man, Colonel Purohit. Not for the Mumbai attack, because this was now not possible with the Pakistani Kasab in custody and his links to Pakistan unraveling, but for the blasts in Malegaon and Samjhauta Express. In spite of the media playing along with the narrative that probably Hindus were behind those attacks, there were many indications that those accused were framed. In 2017, after eight long, torturous years in jail, an ill Sadhvi Pragya and Colonel Purohit got finally out on bail. The army gave the Colonel a hero's welcome. It showed that they never believed he was guilty. Though some charges were dropped, the case is still in court. Regarding another bomb blast in Hyderabad, only in April 2018 the Hindus accused were acquitted.

The accusations against Hindus in those years of the UPA government were unproven, yet unrelenting. Since the Congress traditionally depended on Muslim votes, there may have been a temptation to play to the gallery. The Indian Express reported that Digvijaya Singh, during the release of the book said to a cheering audience, "Hemant Karkare had come forth as a form of Ishwar

(God) for Muslims in this country… he saved a community from being defamed." And then went on to accuse the BJP ruled states as becoming bastions of majority (read Hindu) terrorism.

Only when Karkare's wife suspected him of playing politics with the death of her husband, did Singh acknowledge that in the case of the Mumbai attack, there was no doubt that Pakistani terrorists were behind it.

I wondered, why 'Hindu' could be freely associated with terror without evidence, yet 'Muslim' would be disassociated from terror even when there was evidence. "Terror has no religion" is worldwide the official formula when Muslims are the perpetrators. Was the invented Hindu terror an attempt to make Islam, Muslims or maybe Pakistan look better? But why is so much care taken to protect Muslims from possibly unfair accusation, at the cost of unfairly accusing Hindus? Nowadays, after terrorism has reached the West, many people anyway suspect that terror has something to do with Islam, never mind how strongly political leaders deny it. After all, the exhortation to do Jihad is clearly part of the Quran.

Hindus, however, were not only unfairly blamed for terror attacks. From 2012 onwards, there was a malicious, still on-going attempt to portray Hindus as having a rape culture and being the worst offenders when it comes to the treatment of women.

It started with the brutal rape and murder of a student in Delhi. She and her friend were encouraged to enter a bus which was plying off duty with six men on board. Once inside, her friend was beaten up and the girl gang raped. Then they were thrown on the road. Five of the six rapists had Hindu names. One name was withheld, as he was six months short of his 18th birthday. The young woman later died in hospital. Media named her Nirbhaya (fearless).

The outcry over this dastardly act was massive. People came out on the Delhi streets demanding death sentence for the rapists. International media not only highlighted the rape in a big way but also made unsubstantiated insinuations. The Washington Post proclaimed that sexual violence was endemic in India. The Reuters Trust Law group named India one of the worst countries in the world for women. A Harvard committee crafted strategies for 'adolescent education' to change the Indian mindset about gender. Suddenly, not so much the rapists, but India stood accused. The street protests should have made clear that Indians consider rape as completely against their culture. But the opposite happened. Hindu culture was held responsible, and many of those who wrote those articles had Hindu names.

When I was in Germany one year later, the local Nuremberg paper dedicated half a page to Nirbhaya on the anniversary of the rape. This surely was startling. About a week later, the Tagesschau informed its viewers about "another gang rape in India". Even my sister wondered how a gang rape in India made it to the most watched TV news bulletin in Germany, when local rapes (a girl had been raped and killed by throwing her into a lake at that time) were not reported. On any given day in a conservative estimate, over a thousand rapes are perpetrated worldwide. In the USA some 200, in South Africa some 170. With so much crime happening everywhere, why was India singled out and shamed with "another gang rape"? Was it again about saving the reputation of Muslims and in the process sullying that of Hindus?

I felt this was indeed the case. Some months before Nirbhaya was gang raped, the Rotherham grooming gang scandal had broken with thousands of young white girls as victims. Especially Pakistani men were in focus. Yet media called and still calls them 'Asian' gangs. Hindus are also Asians. Was there an attempt to blame the race and divert from religion? Was this the reason that media almost gleefully spread the news about Nirbhaya to every nook and corner of the globe?

How successful the relentless "rapes in India "campaign was, I realised, when I got a tweet in March 2015 that a biochemistry professor at the university in Leipzig, Dr. Beck-Sickinger, had refused admission to her course to an Indian student because of India's "rape problem". The tweeter asked me to contact the German embassy as this was outrageous. I could not believe it was true. Yet soon after, the email from the professor to the student was shared on twitter. It was true. And it even was not the only case.

The German ambassador Michael Steiner intervened promptly, maybe because only a month later Prime Minister Modi was to visit Germany. He strongly criticised the professor, called it an unfair judgment and wrote "Let's be clear. India is not a country of rapists."

Of course, India is not a country of rapists. In fact, India is way behind America, Europe or Africa when the number of rapes is put in relation to the population. This is precisely because the Hindu culture is still alive. And when nowadays far more crimes happen than in earlier times, it is because many Indians have discarded their culture—not only the 200 millions who converted to Islam and the 50 millions who converted to Christianity, but also many Hindus.

Contrary to what the world is made to believe, the ancient Indian culture treats women well. This will be obvious to anyone who cares to find out what the Vedas say about women. Feminists may not agree, because Indian culture stresses more on duty and not so much on rights; more on what one can give and not so much on what one can take. This approach is the healthier one and ultimately leads to more contentment—paradoxically. Maybe we in the West should give it a try.

Strangely, it is also the approach which is dismissed as out of sync with modern times. It requires a husband to see, apart from his wife, other women as sisters, or for a wife to see, apart from her husband, other men as brothers. Is rape possible in such an atmosphere? Is free sex possible? Yet free sex is being propagated as 'modern' in India, while in the West many realise its shallowness and pledge to remain celibate till marriage.

If worldwide rape statistics mentioned the religion of the rapists, in all likelihood Hindus would be at the bottom of the list and Muslims on top. Why? Not because Muslims are bad and Hindus are good, but because the values which guide their lives are different. The Quran allows taking advantage of non-Muslim girls and Mohammed himself showed the way. Is it then a surprise when especially devout Muslims have no feeling of guilt or regret? Incidentally, the juvenile, who was the most brutal and responsible for Nirbhaya's death, was a Muslim. He is meanwhile free after three years in a detention home amid concerns that he has been 'radicalised'. The other rapists of Nirbhaya are on death row in jail, except one who is already dead. He either committed suicide or, more likely, was murdered by other inmates.

In April 2018, a supposed rape (rape was not confirmed by autopsy) and murder of an 8 year old Muslim girl again went viral. Typically, the eight accused were all Hindus. They claimed they were framed, demanded a narco test and an enquiry by a central agency. Their families sat on hunger strike demanding a fair probe. Yet umpteen media channels projected the demand for a fair probe as "shielding the rapists". The TV anchors were shrill and unreasonable, and protests on the streets demanded the death penalty for the rapists. As a result, the government promulgated an ordinance which provides now minimum 20 years and maximum death for rapes of children under 12.

If it turns out that the accused were not guilty, which may well be the case, the world won't come to know of it. The intended damage to the image of India has been done, like it happened in the case of a gang rape of a nun in West Bengal. World media and the Church immediately accused 'Hindu fundamentalists'. When it turned out that the culprits were Muslims from Bangladesh, media fell silent. The world media is overly interested in negative stories about India, especially about rape, but only if the culprits are Hindus or if they can omit the name, like in the case of the juvenile. And the Indian media obliges and provides them every day 'with another rape', even before any enquiry started.

Ever since 2013, when the definition of rape was expanded by law, false allegations skyrocketed. One reason may be that the law is clearly in favour of women, and allegation of rape is worldwide used as a means to discredit or blackmail somebody. Even the courts and BBC acknowledged that India has a problem with fake rape cases. The ordeal for the falsely accused is long and damaging to their standing in society.

There were insane stories, too, and they show how far distrust has already grown between men and women due to the relentless, unfair media campaign on 'predatory Indian males'. For example, two young women claimed that during Holi festival in March 2018, when balloons with coloured water are thrown, a balloon filled with semen was thrown at them. Incredibly, media took it up. The lab test showed it was coloured water.

After the massive influx of Muslim migrants into Western Europe, the natives there suspect meanwhile that the huge increase in rapes has something to do with the mind-set which Islam produces. Strangely, media and politicians call such suspicion Islamophobia, instead of analysing the religious texts and the resulting mind-set. They prefer to stick to the narrative that "Muslims have grievances and need our sympathy". This doesn't hold water, as Hindus have even more grievances. While the West indeed rode roughshod over Muslim countries, yet over India, not only Western colonial powers but also Muslim invaders rode roughshod. Millions of Hindus were killed by Muslim invaders. Yet Western academia in spite of their fancifully named studies (subaltern, postmodern, postcolonial, etc.), ignore that Indians greatly suffered at the hands of both the West and Muslims. Instead, they keep hitting out at Hindus, accusing them unfairly of terror and rape-culture. Yet the stick, they mostly use to beat Hindus and especially Brahmins with, is the caste system.

CHAPTER 43

Caste system—stick to beat India with

If there is one thing the whole world knows about India, it is this: 'India has an inhuman, oppressive caste-system which is an essential part of Hinduism'. How this questionable notion spread so far and wide is a mystery. I also knew about it already in primary school in the early 1960s in Germany. We children were shown pictures of poor, wretched untouchables, and the term "Unberührbare" left a deep impression on my mind.

At that time I knew nothing about what had happened in the concentration camp Dachau not far from my native place. I didn't know that Germans had murdered millions of Jews and gypsies only 15 years earlier. But I knew that in India, the highest caste, Brahmins, snubbed many of their countrymen by not even touching them. It looked like the worst possible human behaviour. Of course it was not the worst possible human behaviour. So why was it made to look like this?

Indian leftists even with Brahmin names may come down heavily on me, a foreigner, for not knowing anything about the ground realities of Dalits (oppressed), as members of the lowest section of Indian society are called nowadays. The atmosphere is vitiated with fanatical anti-Brahmanism in academia all over the world. Yet from my outsider position, I would like to share some observations.

Yes, the caste system exists. Right in the beginning in Anandamayi Ma's ashram in 1980, I was confronted with it. Orthodox Bengali Brahmins were running it and Melita, the German journalist, who lived there for years, briefed me that we foreigners are outcastes and have to sit separately for food and must not go near the kitchen. I could also sense that some ladies were careful that their sari didn't accidentally brush my cloth while passing. I took it as a mild reciprocation for what the British had done only a few decades earlier. There had been boards at clubs or parks which read, "Dogs and Indians not allowed". How would Indians have felt in their own country? Especially when those British officials were uncouth adventurers who plundered Indian riches? Moreover, the exclusion from clubs was only a minor issue, compared to what else the British did.

I also didn't mind not being allowed into Jagannath Mandir in Puri; I rather felt it was a good thing not to allow tourists with no understanding of the indigenous culture into spaces which were sacred. And compared to Germans, Indians are surely flexible regarding rules. I went to see the Shankaracharya of Puri, one of the pillars, who uphold the purity of Hindu Dharma. He gave me time, showed me even how to do japa and then asked whether I have been to Jagannath Mandir. I was puzzled, "Well, of course not." Then he said something, which now, after almost 40 years, sounds unbelievable, but I couldn't have made it up. He said, "You know when a woman is newly married, she pulls the end of her sari fully over her face and nobody will ask her to lift it. You could do this".

I didn't do it. Yet over the years, I went into a few shrines where there was a board "only for Hindus" without being stopped.

I wonder why there is such bigoted condemnation worldwide of the structure of Indian society, as if other societies are equal, and why Hinduism is blamed for it. Are people not aware how much affirmative action India has done right since Independence in favour of Dalits? Are people not aware, that insulting a Dalit results in immediate arrest? Are people not aware that India presently has a president, had a chief justice, a chief minister, who all came from the Dalit community? Don't people know that jobs in government and seats in educational institutions are reserved for them? Dalit students even need much fewer marks to get admission. It has reached a point where it has become reverse discrimination.

Naturally, this creates resentment among the upper castes which are often poorer. The son of our watchman, belonging to the Kshatriya caste, won't get any concession, whereas his friend will get. For example to pass the prestigious JEE entrance test for the top engineering colleges, he needs 90 marks and his friend only 35. Both boys were doing well in school. His mother told me once that if she had a chance to meet Prime Minister Modi, she would like to tell him: "Please stop this inequality".

Yet so far no government dared to tinker with the concessions to the lower castes even though the Constitution had envisioned them only for the initial ten years. That means that even the daughter of a former president is entitled to preferential treatment. The result is that some upper castes agitate on the streets to be categorised as lower castes. Where else does it happen that people want to be downgraded socially? Especially in Tamil Nadu, Brahmins are badly discriminated against and many emigrate for education and jobs. Silicon Valley is the beneficiary.

Every society has a structure. Every society has people on top and people at the bottom. Equality is not possible in this world. Communism promised it and failed miserably. Different jobs, including cleaning the sewers, need to be done. But discrimination against certain occupations needs to go. No job must be seen as lowly. Yet is there one country where people have reached the state of a yogi who sees all with an equal eye, whether it is a beggar or a king, whether it is a stone or a diamond? In all likelihood the most ideal society was the ancient Indian society where the ideal of a yogi was alive, and where the knowledge that our life is only one of many, puts one's position into a broader and more relaxed perspective.

The Vedas do not mention caste. The Rig Veda, the oldest text in the world, talks of four varnas which depend on the inclination and work of a person. It compares the different Varnas to parts of a human body. The head stands for the thinkers and teachers (Brahmins), the arms for the army and administration (Kshatriyas), the thighs for the traders and farmers (Vaisyas), and the feet for those who serve (Shudras). Isn't it a beautiful analogy? The head may get more respect, but will the feet be abused? Each part has its own value and all are necessary for society. In India, to show respect to a person, one touches his or her feet.

It was the British, who introduced the term caste, taken from the Portuguese 'casta' (class, race), and fixed the castes in their Census from 1871 onwards. Indians, who did not know their caste, were allotted one by the census officer. Shockingly, the British even declared several tribes as 'criminal by birth', and thereby made sure that millions of people were ostracised. Yet did you ever hear any outrage on this? Further, in the 1901 census, over 2000 castes denoting different occupations were added, and put into a hierarchical order. Sure the British knew how to divide and control a society.

Politically aware Indians realised their devious strategy and prior to the 1931 Census, leaflets were distributed by Arya Samaj, asking people to write 'NIL' into the rubric of 'caste'. And yet, the British brazenly accuse Indians not only for their 'inhuman caste-system', but made it the defining feature of their religious tradition. Isn't it duplicitous?

I have the suspicion that the British and especially the missionaries attacked and still attack the caste system so ferociously, because they did not find much else to attack India and Hinduism with. Yes, Indian kings fought wars to expand their territory, but they stuck to rules of fair warfare. They did not brutalise the civilians, did not rape their women, did not destroy temples, did not force conversion.

Their fairness proved to be a great disadvantage when the Muslims invaded India. Prithviraj Chauhan would have never imagined that other kings could be so devious. He defeated Muhammad Ghori several times around 1200 AD, but when Ghori pleaded for it, always showed mercy, and let him go. Yet Ghori kept coming back and when he finally defeated Prithviraj, he showed no mercy, tortured him and blinded him with red-hot iron. The Islamic invaders were brutal. They killed millions of Hindus for being Hindus and did not follow any rules of war. Even today, a Muslim nation like Pakistan does not follow rules of fairplay. Several Indian soldiers who had fallen into Pakistani hands were pitilessly tortured before being killed.

Strangely, such atrocities are not blamed on Islam even though the Quran declares infidels as the 'worst of all creatures' (Q 98.6) for whom eternal hellfire is destined. When believers are encouraged "to smite the neck and cut all the fingertips" (Q 8.12) of the unbelievers, do such verses not serve as incitement and justification for torture and killings?

Christians have done similar atrocities in the name of their faith. The Inquisition of course comes to mind which was most brutal also in Goa; or the conquest of South America, where the Pope had ordered the Spanish invaders to convert the natives. When in 1520 thousands of Aztecs celebrated a festival for their god with song and dance in front of their temple, the Spanish under Governor Alvarado closed all exists and brutally massacred almost everybody of the unarmed men, women and children, similar to what the British did in Jallanwalia Bagh in 1919, only that the Spaniards didn't use guns. They slaughtered with knifes, daggers and swords.

Indians never did anything of this sort. Yet the Churches, media and NGOs call Hinduism violent and vitiate the atmosphere with an inexplicable hatred for Brahmins. A friend, who has intimate insights into the evangelical scene in America, said that the discourse in those circles is frightfully anti-Brahmin. She even felt that if there were genocide of Brahmins today, the West wouldn't react, as people there are already brainwashed enough to see Brahmins as devious and despicable.

Have those people never met any Brahmin?

What she said, however, explained a question on Quora internet forum to which I had replied. The question was, "Do Brahmins feel guilty for what they have done and are doing to India?" I was puzzled and started my reply with "Why should Brahmins feel guilty? They should feel proud. It is because of them that India and the world still have at least a part of this most precious wisdom that is contained in the Vedas, because they painstakingly memorised them and passed them on over many thousands of years." My post got many comments and they showed how much Brahmin youth suffer. Many have internalised this guilt.

Memorising and preserving Vedic wisdom in their brains and not only in writing was a great service, because when the centres of learning were set ablaze by Muslim invaders, a lot of knowledge was still alive in many Brahmins as they couldn't kill them all. This knowledge is precious. Yet missionaries and mullahs see it as dangerous.

Imagine the plight of the Church: After the Vedas reached the West in the 18th century, the intellectual elite there was greatly impressed. Right from Voltaire to Einstein to Steve Jobs, many great minds were inspired by Vedic wisdom. To keep her flock under control, the Church needed to make sure that this knowledge didn't spread and more important, was made to look primitive.

How to go about it? The name 'Hinduism' was given to India's religious tradition whose main feature, so was decreed, was an 'inhuman caste system' and 'idol worship'. The Church was successful in changing the perception of the Indian tradition. I asked recently three German girls in Rishikesh what they associate with Hinduism. Promptly they replied "caste system", and after a while "many gods". The Vedas or even yoga didn't cross their mind.

Back to Brahmins. Being the head of the body, they had the greatest responsibility and had many rules to follow. Brahmins were supposed to live on donation and not hoard any wealth. They had to live pure, devoted lives. And they had to be exceptionally careful regarding food. Food is enormously important not only for our body, but even more for our mind. The West has forgotten this truth. Brahmins, who had to preserve the purity of the Vedas, were required not to eat stale food, and of course no meat. They also could not eat with somebody who ate meat. Can such persons be wily, devious and mean to others? Yet they were accused: 'What despicable behaviour! They refuse to eat with others!'

There is no doubt that Dalits were often badly treated by castes above them, though least likely by Brahmins. But the point is—the discrimination is not part of Hinduism. The British had institutionalised the hierarchy among castes in order to divide the society.

New generations should not be held responsible for the sins of their ancestors, is the general rule. Yet this rule is not applied to Hindus. Moreover, many of those sins may be exaggerated, because the picture is far more complex than what is presented by vested interests.

Recently for example the newspaper carried an item that a Brahmin youth was killed allegedly by the family of a Dalit girl for marrying her. In another instance, a Dalit school teacher rammed a wooden stick down the throat of an 11 year old boy because he couldn't answer a math question. His food and wind pipe got severely damaged. Even among the 'self-styled godmen' as media likes to call gurus with a huge following, immeasurable wealth and often shady if not criminal behaviour are Dalits.

Yet such news will not reach an international audience.

Once, in Pondicherry near the sea, an old man hesitantly approached me. He pulled from under his shirt the Brahmin thread and then stretched out his hand for begging. If I had been a normal tourist, I wouldn't have known what he wanted to convey by pulling out the thread.

There were many Rajas (kings) from among the Shudras and many Shudras were far richer than Brahmins. It was again the British who pushed many professional groups, like weavers or Ayurveda doctors, into abject poverty due to colonial policies and exorbitant tax rates of up to 85 per cent. Yet times are changing. I asked recently the owner of an Ayurveda Resort to which caste he belongs. "Shudra" he replied.

It is truly unfortunate that English education brainwashed Indians that Hindu tradition deserves contempt. It can be safely assumed that the British purposely made wrong translations, apart from genuine mistakes, and inserted false passages into the ancient texts to make Hindus feel ashamed of their tradition. For example you may come across the claim that in ancient times the Brahmins ate meat and even cow. Yet there are so many passages in the ancient texts which make it highly unlikely that this could have been the case.

Another dubious claim is that Manusmriti mandated molten lead to be poured into the ears of a Shudra who listened to the Vedas. This claim has been thrown at me umpteen times to make me realise how violent the texts are which I defend. I am sure this claim is interpolated and not genuine. Can I prove it? No, I can't. But neither can the other side prove their point. Is there any documented incident that this has happened? If there was, it would have been broadcasted all over. This claim fits too well into the agenda of trying to demean Indian tradition and portray it as violent.

Still, even today true Brahmins exist and they are like a thorn in the flesh of those who want to weaken India. Vedic wisdom makes people internally strong, because they know that Brahman is within them. And it makes them kind to others, including to animals and nature, because they know that Brahman is in everyone and everything. It makes them self-sufficient, because they know that true happiness needs to be discovered within. Followers of Vedic wisdom don't need enemies to define themselves. They pray for the welfare of all. And this wisdom has the potential to challenge blind belief, because it shows the way to directly experiencing the truth of oneself.

Isn't it about time to realise that Vedic wisdom is beneficial for all of us and stop this unfair Brahmin bashing? Isn't it about time to stop portraying them as villains when they are not? The outrage by Western and also Indian academia and media about Brahmins and the caste system is so fake, especially when seen in comparison how media report about the atrocities of Islamic terror and how much care they take to dissociate those atrocities from Islam. Yet Hinduism is a free for all.

It is a pity that many Indians nowadays debunk their traditional varna system due to the constant criticism. Discrimination is bad. It needs to be overcome—worldwide. Yet belonging to a bigger group has advantages. In recent years, there are voices even among foreign correspondents, who find advantages in the caste system. Highly skilled craftsmen in many different fields for example owe their skills to a tradition that goes back for generations.

Further, members of the same caste feel a certain familiarity towards each other. If someone moves from his village to a city, he finds support from among his own caste. Compared to those huge caste families, we in the West are lonely. We hardly know our cousins. If we need support we depend on a cold construct—the state. Hopefully Indian society does not become as lonesome and individualised as Western societies. Attempts to break it are surely on.

CHAPTER 44

Baba Ramdev—a Yogic powerhouse

I wonder who spread this rumour that yogis take no interest in the affairs of the world. In 2001, when the airplanes were crashed into the World Trade Center, I happened to be in Gangotri. We came to know of it rather late, but once the news had spread, groups of sadhus gathered around transistor radios, intently listening and discussing whether the USA will invade Afghanistan or not.

Yet the best example of a yogi not only taking interest, but shaping India and maybe the world is Baba Ramdev.

I heard about him at the end of 2005 thanks to a controversy. Ramdev was accused by a woman politician of the Communist Party that his Ayurvedic medicine contained human bones. Media made much of it, yet the laboratory tests did not confirm it. While I searched on the net I noticed that a huge number of people had reacted to the news and the majority took the side of Baba Ramdev. People assumed that the Pharma industry was after him, as he was harming their business.

Obviously, he was already well known and I wondered how I had missed out on him. I wanted to add at least a few paragraphs about him in my German book, which was about to go into print, and visited his Centre for Yoga and Ayurveda, some 15 km outside of Haridwar. It was still under construction and I was stunned by the sheer size of the site. I wondered who would come to this rather unattractive, flat place on both sides of the Haridwar-Roorkee road and fill these huge buildings—a yoga hall of 25.000 square meters, thousand apartments for guests, conference halls, cafeterias, a university, a hospital and several apartment blocks for permanent residents. I was amazed at his courage. Ramdev obviously did not just think big, he thought vast.

Five years later, in January 2011, I was there again to attend an international yoga conference that was organized by Patanjali University. The transformation of the construction site was unbelievable. Two thousand delegates had arrived. We were accommodated in luxurious apartments, fitted with flat screen TV and AC. Patanjali Yogpeeth, named after the compiler of the Yoga Sutras, was now the biggest Centre for Yoga and Ayurveda worldwide. Not only this. Ramdev forayed also into big business and his Patanjali brand of natural foods and cosmetics produced in state-of-art food parks is meanwhile one of the top MNC in India and forced Unilever, Nestle and others to adjust their policies.

"Enjoying inner peace does not mean you sit around doing nothing. Be fearless. Whenever a good thought enters your mind, follow it immediately," Ramdev apparently summed up his own approach at the conference.

During my first visit in early 2006, the building of the hospital was completed, but still empty. In a corner of the entrance hall, forms were lying on a window sill and some villagers were filling them in. Those were applications for membership at Bharat Swabhiman, which means self-respect for India. A nominal fee and some vows were demanded: the person had to promise to practice yoga, not to smoke, not to drink alcohol and to be vegetarian.

I felt it was a good thing to encourage Indians to value and follow their tradition. However, I doubted whether Bharat Swabhiman could become a worthwhile movement, when here in a corner some forms were lying around. I had gravely underestimated Baba Ramdev—his passion to work, his talent to organize, his energy and his effectiveness in making a vision reality— and probably also his direct connection to Bhagawan. In only five years, Bharat Swabhiman became a national movement that instilled fear in the government. When in June 2011 Baba Ramdev asked to support his fast against corruption with a missed call, over 11 million Indians responded.

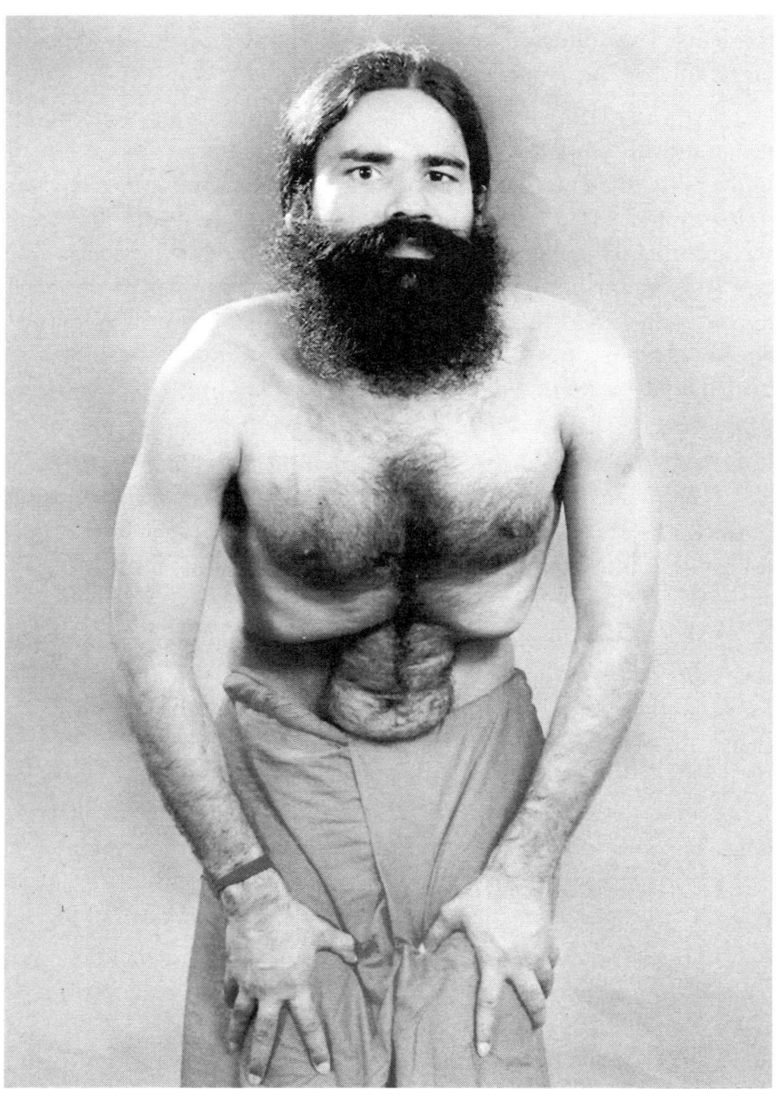

Baba Ramdev, the accomplished yogi.

Ramdev came from a simple farmer family. He went to a government school for eight years and then studied in one of the traditional Sanskrit gurukuls.

In the mid-1990s, he taught yoga in Haridwar to small groups, and produced together with Acharya Balkrishna, a friend from his studies, Ayurvedic medicine on a tiny scale. Yet from 2003 onwards, when he started to demonstrate and explain yoga and pranayama on Astha TV, his fame shot up exponentially and he gained plenty of admirers. And detractors. He was heavily criticized by the medical fraternity for his claim that yoga can cure 99 percent of all diseases. Yet he spoke with certain authority, because he had experimented and had healed himself from a partial paralysis which had affected his face.

"Everyone should practice yog—in India and in the whole world," he stated his goal and explained why. "Yog makes you healthy, happy, peaceful, enthusiastic and prosperous and also leads to Self-realisation. Yog is not only asanas and pranayama. It is a complete lifestyle and a complete philosophy. Shri Krishna exhorted Arjuna to be a yogi thousands of years ago. Yog means joining—joining with the real Self, joining the whole world. Everything is inside you. The whole universe is inside you. God is inside you", he explained.

Baba Ramdev has given a tremendous boost to yoga in India. Even his critics won't deny this. He is the proverbial yogi, fully in control of his body and mind. Early morning, at 5 degree Celsius, he was teaching yoga in the imposing, huge Yog Bhavan to the delegates with only a cotton cloth wrapped around his hips, while I was packed in several layers of woolens and still felt cold.

"Whatever I have achieved has been given to me by pranayama", he claimed. "Partially, I have been able to attain that extraordinary power and that extraordinary knowledge that is within each one of us. I have felt what is eternal and real. Sages before me, too, have felt it. And I don't say this to praise myself, but to give you an example and inspiration."

Yet Baba Ramdev taught not only yoga and a dharmic, healthy way of life, he also thundered on TV against multinationals, which drained India's wealth and ruined the health of Indians with medicines, pesticides and fertilizers, and with junk food, which had flooded the Indian market after the opening of the economy in the 1990s. He propagated Ayurveda, claimed that Coca Cola is useful as toilet cleaner, but unfit for drinking, and explained to farmers how they can make enough fertilizer and pesticide for two hectares of land with the dung and urine of only one cow.

In 2009, after a number of scams of unprecedented magnitude by the government had come to light and also information about mountains of black money hidden abroad by the political elite, Baba Ramdev became even more forceful. He travelled now all over the country, and informed the villagers about the benefits of yoga on one hand and about the brazen corruption and the loot of natural resources on the other. "If your mother is robbed, will you sit quiet?" he asked. "How can I watch when Bharat Mata (Mother India) is looted?

The mainstream media ignored him, yet his yoga sessions around the country were aired daily for 3 hours in the morning and his talks for 2 hours at night on a spiritual TV channel. My Hindi improved a lot because I keenly followed his talks. Wherever he went he spoke to mammoth gatherings. He had clearly the gift to inspire and motivate his listeners, passionate, full of energy, connected to his roots and with a lot of humour. He enlivened his talks with spiritual and patriotic songs and aroused his audience against the corrupt government of the day. No surprise that within a short time, he became the government's enemy and the hope of the poor.

On 4th of June 2011 he started his fast against corruption on Ramlila Maidan, a vast open ground in Delhi. It was well organized: a huge tent of 30,000 square metres was put up, 1000 toilets and 7000 taps with drinking water were installed and in spite of the tremendous heat of over 40 degrees Celsius, the ground was packed with over 100,000 people. Some 30,000 people had committed themselves to fast together with Swami Ramdev for an indefinite period. They spent with him the night in the tent.

Next morning, I switched on Astha TV and could not believe what had happened: in the middle of the night, 5000 riot police with helmets, lathis and teargas had stormed into the tent where some 30,000 fasting people were sleeping. TV cameras were still there and started rolling. Teargas shells were shot, the canvas caught fire at some places, and those who tried to extinguish the fire were beaten by the police. Swami Ramdev jumped from the high stage, was hosted onto the shoulders of one of his followers, appealed to the police to spare at least the women and children and then disappeared in the chaos.

On June 5th, he reappeared. He had been arrested when he tried to escape early in the morning, wearing a white salwar kameez. He was flown to Haridwar and not allowed to enter Delhi for 15 days.

The whole of India was shocked over the police action. It was compared to the brutal methods of the colonial rulers. 79 persons were injured. A 51-year old woman, Rajbala, died from her injuries. Thousands were stranded in the night in an unknown city, their bags and sandals lying in the tent. Others wandered from one hospital to the other to find their relatives. The Supreme Court demanded from the government an explanation for the action against peaceful, fasting citizens.

Media ridiculed Ramdev for trying to escape in women's clothing. Yet he felt that the ruling dispensation wanted him to get killed during the police action, and his feeling may not have been wrong. He was definitely a headache for the corrupt government which now went after him with over 100 notices from its institutions to harass him. He vowed to fight against corruption till his last breath and also vowed to get rid of the Congress led government and save the country. 'Congress hatao, desh bachao' was the slogan. He pitched strongly for Narendra Modi, who was at that time the chief minister of Gujarat, to become prime minister in the 2014 election.

Narendra Modi did become prime minister—in spite of a massive worldwide media campaign to prevent this from happening. It reached even my mother, 95 at that time, and she also fell for it. When I told her that Narendra Modi will be good for India, she objected, "But media must know why they portray him so negatively. They would not do it without reason." She was right, they did it for a reason, but the reason was not honorable. They didn't want India to come up.

Narendra Modi's party, the BJP, even won an absolute majority in Parliament. The Congress party was almost wiped out with only 44 seats in the 543-member parliament. There is no doubt that Baba Ramdev played a major role in this rout.

He is no doubt an organizer par excellence and his Bharat Swabhiman reaches down to the village level. Everywhere he motivated especially the young to do yog, live a dharmic life, use only Indian products and dedicate some of their time to Mother India. He trained them in Patanjali Yogpeeth and they came in big numbers, easily filling the huge Yog Bhavan.

Ramdev has set now his sight on 2050. By that time he wants India to be again an economic and spiritual super power and he is actively working towards it in many areas—from Vedic plus modern education to protection of indigenous breeds of cows. "In some 20 years Patanjali will produce everything, from a pen to a car" he even promised recently on TV. Already now his range of products is impressive. His company 'Patanjali' had in 2017 a net worth of 6,4 billion dollar and his associate Acharya Balkrishna (Swami Ramdev as a sanyasi doesn't own anything) is on the Forbes list of the rich. However, profit will be fully used for charity, they declared.

"English education has spoilt our character", Ramdev claims and he has a point. He is surely not worse, rather much better off, for having missed out on English education. "We must strengthen our character, only then we can strengthen the country and make it free from corruption, poverty and illness", he tells the youth. And in case they consider the task too difficult, he fires them up, "we are the offspring of the Rishis. Ram and Krishna were our forefathers, never mind whether today we are Hindus, Muslims or Christians. Our history goes back millions of years. Our country was the cradle of civilization. For us the whole world is one family", he said, and continued "Never think that you alone can't do much. Bhagawan is in you and his limitless power and intelligence. Connect with him through yoga. A single yogi can do superhuman things. —How much then 1000 yogis can do?

I truly admired Baba Ramdev, but there was one point, I felt a little uneasy. Like Hindus generally, he also would refer good-naturedly to all religions as brothers and on the same beneficial level as Hindu Dharma. However, from my Christian background, I know that this is not the case. Christianity and Islam do not see Hinduism as equal. On the contrary, they consider Hinduism with its many gods even offensive to their respective god, as it violates their most important commandment "Thou shalt not have any other god beside me."

So when I had a chance to meet Baba Ramdev in person, I wanted to bring up this issue. I came much too late for the appointment, as I had not seen the message that there was a change in the timing, yet he had waited for me, was very kind and seemed like an old friend, natural, calmness personified, even though he has so much on his hands.

Afterwards I however regretted one thing: I had talked more than he had. I was eager to put my concern across, yet may not have

Baba Ramdev poses with me for a photo after our meeting where I unfortunately talked more than he did.

done it successfully. My Hindi was far from perfect. Also, it felt a bit bad to endeavor to make his generous, trusting attitude less generous and less trusting. On the other hand, I am an insider of Christianity and know that missionaries have a mischievous agenda which of course they don't tell into the face of others. Islam, too, has the agenda to bring the whole humanity under Islam. In fact, missionaries don't see conversion even by devious means as a mischievous agenda but as a divine command. They claim they save Hindus from eternal hellfire, which would be, according to both the religions, their destination if they remain Hindus. It is a tricky situation, because against strong, blind belief, reason has little chance. But we need to try making them see sense and discover and experience truth. Truth is not in a book. It is that what is.

Baba Ramdev had listened attentively.

CHAPTER 45

The world is in need of Indian wisdom

Meanwhile my stopover in India lasts over 38 years. I still have not been in Australia and have no intention to go. I never thought I would live my life in India, yet I am so glad, it happened; glad and grateful, especially for becoming familiar with India's wisdom. I couldn't imagine how I would live my life without being familiar with it, and wondered why we in the West don't hear about this profound philosophy.

I love India and while still in Germany, I wouldn't have guessed that one could love a *country* so much.

Maybe this is the reason why I feel so incensed when India is under attack. It touches me personally. My sense of fairness is violated. And India and Hinduism are often under heavy attack. The best option for humanity, which is Hindu Dharma, is made to look as if it is the worst. I realised it only after I started following the news. I didn't understand why it was happening. All the big media outlets seemed to go after India.

I also didn't understand why Hindus went on the defensive instead of exposing those who maligned their tradition. The reason may be that the majority of Hindus has little knowledge and never deeply reflected on Vedic wisdom and therefore is not sure whether those, who attack, have a point.

So far, I had written mainly spiritual articles, but from 2009 onwards I wrote more forcefully and from 2013 onwards, my articles got a wider circulation thanks to a surprise gift from a reader of Life Positive. He had made a blog for me. I only had to change the password and could start posting write-ups which mainstream media did not take. I posted on different topics, but many of my articles dealt now with religion and the comparison between them. I wanted to counter the rampant misinformation regarding Hinduism.

In the Germany of the 1970s, religion seemed on its way out. People went for a picnic instead of Sunday mass. The unfortunate aspect of this development was that many people threw out not only Christianity, but also any belief in a higher power. People (wrongly) felt that life has no meaning other than to be enjoyed as long as it lasts. Yet Western societies are not happy—because of this focus on mere enjoyment. They lack wisdom.

I never expected that some 40 years later, religion would again be centre stage even in the West. Yet now it was not Christianity, but Islam, due to Islamic terrorism. India of course was since long familiar with terror committed in the name of Islam. Yet after 9/11, terrorism ('Islamic' is usually dropped) became a big problem worldwide.

But something strange happened. In the 1970s one could freely criticise religions and blame them, together with communism, fascism and Nazism, for the greatest genocides on earth. But now, 40 years later, Islam was out of bounds for criticism not only in the Muslim countries with blasphemy laws, but surprisingly also in the liberal West. To criticise Islam was labelled as Islamophobic or racist and meanwhile can even land one in jail for insulting a community, never mind that Islam is not a community.

A huge propaganda machine seemed to be involved in fiercely projecting Islam as a religion of peace. 'The terrorists are misguided youth. Islam is a religion of peace,' was regularly stated by whoever stood in front of a TV cameras after yet another attack. President Obama also stated it. And I wondered if the massive opposition, which Donald Trump faced, had something to do with his sceptical view of this enforced political correctness.

Strangely, nobody asks who or what misguides these youth who killed and maimed at random numerous people, though this question can easily be answered. "Fighting is prescribed for you though you may dislike it…." says Quran 2.216. It is obvious from history as well as from many verses in the Islamic texts that a good Muslim has the duty to spread Islam, till it dominates over all other faiths. When every human being is Muslim, then maybe it could become a religion of peace. But even then, a peaceful life on earth is not the goal—the real goal is paradise.

In spite of the incredible and inexplicable support for Islam by leftist media, politicians and academics, common people meanwhile suspect a link between terror attacks and Islam. Why? Because then the motive at least is clear.

Why does hardly anyone point to the violent passages in the Quran and the Hadith? Talk shows debate on terror, and not once Quran or Hadith is mentioned. On a German talk show, an Ex-Muslim who was about to give examples from the Quran, was obstructed even by the anchor. He stood his ground, said, he would leave if not allowed to bring facts to the table. These facts are all available on the internet. Hiding them won't work. If some Muslim youth or a convert reads them and takes them seriously, he becomes 'radicalised' and then we condemn him as misguided and a monster.

Don't we have a responsibility for those youth who wrongly believe that Allah will give them paradise if they kill infidels, because he likes only Muslims? Forget about these youth troubling non-Muslims, even Muslims suffer under those who follow the texts literally. And, of course, there won't be paradise waiting for them. They will come back in another body and reap their karma—'every action has an equal and opposite reaction' is valid for them, too.

How can we stop this madness of killing in the name of Allah?

Christian leaders are in a weak position, as till some 250 years ago, Christians, too, killed in the name of their god. Christianity, too, like Islam, demands that the doctrine is followed over one's conscience if the two are in conflict. Maybe that is the reason why the West is so confused and tries to absolve religion from terror.

Or could there be another reason? One day a thought struck me while I was watching the massive immigration influx of Muslim youth into Germany. Is it possible that there is an attempt to host Islam on the populace, as Islam and sharia are capable of enforcing submission with ease or rather with threats and blasphemy laws, whereas Christianity has lost its power to subdue people? The Holy Roman Empire had established a profitable collaboration between the king and the Pope. A German saying goes: the king made the common people poor and the Pope made them stupid. Is a future Caliphate meant to keep people poor and stupid?

Whether it is confusion or a mischievous agenda, India has a great responsibility to prevent another dark age for humanity. India was in ancient times the guru of the world. She needs to carry this mantle again. Indian wisdom needs to spread because the world is in need of it.

There is only one problem: Islamic clergy are adamant that Islam alone is the true path because Allah, the Supreme Being, has personally dictated it. Therefore all humans need to follow this path. Criticism is not allowed because this would amount to criticising the Supreme Himself.

However, there is a flaw in this argument and it is the duty of Hindus to expose it. The flaw is that neither the so-called revelation of Islam, nor that of Christianity, is original, nor do these revelations stand the test of reason or common sense.

The most ancient, original revelation regarding the ultimate truth, are the Vedas. The Rishis did not create the Vedas. Thanks to their tapas (austerities) they 'saw' them in cosmic consciousness through the veil of thoughts that hides the truth from ordinary eyes.

The Vedas are about the eternally valid, universal laws, about Dharma, and they are also a goldmine of knowledge in all fields. This knowledge has never been proven wrong. On the contrary, it has inspired even quantum physics. It is thanks to the Vedas that

India has contributed maximum to human civilisation over the millennia. Unfortunately, even this fact of India's immense contribution is not common knowledge, because for Westerners, the world ends in Greece and nobody tells them that even the Greek were greatly influenced by India with many of them, including Pythagoras, visiting there.

The Vedas declared the existence of one, great Brahman that is the cause for this universe ages before the Abrahamic religions were founded. Judaism took over the concept of one great God, and Christianity and Islam, too, yet they got something wrong:

These religions made the all-pervading absolute Truth into a separate, male, all-powerful entity with strong likes and dislikes and declared that entity as the 'one true god'. These religions don't realise that they dropped the absolute oneness level, and are left only with the relative, duality level. So the highest god of those religions is more in tune with the 'gods' of Hinduism whom they so despise. Yet with one significant difference: Hindu Dharma declares that Shiva, Devi, Ganesh and others are ultimately only Brahman—pure, infinite consciousness. Everything, including us, is one with Brahman, the absolute truth. This knowledge is lacking in the Abrahamic religions.

This lack alone would not matter much, as mystics could retrieve this knowledge through an intense inner search for truth. But unfortunately, the Christian Church invented a highly effective strategy for world dominion: it declared that the one, separate god wants all to believe only what the Church says, and those who don't believe will be thrown into hell. A few hundred years later, Islam copied this strategy and declared that the one, separate Allah wants all to believe only what Prophet Mohamed said, and those who don't believe will suffer in hellfire if not already on earth.

Those claims "THIS alone is the full truth, believe it or be damned" are the basis for divisiveness and hatred, which has caused so much bloodshed over many centuries. Those claims make those, who want to be good Christians and good Muslims, into very unpleasant human beings. Any religion where human beings are better when they don't follow it and worse when they follow it to the letter needs to be scrutinized. Such religion does great harm to any society, whether in India or Europe. Those unfounded claims need to be given up, as they made the faithful go wild, destroy temples and kill those who did not convert. The list of atrocities is long. ISIS is only one recent example.

If truth is to win, we need to be truthful. We must not shy away from exposing unacceptable passages in the scriptures which proved to be a bane for humanity. Especially Hindu leaders must not only spread the knowledge about dharma, they must also question adharma in the name of religion.

Indian wisdom is the beneficial guiding light for all humanity. It has been carried over to us from a time, when the world was still more transparent, more spirit, where everything was sacred and miracles were possible anytime. Devas (superhuman powers who support our life on earth, wrongly translated as gods) could appear in the human dimension easily. In India, even now it feels as if only a curtain separates our material world from subtler worlds, while in the West, a brick wall is between them.

Indian wisdom is practical and needs to be experienced. It is a genuine enquiry into truth. It is about discovering what we really are, apart from the ever-changing body and mind, and the ways for this discovery are manifold and joyful. No book is even needed, nobody needs to come and tell a story about what happened 2000 or 1400 years ago. The knowledge of truth is deep inside us.

Conscious, blissful oneness is not somewhere up in heaven. It can be felt as one's own essence. This essence can be called by different names, but the main thing is, that it is within everyone, including in animals and nature. So, we are all children of the same infinite Divine Presence. This truth provides the basis for a harmonious world, and it has another important benefit: it gives meaning to life. Life is about discovering our blissful essence.

The motto of the Indian Republic is the Vedic dictum "Satyameva Jayate"—Truth alone triumphs. Many of India's great personalities like Swami Vivekananda or Sri Aurobindo predicted that India will be again the guru of the world, as it was in ancient times before the dogmatic religions mixed the truth of "there is only one Supreme Being" with untruth like "this Supreme Being likes some and doesn't like others."

Truth *has* to triumph. Humanity needs to win over inhumanity. Imagine if the great majority of human beings would follow the Golden Rule again—don't do to others what you don't want to be done to yourself.

We could leave our doors and hearts open...

Lokah samastah sukhino bhavantu

May all beings everywhere be happy.